ISBN: 9781290538572

Published by:
HardPress Publishing
8345 NW 66TH ST #2561
MIAMI FL 33166-2626

Email: info@hardpress.net
Web: http://www.hardpress.net

Presented to

The Library

of the

University of Toronto

by

Mrs. Graham Sinclair

Church History from Nero to Constantine

BY

C. P. S. CLARKE, M.A.

Rector of Donhead St. Andrew
Author of " Everyman's Book of Saints "

A. R. MOWBRAY & CO. Ltd.
London : 28 Margaret Street, Oxford Circus, W. 1
Oxford : 9 High Street
Milwaukee, U.S.A. : The Morehouse Publishing Co.

First impression, 1920

Viro Praeclaro
Benigno, Dilectissimo
CAROLO GORE, S.T.P.
Gregis fidelium summo Pastori
Hoc opusculum dedicavit
Philippus Clarke, A.M.
Discipulus et quondam curarum pastoralium
Particeps indignus
Amicitiae et venerationis
Quantulumcunque Testimonium.

PREFACE

THE modest aim of this book is to set forth for the benefit of the general reader facts already known to scholars concerning the life of the Church in the age of persecution.

The words *facts* and *life* are used advisedly. The book is written to interest the layman, and by the layman I mean not the unordained but the non-specialist. Now English people are not as a rule much interested in opinions. This is, perhaps, a pity, but it is so; they are as God made them. They are not, therefore, interested in theology, especially if by theology is meant, not the bare statements of the Creed, but the elaborate explanations of such statements extracted from theologians under the pressure of the questionings and denials of the heretic. But they are interested in the Church as a living and working society, and it is the history of the Church under this aspect that I have attempted to write. After all the Church has always been a way of life rather than a system of thought. It is a way of life, it is true, based on certain fundamental assumptions of God and man's relation to God, and, in consequence, of man's relation to man, but it is always thought translated into action, a way of life, that is, involving certain assumptions in thought, but never a mere school of philosophy. I have therefore attempted to show what the Church was like as a living organization. I have tried to describe on the one hand its life, its organization, its officers, their duties and the method of their appointment, its sacraments, services, its social services and welfare work, its discipline, as well as the main points of its teaching, both moral and doctrinal ; and, on the other, its relation to the heathen world, its persecution, its unpopularity, the rivalry of popular religions like Mithraism, and the vain attempts at counter-propaganda by emperors and philosophers.

I find after writing it with these objects in view that the book seems to be marked by three special features.

1. A far more considerable use is made of the so-called Church Orders, those early disciplinary manuals which Dr. Frere, Dom Conolly, and other scholars have done so much to elucidate, than has been done by any existing Church history, so far as my knowledge serves.

2. The persecutions are also described with some particularity and detail. It is impossible to understand the conditions under which men and women professed Christianity, or the temper of their heathen contemporaries, or the reaction on the Christian character, unless we understand the ferocity of the persecutions, which we can only do by reading the first-hand account of them, or the nearest we can get to first-hand, with all its horrors. One doesn't write about

horrors for pleasure, but because they are a prominent part of the history.

3. The number and length of the quotations. This may be considered good or bad. It was adopted deliberately, as the object is to give an idea of Church life as it was, and for this some knowledge of the original documents is indispensable. It would have been possible to relegate the quotations to notes, but that expedient has its drawbacks; or they might have been published in a separate volume, as was done by Professor Gwatkin. One friend advised this, but added with a flash of candour, "Of course no one would look at it." On the whole the method pursued is the only one likely to bring home to the average reader what I wanted to bring home. The events are so far away, the details so few, that one cannot afford to lose the least touch that helps to lend a sense of reality, and there is no doubt that a quotation from a contemporary writer does help to do this. To be told once more that the early Christians loved one another, or were kind to widows and orphans, or cared for the sick, can hardly hold the most alert attention. If one could truthfully write that the early Christians habitually beat their wives it would be different. A reference in a footnote would be enough. A fact so new and startling would arrest attention. But as it is, while the general statement that Christians were kind to orphans may be very flat and stale, it seems not unreasonable that the precise directions in the words actually used, or

at least a translation of them, may appeal with a certain freshness and reality.

The labours of many scholars have left me in their debt. I must first of all acknowledge the very great kindness of Dr. Darwell Stone, Principal of the Pusey House at Oxford, who has read the proof-sheets and made many valuable corrections and suggestions. As to *published* works, I have used the ante-Nicene translation of the Fathers, though I have been at some pains to compare the translations with the originals, as published in the Migne edition, and in most cases have given my own. Bishop Lightfoot's great work on *The Apostolic Fathers* is a storehouse of learning, and has been invaluable. I have, however, used Professor K. Lake's text in the Loeb edition, but am myself responsible for the translations. The late Dr. Bigg's works on *Neoplatonism*, the *Christian School of Alexandria*, and the *Church's Task under the Roman Empire* have all been consulted, and never in vain. That brilliant and suggestive writer sends no one away empty. The volume of Essays on the *Early History of the Church and the Ministry*, originally edited by the late Dr. Swete, has been of great help, principally because it introduced me to that body of interesting literature known as the Church Orders. For further enlightenment on them I am deeply in debt to the Rev. W. H. Frere, C.R., and Dom R. H. Conolly, O.B.S., and to the translations of the first Church Order by the Rev. G. Horner in his *Statutes of the*

Apostles, and that of the Syriac version of the *Didascalia*, by Miss Margaret Gibson. The latest edition of Bishop Gore's *The Church and the Ministry*, revised by Mr. C. H. Turner, appeared after the chapter on the ministry was written, but not too late for me to benefit by its learning and illustrations. For the chapter on Mithraism I am indebted to the monumental volumes of M. Cumont. I used Berwick's translation of *Philostratus's Apollonius of Tyana* before I discovered Professor J. S. Phillimore's, but I have since made considerable use of that scholar's most learned and suggestive introduction. Sir William Ramsay's works, especially *The Church in the Roman Empire*, have been of great service; so have the *Texts and Studies* edited by the Dean of Wells. For the rest I have relied mainly on my own studies of the Fathers, and other contemporary documents, and drawn my own conclusions.

I should like also to acknowledge the kindness and attention of the Librarian of the London Library, without which the book could not have been written. Mr. Gordon Crosse has given one more token of an old and valued friendship by reading the book in proof. Finally, I should like to express my grateful thanks to Miss Flora Hill for her most valuable assistance in preparing the volume for the press.

C. P. S. CLARKE.

DONHEAD ST. ANDREW,
All Saints' Day, 1919.

INTRODUCTION

THE Christian religion has been the great constructive element in the formation of Western civilization. It is true that Roman law and Greek letters have had an enormous influence, but the effect of Roman law and Greek letters would have been very much diminished without the humanizing and preservative forces of the Church. If Christ had not been born, life as we know it to-day would have been very different—less civilized, less humane, altogether rougher and more barbarous, though possibly in some ways more efficient : at any rate different. Since 1760 another force has come into action. The discovery of the uses to which steam might be put and the invention of machinery have already produced a social and industrial revolution, and seem not unlikely to produce a political revolution as well. This new force, *industrialism*, to give it its ugly but convenient label, has reached the East, and is domiciled in India and Japan. Without it the great European war could not have been fought on so gigantic a scale, for armies are always limited by the power of nations to feed and munition them, and it is only through industrialism that it has been possible to feed and equip millions at a time. In the eyes of the world it seems to-day to be even more important in its effect on civilization than religion, which does its work for the most part beneath the surface in comparative silence and obscurity. The influence of religion must not, however, be measured by its apparent effect. Now, as always, unless it speaks through the megaphone of loud and noisy advertisement, it receives little attention. It may seem to have no more effect to-day than it had in the reign of Marcus Aurelius or Philip the Arabian, and in Russia it is persecuted, or was recently,[1] as in the days of Diocletian. Yet in those days it was religion that had the last word, and so it may be now. But however we may regard its present importance, it is not unworthy of the attention of the intelligent person with a proper scientific curiosity in beginnings to watch, if not the birth-throes, at least the infancy and growing-pains of the Christian Church, which has had such a vast and preponderating influence in the past.

It has been objected that Church history should not be separated from secular history, and that all history is one. This is at once a truism and

[1] The Archbishop of Canterbury received the following telegram from Platon, Metropolitan of Odessa, December 20, 1918 :—

"I fervently beg Your Eminence to protect the Orthodox Russian Church. The Revolutionary Government is subjecting it to cruelties by the side of which the persecutions of the Christians in the first three centuries pale. Many archbishops, hundreds of priests, have been martyred and shot. The churches are profaned and pillaged."

untrue. History is one, but man's life is a big theme, and history is forced to select and discriminate, and it is convenient to write it in parts. One used to be told that the division between ancient and modern history was artificial and unreal for the same reason. This also is true; and Sir Walter Raleigh, anticipating this verdict, wrote a *History of the World*, beginning with the Flood; but he has had few imitators. Most of us have to cabin, crib, and confine ourselves within a period and within a subject. One cannot have even an adequate general knowledge of the whole unless one is intimate with at least some of the parts. Church history, after all, is only the history of one of the biggest, if not the biggest, single factor in universal history, and no one who wishes to have a grasp of how modern conditions came into being can afford to neglect it.

Now the history of Christian religion, at any rate in the first centuries after Christ, is the history of the Church. It is true that some scholars hold that Jesus did not intend to found a Church. But such views can only be regarded as the unaccountable vagaries of scholarship. If Jesus did not found a society or Church to carry on His work, if He was merely a voice, a message, and a witness, it would seem that either the evangelists woefully misunderstood Him or very much of what He did was beside the point. It was in that case a misdirection of energy to concentrate as He did on His disciples, instead of endeavouring to let His message reach as wide a circle as possible. The preacher or messenger requires a large audience. He desires a platform, whether it be a rostrum in the market-place, a pulpit, or the columns of a daily paper, by which he can reach as many minds as possible. But the founder of a society is indifferent to numbers. Everything depends on starting on the right lines and with the right people. Numbers can be left to the future. So Jesus was indifferent to numbers. He concentrated more and more on His immediate followers. Much of His teaching bears on the future problems that the society will have to face. The power to bind and loose given to S. Peter was the regular Jewish expression for making the rules or bye-laws of the synagogue—in other words, for legislation; the problem of the unworthy member and of discipline was touched on in the parable of the field with wheat and tares growing side by side, and in the parable of the draw-net. Authority to exercise effective discipline was conferred when power was given to the Church to forgive and retain sins. He ordained also a formal sacrament of admission to His society and one of union for those who were already members. Unless we tear fragments out of the text to suit preconceived theories, like the Gnostics, who were " ever mending the Gospels," it seems merely perverse to accept Christ and deny the Church as His creation and bequest to the world.

We see the Christian society first as a tiny

group of men and women in an obscure corner of the Roman Empire, waiting for their Master to reappear, and almost feverishly eager to proclaim Him as the Saviour of mankind before that event should happen and the world in which they lived come to its appointed end. That hope gradually receded into the dim future, but the members of His Church were none the less fired with the desire to proclaim their good news throughout the world. They did not arrive at this stage in a moment. It is probable that the Apostles remained twelve years in Jerusalem after Pentecost, that is until A.D. 41, and S. Paul's first missionary journey did not take place before A.D. 46. But by the Council of Jerusalem, A.D. 48, when the reports of S. Peter and S. Paul were received and an agreement arrived at about the treatment of Gentile proselytes, the general policy of the Church as a world-wide and not a national movement was settled. At first the most formidable opponents were not the heathen, but those of their own household, the Jews. The Roman authorities appear rather as the protectors than persecutors of the Christians. Gallio drove the Jews out of his court and would not listen to their charges against S. Paul, and S. Paul himself appealed to Caesar when accused by his own nation. As far as possible they held aloof from what they regarded as the internal squabbles of a fanatical and disagreeable nation. But the Jews became implacable adversaries when they once realized the content of the Christian message, namely, that the Messiah had come already in the person of the crucified Jesus, and that salvation was to be through the Cross and no longer by the law. As soon, however, as the Roman government discovered the existence and vitality of this new sect it began to persecute with fire and sword, with torture, and all the terrors of wild beasts. The persecution, sometimes more, sometimes less energetically carried on, lasted for one hundred and forty years. It is easy to exaggerate its ferocity. Pliny, an anxious and over-conscientious official, went to govern Bithynia without having informed himself as to how Christians were to be treated if brought before him for judgement. It had not occurred to him that their treatment might be an important detail in the administration of his province. Moreover when anonymous accusations were forbidden persecution lost its chief terrors. The rôle of an accuser is not popular. Few people like to come forward to denounce harmless and inoffensive neighbours, and when Christians grew in numbers it is possible that reprisals were feared. Still the fact remains that Christians were outlaws. They were never safe. The writings of Tertullian show plainly that torture and death were possible contingencies that no Christian could safely leave out of his calculations.

The persecutions of Decius and Valerian were altogether more serious affairs. They were determined attempts engineered from head-quarters, striking first of all at the heads of the new religion, to destroy it altogether. They failed, to be renewed on a more thorough scale by Diocletian forty years later, and with the same result. This was the most serious effort at suppression the Church ever had to face, and showed by its failure that no attempt in the future was likely to be more successful, and anticipated in effect the words of a later persecutor—the apostate Julian—when he exclaimed " Galileean, thou hast conquered."

Besides the official power of the State, the Church had other foes to contend with. It was long unpopular, as being unsocial, since Christians were cut off from popular amusements which centred in the theatre, and from most social festivities as being involved in pagan observances. It was also attacked by the philosophers, who were the self-appointed preachers of their time, a function in some measure discharged by journalists to-day.

Unfortunately very little has survived, except the great attack of Celsus preserved for us by Origen. The effect of these attacks must have been confined to the few, whether heathen or Christian ; they could have had no more effect on the multitude than a leading article in *The Times* or the *Spectator* would to-day. The more ambitious attempt of Philostratus to supplant Christ by Apollonius of Tyana must have been even more ineffective.

Far more formidable than the attacks of

philosophers were the attractions of popular religions. Besides conventional paganism, there was the appeal of Isis to the sensuous and the sentimental, and that of Mithras to those of a more dour and sombre type. The attraction of both was real enough. For one who deliberately rejected the Gospel through the arguments of Fronto or Celsus, there must have been fifty who preferred the worship of Isis or the cult of Mithras. Mithraism alone was a far more serious danger than all the philosophers with whom the Apologists argue. It is, therefore, rather puzzling to find hardly more than a few incidental notices of Mithraism in the works of the Fathers. Attacks on an effete paganism abound. Mockery of idol-worship is common form. But the living and triumphant religion of Mithraism is left alone. Probably the reason was that most of the apologies were pleas for toleration addressed to the persecuting Government, whether emperor or proconsul; and the persecution was based on the Christian "atheism" or rejection of the official gods. Christians were not persecuted for refusing to adore Mithra, but for refusing to sacrifice to the emperor and the gods of ancient Rome. Other apologies were addressed to philosophers, and the philosophers, so far as they were anything, were pagans. Mithraism, like Christianity, was a popular religion; it appealed to the common man and woman. If it attracted a philosopher or ruler, it did so by virtue of its appeal to the common humanity in them, not to their extra portion of brain or cultivation. It would have been waste of time for Origen to address elaborate philosophical treatises to Mithraists; they would neither have been read nor understood. The people for that work were the plain men who talked to the ignorant, and rather avoided philosophers than otherwise. The real work of conversion was done then as it always is—unless, as in the Saracen invasions, it is effected by force—by those who talked to little groups of people at street corners, or to labouring men at their work, or even lowered themselves so far as to carry the good news to women and children. The Church, as a living society, did not trouble itself specially about philosophers. It was more concerned with the conventional and carnal person outside its gates who was indifferent and contemptuous to religion, or, if inclined to take religion seriously, was in danger of being attracted by Isis or Mithra.

That is where the real fight must always go on. The philosophers now, as then, have their work to do. They are the staffs of the contending armies, but the fighting of which we hear and read so little is not done by them, but by those who are in the line, the men and women in the home and the streets.

The Church had other troubles. It had spiritual and intellectual dangers as well as those threatened by the secular arm. The great foe of this sort was Gnosticism, that "knowledge falsely so-called" of which S. Paul wrote. Gnosticism seems to us wild enough, considered either as religion or philosophy, but it had an attraction for a certain type of the more intellectual, and won over some who were, or might have been, Christians. Gnostics may be roughly divided into two kinds, namely, the pagan Gnostics, who borrowed as much of the Christian theology as suited them, and attacked from outside, and the Christian Gnostics, like Marcion, who tried to twist Christianity into conformity with Gnostic ideas. They probably stood in much the same relation to the Church as Theosophists and Spiritualists and the votaries of Christian Science do to-day. Some were in the Church but most were outside, and nearly all were rather superior and inclined to be contemptuous and patronizing. The real danger was not that any considerable number of Christians, or pagans inclined to accept Christianity, should be led away into Gnosticism, but lest the authorities of the Church should be deceived or bullied by the intellectual pretensions of the Gnostics and alter the creed to suit their fancies.

The danger was averted, and, in spite of very considerable intellectual pressure, the main doctrines of the Church, as imbedded in its baptismal creed, were unaltered, and remain unaltered to this day. *Explanations* of the doctrines have changed, but not the doctrines themselves. That God created the world; that Jesus was God and also Man; that He was born of the Virgin Mary, was crucified, rose again from the dead, ascended into heaven; that He will come to judge ; that the Holy Ghost is also God. All these doctrines were held from the first. They are found in the New Testament, in the Roman baptismal creed, and in the earliest Apology that has survived, that of Aristides. The explanations came later. If Jesus was God, how and in what way could He be also Man ? Many explanations were evoked by Gnostic and Arian speculations before one was accepted. So with the doctrine of the Trinity. From the beginning the Church believed that the Father was God, and the Son God, and the Holy Ghost God, yet not three Gods but one God ; but—to use a word somewhat overworked to-day—it was long before the Church found a satisfactory formula in which these apparent contradictions could be reconciled.

Nevertheless the Church triumphed. In spite of fightings within and the frontal attack of the Roman Empire, the most perfectly organized instrument of government on the grand scale that the world has ever seen, it survived and conquered, and the head of the Empire, as much perhaps out of interest as conviction, became the official patron of the new religion, so long despised and persecuted. The extent and numbers of the Church when the last persecution broke out has been the object of a careful and exhaustive examination by Professor Harnack in his *Expansion of Christianity*, for which all students owe him a deep debt of gratitude. It seems safe to say that the Church extended as far as the Empire, and sometimes further. It was weakest in Germany, where we only know of one bishop, the Bishop of Cologne. It was strongest in Asia Minor, where perhaps nearly half the population was Christian. There the Church was not only strong in the Greek-speaking cities on the coast and the great trade routes, but was firmly established in the interior. Firmilian was Bishop of Caesarea in Cappadocia, in the very heart of what is now [1] Asiatic Turkey, and exercised a wide influence. By the middle of the third century Dionysius of Alexandria was able to write [2] that Mesopotamia, together with the provinces of Syria, Bithynia, Arabia, and Pontus, was rejoicing in the brotherly love then prevailing. In the West bishops from every province in Spain were present at the Council of Elvira, A.D. 305, while the North sent three bishops to represent the British Church in the Synod of Arles, A.D. 314. Beyond the frontiers of the Empire the kingdom of Armenia had been converted by Gregory the Illuminator, and was the first nation to adopt Christianity as its official religion. In the South the Ethiopian version of the Hippolytean Church Order points to the early spread of Christianity in that region. In the East Origen tells us that S. Thomas preached in India and S. Andrew in Scythia, which at least shows that there were Christians in those countries in his time.

Such a marvellous growth in the face of persecution has no parallel in history. Gibbon has attempted to account for it in his famous

[1] August, 1919.   [2] Eusebius, *H. E.* vii. 5.

fifteenth chapter, and has enumerated five causes, namely :—
1. The zeal of the Jews.
2. The doctrine of the immortality of the soul and the promised rewards and punishments of heaven and hell.
3. Miraculous powers, real or pretended.
4. The virtues of the first Christians.
5. Their activity in the government of the Church.

But it is not very easy to see what the zeal of the Jews had to do with it. It is true that the first Christians were Jews, but there was soon a preponderating majority of Gentile Christians in the Church, and it is more natural to attribute their zeal to their religion than to Jewish infection or heredity. As to the doctrine of immortality of the soul, it is true that philosophers scoffed at the resurrection of the body, and their views on the immortality of the soul were timid and lukewarm compared with the confident affirmations of the Church. But Mithraism also taught the resurrection of the body and the immortality of the soul, and Mithraism was a far more serious enemy to the Church than philosophy ever was. As to the third cause, miraculous powers, no doubt, play no small part in accrediting the first preachers of the Gospel, but we hear very little of them in the second and third centuries, when the Church was advancing by leaps and bounds. The question of organization was important; but organization by itself can accomplish little. Four, therefore, out of the five causes amount to little, and we must seek further for the real ground and root of so rapid and overwhelming a success.

It will be well to begin by reminding ourselves that men and women change their dress, their ways of speech, their weapons of war, their means of transport from age to age, but not their essential humanity. That is why the best literature never grows old. Take the picture of Ahab coveting the vineyard of Naboth, and coming home heavy and displeased and refusing to eat, while Jezebel, a far stronger character, regarded him with mingled pity and contempt. If he wants it, why doesn't he take it? However——; and with contemptuous good nature she undertakes to arrange the matter for him, and does so with an efficiency and ruthlessness which would do credit to a twentieth-century heroine. It is a wonder that a celebrated modern playwright has not built a play round this exponent of his favourite theme. What could there be more modern?

Or take the poignant farewell of Andromache and Hector in the sixth book of the *Iliad*. There is first the appeal to Hector not to go out to meet Achilles, but " to stay thy folk beside the fig-tree, where best the city may be scaled." He is not, so to speak, urged not to join up, but to join something comparatively safe. Hector's reply would be impossible for a tongue-tied, self-conscious Englishman, but not for a Frenchman, and an Englishman would feel the same even if he could not express his feelings. "' Surely I take thought for all these things, my wife; but I have shame of the Trojans and the Trojan women, if like a coward I shrink away from battle. Moreover, mine own soul forbiddeth me, seeing I have learnt ever to be valiant and fight in the forefront of the Trojans.' So spake glorious Hector, and stretched out his arm to his boy. But the child shrunk crying to the bosom of his nurse, dismayed at his father's aspect, and in dread at the bronze and horse-hair crest that he beheld nodding fiercely from the helmet's top. Then his dear father laughed aloud and his lady mother; forthwith glorious Hector took the helmet from his head and laid it all gleaming on the earth; then he kissed his dear son, and dandled him in his arms and spake in prayer to Zeus and all the gods." In his prayer he asks that men may say of his son, " Far greater is he than his father." [1]

The expression, like the arms, is different, but the feeling has not changed in three thousand years.

The fierce, unreasoning enthusiasm of the mob in the great towns of the ancient world for their favourite charioteers, their passionate interest in the victory of the white or the red, has its parallel in the crowds at a modern football match, or the even greater masses who read the results in the evening papers. A modern boxing-match is tame

[1] *Iliad* vi. Translation by W. Leaf.

compared with the bloody spectacle of the Games, but it is doubtful if these combats would be less popular if they should become more dangerous to those who take part in them. In spite of civilization and education man retains his strong affections, his fierce desires, passions, and instincts, which may be controlled by public opinion, by law, or by religion, but are not eliminated. The highly educated may change, at least on the surface, but human nature as a whole remains much the same. So that we shall not go far wrong if we assume that the raw material with which religion had to do in the second century was not so different from that with which it deals in the twentieth, as we sometimes like to think. The conditions of Christian success have not altered. If the Church is to win its way to-day it can only do so by reason of its inherent attractiveness, because it can offer men and women something that corresponds to a vital need in their nature. The Church had to draw men almost in spite of themselves. What was there in it to attract?

1. *The life of believers*. This is in effect Gibbon's fourth cause. The Apologists appeal confidently to the superior morality of Christians, to their moral purity, their inoffensiveness, their spirit of brotherhood and mutual service. They relieved the widow and the orphan, they nursed the sick, ransomed the captive, and buried the dead in a manner neither paganism nor any other religion could rival. The mass of mankind, then as now, led hard and suffering lives, and craved

as they do still for sympathy and kindness. The Church gave it as no other religion did, and, it must be admitted, as it has never done since. It was, in fact, part of its "expression work." We see it in the claims of the Apologists, in the sneers of Lucian, in the provisions of the Church Orders, and in the instances that have come down of the practical care for widows, orphans, the sick, the prisoners, and the dead. The present writer remembers being present at a meeting in the East End of London of a number of working men who were members of the Church of England Men's Society, when the subject of the discussion was "What brings men to Church?" Not a man present had been a professing Churchman from his youth up. All had come in from outside, some from other religious bodies, but most from nothing at all. Every man present gave his own personal experience. Some said they had been drawn by the kind of religion taught, others by the kind of worship practised. No one said he had come because Church people led better lives than other folk, and no one hinted that he had joined because the Church believed in a life after the grave. Most gave as their motive some act of kindness that they or their families had received. It might be a visit during sickness, or a friendly welcome in church or at a social gathering, or attention to a sick child, and in one case the only reason given was "Your people seemed so kind to one another." There was no question of bribery or coming to church because it paid. These were not "rice-Christians" who came for what they could get. The acts of kindness were in most cases mere acts of courtesy and brotherhood that had no expression in currency. This seems to give a clue to the attractiveness of Christianity in the first centuries of our era. The heart of man craved for a religion of sympathy and brotherly love, and he found it in the Church.

2. *The doctrine*—especially the doctrine of a God of love—that God so loved the world that He became Man and died on the Cross. This was anathema to the philosopher, but appealed to the weak, the fallen, the poor in spirit, the broken in heart, and in fact to all the wayfarers who had to trudge on life's dusty high road, though perhaps not to the few who, by reason of birth or fortunes or superior abilities, were able to make the journey in greater comfort.

"Why did He do it?" was the exasperated cry of Celsus. But the bereaved, the sufferers, the hungry, and the wretched crave for that divine sympathy of which they can only be assured by belief in a suffering God.

3. *The discipline.* Men and women who do not seriously feel the need of religion only ask that whatever religion convention brings in their way should make little demand on them. The serious seeker after God desires not only to receive but also to give. It is doubtful if Isis made a sufficient moral demand on the general body of her votaries to attract the more earnest.

It is certain that paganism did not. The Church exacted a high moral standard, and though no doubt when persecution slackened that standard could not always be preserved, and the crop of tares growing up with the wheat was perilously large, there seems little doubt that there was a real attempt to exclude insincere persons from joining the Church, to remove those who fell back into heinous sin, and to spare no effort to restore to penitence and communion those who had so fallen.

The seeker after God in East London to-day looks to see if those who profess to have found Him show by their lives the greatness and reality of their discovery. He asks for much and is ready to give much. There is no reason to suppose that such a man would have been very different then, and there is certainly no comparison between the demands made by Isis or Mithra or paganism and those made by the followers of Jesus Christ. He was offered the pearl of great price, but he had to pay the price and he valued it accordingly.

No doubt there were other reasons as well. The organization of the Church was admirable. Each local Church, under its bishop, preserved enough autonomy to give it the spirit of energy and initiative. There was as yet no papalism. The idea of Caesarism had not been transferred from the Empire to the papacy. But regular and frequent communication with distant Churches, the gatherings of bishops, the need for the local

Churches to remain in communion with the rest of the Catholic Church, and the value attached to the Apostolic Scriptures and rule of faith were sufficient to preserve the unity of the whole. No organization, however, would have helped without the antecedent causes of growth.

Finally, the believer, to-day as then, will believe that though Apollos may sow and Paul may water, it is God that giveth the increase, and that all the efforts of the early Church would have been barren but for the life-giving power of the Holy Spirit.

CONTENTS

		PAGE
	Preface	v
	Introduction	xi
I.	The Preparation of the World for Christ and the Beginnings of the Church	1
	Religion	3
II.	Persecution—From Nero to Marcus Aurelius	15
	Trajan, A.D. 98–117	22
	Hadrain, A.D. 117–138	28
	Antoninus Pius, A.D. 138–161	29
	Marcus Aurelius, 161–180	36
III.	Gnostics, Montanists	46
	The Gnostics	46
	The Montanists	54
IV.	Some Christian Writers from Clement to Tertullian	61
	Tertullian	75
V.	The Church and the World	84
	Family Life	85
	Business	90
	Amusements	93
	Citizenship	95
	Military Service	99
	Slavery	103
	Conclusion	104
	The Way of Light	107
	The Way of Darkness	109
VI.	The Church under Foreign Emperors	111
	Slackening of Persecution	111
	Commodus, A.D. 180-193	114
	Severus, A.D. 193–205	117
	Caracalla, A.D. 211–217	128
VII.	The Catechetical School of Alexandria	133
	Clement of Alexandria	133
	Origen	142

Contents

		PAGE
VIII.	PAGAN ATTEMPTS AT RECONSTRUCTION	152
	Apollonius of Tyana	160
	Neoplatonism	169
IX.	RIVAL RELIGIONS	173
	The Worship of Isis	174
	Mithraism	177
X.	THE PERSECUTIONS OF DECIUS AND VALERIAN	185
XI.	THE ROMAN CHURCH	203
XII.	LIFE IN THE CHURCH	218
	Baptism	219
	Confirmation	226
	The Eucharist	227
	The Agape	232
	Fasting	238
	The Sick	241
	Marriage	242
	Organization of Charity	243
	Discipline	249
XIII.	THE OFFICERS OF THE CHURCH AND THEIR DUTIES	259
	The Bishop	259
	The Presbyters	263
	The Deacon	267
	The Minor Officials	269
	The Subdeacon	270
	Acolytes	271
	The Widow	271
	The Deaconess	275
	Virgins	276
XIV.	MINISTERIAL AUTHORITY AND ITS TRANSMISSION	279
XV.	THE TRUCE, A.D. 260–303	299
	Dionysius of Alexandria	299
	Paul of Samosata	304
	Gregory Thaumaturgus	306
	Gregory the Illuminator	313
	Manes and Manicheeism	315
XVI.	THE FINAL STRUGGLE, A.D. 303–313	317
	LIST OF CHIEF MODERN AUTHORITIES CONSULTED	335
	CHRONOLOGICAL TABLE	337

CHURCH HISTORY FROM NERO TO CONSTANTINE

I

THE PREPARATION OF THE WORLD FOR CHRIST AND THE BEGINNINGS OF THE CHURCH

SAINT Paul says that "when the fullness of time was come" Christ was born. When the world was ready. There has never been a time when the world was more ready for the coming of a Saviour and the founding of a religion intended to embrace all the nations of the earth.

For almost the only time in the world's history there was peace. The civilized world, and a considerable fringe that was not civilized, owned the Roman power. Such wars as there were were affairs of outposts. "Internationalism" was a fact. There were no hard and fast barriers between country and country. All were parts of the Roman Empire. There does not seem to have been any colour bar. It was probably easier for S. Paul to have gone on his journeys and at last get a hearing in Rome when he did, than it would be to-day or ever has been since. The means of communication, whether by travel or by letter, were far better under the Roman Empire than they were up to the middle of the nineteenth century, that is in a region comprising what we mean to-day, or did mean till lately, by Italy, France, Spain, Austria, Western Germany, Switzerland, England, the Balkans, Turkey in Europe and in Asia, Egypt, and North Africa. Over this country there was a net-work of roads and sea-ways connecting the chief towns, and made reasonably safe for travellers. On them there was a constant traffic of imperial officials, merchants, tourists, actors, musicians, athletes, itinerant professors of rhetoric or healing, and teachers of religion. The scene must have been something like that presented by the great Trunk Road in India as pictured in *Kim*. " During Galen's stay in Rome (A.D. 162–166) he was consulted for ophthalmia by letters from Asia, Gaul, Spain, and Thrace. Every year he received parcels of medicines from friends in Spain, Syria, Palestine, Egypt, Cappadocia, Pontus, Macedonia, Gaul, and Mauretania."[1]

" Day after day," says Aristides, " merchant ships and merchants sail both seas—the Mediterranean and the Atlantic—and to Britain; not only officials and troops go, but countless private

[1] Friedlander, *Roman Life and Manners*, i. 303.

people."[1] Nor was traffic confined to the Empire. "Merchants have learned the shortest way and commerce has brought India near to us."[2] They got as far east as China, and as far south as Zanzibar.[3]

Religion

It is sometimes thought that Christianity found its opportunity in the break-up of paganism; that men had ceased to believe in the old gods, and were ready to embrace a new religion. This does not seem to have been the case. The Roman Empire was a very big concern, and included a vast number of widely-varying races, an even more miscellaneous collection than the British Empire does to-day. Generalisations are therefore to be made with caution. What might be true of North Africa might not be true of Britain. Still the evidence on the whole seems to show that the mass of people everywhere clung to their old gods.

Unbelief there was of course, especially among the educated, as inscriptions and literature show. The elder Pliny was a convinced materialist. "Souls and bodies no more have feelings and consciousness after death than they had before birth. But human vanity imagines a prolongation of existence into the future, and invents a life beyond the grave . . . it worships departed spirits and makes them gods, which have ceased to be even men."[4]

[1] Friedlander, *Roman Life and Manners*, i. 306.
[2] Ibid., 307.   [3] Ibid., 309.   [4] Ibid., iii. 282.

Many inscriptions, though only a small proportion of the whole, have been found in which life after death is dismissed as a delusion.
" After having vindicated absurdities I lie here in a sleep from which there is no awaking."
"There is no boat in Hades, no Charon, no Aeacus who holds the keys, no Cerberus. All of us whom death has carried away are rotten bones and ashes, nothing else."[1]

The followers of Epicurus for the most part shared these opinions, but there is nothing to show that they were more common then than now. The elder Pliny may have been a sceptic, but his nephew built a temple and officiated as a priest.

Lucian was by birth a Syrian ; by education, tastes, and interests a Greek, who lived during the last three-quarters of the second century. He was a teacher of rhetoric and a public lecturer ; by the time he was forty he retired, having amassed at least a competence, and then lived at Athens until near the end of his life. He was himself a sceptic. He scoffed at the tales of Greek mythology and at the gods, and his sarcasms at the expense of Christianity have come down in the story of Peregrinus. But his dialogues do not give the impression of a widespread unbelief. Rather the reverse. In the " Lover of Falsehood " he satirises the credulity of the learned. Tychiades, a sceptic, has gone to the house of Eucrates, "a man of sixty with a full descending

[1] Friedlander, *Roman Life and Manners*, iii. 283, 284.

beard, who has long rubbed shoulders with philosophy," and there meets Cleodemus the Aristotelian, and Deinomachus the Stoic, and Ion the Platonist. The talk turns on magical cures and ghosts, and Tychiades is amused by the amazing tales with which they cap one another's stories. " To me at least it often occurs to blush for the poets when they describe the mutilation of Saturn, the fetters of Prometheus, the revolt of the giants, and all the tragic scenes in Hades ; or, again, when they tell how love turned Zeus into a swan, or how this or that woman was changed into a bird or a bear. Then there are the beings like Pegasus, or the Chimaera, or the Gorgon, or the Cyclops, not to mention others of the same kind. . . . Yet if any one finds these things ridiculous, or discredits their truth, if he exposes them—why, such a man is thought at once impious and senseless for throwing suspicion on facts so well known." [1]

The *Golden Ass* of Apuleius, also written in the second century of our era, gives the same impression. The hero Lucius is transformed into an ass, and in that guise meets with many adventures until he is restored to human shape by the intervention of the goddess Isis. He is then initiated into the mysteries of her cult, and we leave him her devout adherent. In this book we find that magic and witchcraft meet with almost universal belief. If men are not changed into asses, or murdered by magic, people think

[1] Trans. by H. Williams.

they are. This is a warning given by a lady to Lucius about his hostess : " She is a notorious sorceress, and is believed to be a mistress of every kind of incantation. Her rejected lovers she either turns into stones, cattle, and animals of every kind, or utterly annihilates them." [1]

Gods there are of all sorts and kinds, and belief in them is general. There were gods, goddesses, " daemons," genii, beneficent and mischievous spirits of every sort, touching the life of man at every point—in his home, in his travels, in his shop, his hunting, his farming, his health, his sickness, and in fact his whole life. Every nation had its own collection, so to speak, but each was ready to enrich itself by borrowing from a neighbour. Syncretism, as this system of borrowing and mixing divinities is called, was the prevailing tendency. It was the churlish refusal of Christians to worship more than one God which made them so unpopular. " Despising and trampling under foot the majesty of heaven, instead of the true religion she affected to entertain some fantastic and sacrilegious notion of a God, whom she declared to be the only one,"[2] was the sarcastic comment of Lucius on a woman reputed to be a Christian.

Lucian and Apuleius are a hundred years later than S. Paul, and no doubt opinion, especially among the educated, fluctuates and becomes more or less sceptical. But there can hardly have been any very notable revival of popular religion in

[1] Apuleius, *Golden Ass*, ii. 27.   [2] Ibid., ix. 176.

The Preparation of the World for Christ 7

the hundred years after S. Paul. The pagan was not, therefore, disinclined to listen to the preaching of a new religion. He did not object to Christianity on religious grounds at first ; only later on, when he saw that it waged war on all other religions, he came to regard it as a kind of atheism.

But besides pagans there were Jews, and the Jews were very different. They were intensely patriotic, and religious to the point of fanaticism. Besides the Jews in Jerusalem there were Jews scattered over the world. In the Acts we read of Jews " out of every nation under heaven " hearing the Apostles speak with tongues on the Day of Pentecost—Parthians, Medes, Elamites, dwellers in Mesopotamia, Cappadocia, Pontus, Asia, Phrygia, Pamphylia, Egypt, Cyrene, Rome, Crete, and Arabia. Outside the Roman Empire the strongest Jewish element was in the region we now call Mesopotamia, where Babylonia became the centre of Jewish life,[1] and where their numbers were reckoned by millions. Within the Roman Empire Jews were most numerous in Asia Minor, Phoenicia, and Syria. Philo says that there were a million in Egypt, or an eighth of the whole population. The synagogue at Alexandria was so large that an official had to wave a flag as a signal for the congregation to make their responses ![2] They were so numerous in Rome that Claudius ordered their

[1] Friedlander, *Roman Life and Manners*, iii. 174.
[2] Ibid., 176.

expulsion, but without apparently being able to carry it out effectually. They were organized there in seven synagogues; they also had their own synagogue at Jerusalem.

The Jews were then even to a greater degree than they are to-day an international force. Greater because, as we have seen, internationalism within the Empire was in some measure a fact; and because nationalism, as we understand it, was a much weaker sentiment. The Jew in Greece or Italy was less of a Greek or Italian and more of a Jew than he would be to-day. At the same time local patriotism is an ineradicable human instinct, and the Jew was no doubt attached, like S. Paul, to his native city. Pilgrimages to Jerusalem as long as the Temple survived kept the outlying Jews in touch with the centre. Returning pilgrims must have brought the news of the Crucifixion and the alleged Resurrection of One Who claimed to be the Messiah to every centre of population in the known world.

The world then, within and without the Empire, was connected by live wires, and ready, as never before or since, for the speedy promulgation of a new teaching. The very list of nations on the Day of Pentecost, given in the Acts, brings home to us into how many distant parts of the world the news of the new sect must have penetrated.

Now, the Jew believed that he belonged to a chosen race, that he alone possessed the law and was saved by keeping it, and that the Messiah was to come and restore his nation to its rightful place, and prostrate all other nations under his feet. The coming of the Messiah was the hope of Israel. The more the pious and patriotic Jew was humiliated by the oppression of the conqueror, the more did he look forward to this event with a passionate expectation. It was to be the great climax of the long history of his race.

The speculations as to the nature of the Messiah and the manner of His coming were many and various. But among them all it had never occurred to any one that He might come and not be recognized. At the beginning, therefore, the outstanding point of difference between the Jews who were followers of Jesus and the rest was that the disciples of Jesus believed that He was the Messiah, while the bulk of the nation, so far from recognizing Him, had procured His crucifixion, but that God had vindicated His claims by His resurrection.

At first, the Christians were hated by the rulers who had compassed the death of Jesus, but not by the mob. It was not until S. Paul began to lay stress on salvation by the Cross instead of the law, and the consequent admission of the Gentiles on equal terms, and the loss by the Jew of his position of privilege, that the hatred became general. Moreover, the Church claimed to be the real Israel, the legitimate heirs of Abraham and of the promises. "We are the circumcision," said S. Paul, and this "unchurching" of the Jews roused their bitterest hostility. Everywhere the Jew was the enemy. At Antioch in Pisidia "the Jews stirred up the devout and honourable women, and the chief men of the city, and raised persecution against Paul and Barnabas, and expelled them out of their coasts."[1] In Iconium "the unbelieving Jews stirred up the Gentiles, and made their minds evil affected against the brethren."[2] At Lystra, when the people could hardly be restrained from sacrificing to Paul and Barnabas, "there came thither certain Jews from Antioch and Iconium, who persuaded the people, and, having stoned Paul, drew him out of the city, supposing he had been dead."[3] In Thessalonica the Jews imitate the loyalty of the Jews at Jerusalem, who said "We have no king but Caesar," when they took Jason and certain brethren to the rulers of the city and accused them of acting contrary to the decrees of Caesar, "saying that there is another King, one Jesus."[4] And so it continued. The Jews of themselves could not do very much, but they could and did make trouble with the Gentile mob and the Gentile magistrates.

The new Israel, then, consisted, as we have seen, of those who accepted Jesus as the Messiah. But this did not necessarily make them into a visible society, a church, a body with members. Dr. Inge and others have maintained that the creation of such a society was an after-

[1] Acts xiii. 50. [2] Ibid., xiv. 2.
[3] Ibid., xiv. 19. [4] Ibid., xvii. 7.

thought, and no part of the original plan. "There is no evidence that the historic Christ ever intended to found a new institutional religion. He was a prophet, and left no school or church."[1] But the evidence is all the other way. Jesus claimed to be the Messiah and a King, and to have founded a kingdom. He took enormous pains to train disciples who should be the leaders in this kingdom. In His commission to them after the Resurrection He gives them the power of binding and loosing, a power which could only be interpreted by those familiar with the usages of the synagogue as applying to a definite and visible society.

The distinctive belief of this society, differentiating it from the rest of the Jewish nation, was, as we have seen, its acceptance of Jesus as the Messiah, its recognition that His Crucifixion was part of God's eternal purpose, and that the Resurrection was the proof of God's acceptance and approval of His work and claims, and that the Holy Spirit was sent by Jesus to His Church to strengthen, consecrate, and guide. Admission into the society was by baptism, and membership in it was realized ceremonially by the Eucharist, originally celebrated after a common meal. At first the members were known indifferently as the elect, the brotherhood, the believers, the disciples, the saints, but the Church —*ecclesia*—became the most convenient term. It was used to describe the whole body of believers

[1] Dr. Inge in *Quarterly Review*. Oct., 1918.

and also the brethren belonging to a particular place, as the Church at Rome or the Church at Philippi. Its main function was to witness to its Risen Lord. It had no consciousness at first of possessing a superior code of morals, or of being called upon to impress its own idea of righteousness on the world. That was incidental and forced upon it by the contrast between the life of the world and the life that was in Christ. What the Apostles and their first disciples had to tell the world, and in the first place the Jews, was, "The Jesus whom you crucified God has raised up."

They witnessed at first in Jerusalem. And then, when persecution began, they were scattered abroad as far as Phoenicia, Cyprus, and Antioch; and wherever they went they preached the Word.

At Antioch a local Church, the first we hear of outside Jerusalem, soon came into being. The Mother Church at Jerusalem was careful to keep in touch with it. When the rumour comes that a number of Greek proselytes had turned to the Lord, Barnabas was sent forth by the Church which was at Jerusalem. The terms of his commission are not stated, but presumably to investigate and either bless or ban. To Antioch Barnabas brought Saul, and from Antioch the two, accompanied by Mark, went forth on their missionary journey, the first expedition definitely organized for the purpose of witnessing to the Messiah, for which the spring of A.D. 46 may be given as a likely date.

The known history of the Church is during the next ten years the history of S. Paul's great missionary campaigns. He set himself to establish a strategic position in as many Roman provinces as possible, and succeeded in planting a strong local Church in Galatia (Derbe, Lystra, and Iconium), in Asia (Ephesus), in Macedonia, and Achaia.

Besides this we know that the Church was established at Rome. The actual date of its establishment is unknown. But it is not unreasonable to suppose that S. Peter went to Rome on his escape from prison A.D. 42–44. He must have gone somewhere and nowhere could he have found a better hiding-place than in Rome. Moreover we know that there were a number of Roman Jews at Jerusalem, as they were sufficiently numerous to have their own synagogue, the synagogue of the Libertines,[1] and converts from among them could have given him commendatory letters to their friends in Rome. Neither S. Peter or the other Apostles are likely to have been blind to so great an opportunity. If so his visit would not be inconsistant with the very ancient tradition that he presided over the Church in Rome as its first Bishop for a period of some years before his martyrdom. This does not mean of course that his residence was continuous or his supervision unintermittent, nor does it commit us to the support of Vatican claims made later. But whoever first preached in Rome, by

[1] Acts vi. 9.

the time S. Paul's Epistle to the Romans was written, about the year 54, we may assume that by then the Church there was fairly strong. Their faith, we are told, is spoken of throughout the whole world, and he had often meant to visit them but had not had the opportunity. We hear nothing of the Church at Alexandria, but considering the number of Greek-speaking Jews who flocked to Jerusalem for the great feasts there is no reason to doubt the statement of Eusebius, whether or no S. Mark was the founder, that in his lifetime the Church was established there.

The Church spread through official and unofficial missionaries. The Apostles, like Paul and Barnabas, and the evangelists, like Philip the Deacon, went with the express mission of preaching Christ, though not all may have been so aggressive as S. Paul in issuing his challenge first of all in the synagogue itself. But besides these official and recognized evangelists, no doubt every Christian was a missionary. In great centres of population like Rome and Alexandria Christians were there before the Apostle came to organize and establish rather than to found.

II

PERSECUTION—FROM NERO TO MARCUS AURELIUS

UNTIL A.D. 64 the State had no official knowledge of the Church. Judaism was a *religio licita*, that is, a religion which was tolerated by the State, and Christians were regarded as a mere sect of Jews. Of the existence of the Christian Church as a non-Jewish society the State had no knowledge. In the Acts there are two cases of the Church coming into collision with pagans, but in each a private person, not the State, is aggrieved, the motive in both cases being threatened loss of money. There was the slave-girl at Philippi, when " her masters saw that the hope of their gains was gone " ; and Demetrius, the silversmith at Ephesus, fired the mob with the cry, " This our craft is in danger to be set at nought." But unofficially the Christian must have found himself at issue with his pagan neighbours at every turn. He could not go out to dinner, or buy in the market, or attend a wedding, or take a wife, or marry his son or his daughter, or give or receive hospitality, without coming into collision with some heathen custom or observance. S. Paul's advice on marriage by itself would be enough to rouse intense bitterness against those who took it. His counsel, that is, of celibacy as an ideal, and his advice against the marriage of a Christian with a heathen. In the apocryphal *Acts of Paul and Thecla*, which Sir W. Ramsay attributes to the early part of the second century, this appears plainly. Thecla, attracted by the preaching of S. Paul, breaks off her engagement with Thamyris. He, questioning as to Paul's teaching, is told " that he deprives young men of their wives and virgins of their husbands " by inculcating celibacy. Thamyris then resolves to get rid of Paul, and collects a large mob and carries him off to the governor, "and all the multitude cried out, 'Away with this imposter, for he has perverted the minds of our wives, and all the people hearken unto him.'" We are reminded of the cry of the Japanese mob when S. Francis Xavier and the Jesuit missionaries first preached the Gospel there.[1] These things would not all happen to one man in one place, but they were happening to different men wherever Christians had a foothold in any town of the Empire. But for the most part the Roman officials appear as the protectors, not the persecutors, of the Church during the greater part of the New Testament period. The antagonism between pagan and Christian ideals was so great that persecution was inevitable. However, the first

[1] "There go the men who tell us it is wicked to have more than one wife."—Coleridge, *Life of S. Francis Xavier.*

persecution was due to accidental circumstances, namely, the need Nero found for a scapegoat, and the general unpopularity of Christians for reasons already stated.

The fire of Rome occurred A.D. 64. Nero, whether justly or not, was suspected of being the author of the fire. According to Tacitus he screened himself by putting the blame on the Christians. "The infamy of that horrible transaction still adhered to him. In order, if possible, to remove the imputation he determined to transfer the guilt to others. For this purpose he punished with exquisite torture a race of men detested for their evil practices, by a vulgar appellation commonly known as Christians. The name was derived from Christ, Who in the reign of Tiberius suffered under Pontius Pilate, the procurator of Judaea. By that event the sect of which He was the founder received a blow which for a time checked the growth of a dangerous superstition (*exitialis superstitio*); but it revived soon after and spread with recruited vigour, not only in Judaea, the soil that gave it birth, but even in the City of Rome, the common sink into which everything evil and abominable flows like a torrent from all quarters of the world. Nero proceeded with his usual artifice. He found a set of profligate and abandoned wretches who were induced to confess themselves guilty, and on the evidence of such men a number of Christians were convicted, not so much of having set the city on fire as of hatred of the whole human race. Some were covered with the skins of wild beasts and left to be devoured by dogs; others were nailed to the cross; numbers were burnt alive; and many, covered with inflammable matter, were lighted up when the day declined to serve as torches during the night. At length the cruelty of these proceedings filled every breast with compassion. The manners of the Christians were pernicious. Their crimes called for punishment. But it was evident that they fell not for the public good, but to glut the rage and cruelty of an individual." [1]

There appear to be two stages in the persecution. First, Christians are examined by torture, and some confess to incendiarism and reveal the names of other Christians. Secondly, Christians are punished for the crime of being Christians and the hatred of the human race that this crime implied. A great number of people were convicted, not so much on a charge of incendiarism, as on that of " hatred to the human race," that is, presumably for being Christians. No law or edict was necessary for their punishment. They would have come under the head of sacrilegious persons, disturbers of the peace and practisers of magical arts, and their punishment would have been a matter of police administration. [2]

[1] Tac., *Ann.* xv. 44.
[2] For the view that the second stage was not reached until the reign of Vespasian, see Ramsay, *The Church in the Roman Empire*, p. 243.

Christians are evidently not persecuted for the Name, but only for acts of illegality during the time covered by the Epistles of S. James and S. Paul, with the possible exception of 2 Timothy. In 1 S. Peter and in the Apocalypse they are no less clearly punished for the Name.[1]

Among the victims of Nero's persecution were S. Paul, and possibly S. Peter. Caius of Rome, a third-century writer, is quoted by Eusebius as having written: " I can show you the trophies of the Apostles. For if you will go to the Vatican or to the Ostian Way, you will find the trophies of those who have laid the foundation of this church."[2] The tradition is that they perished on the same day, though there is a difficulty in placing the date of S. Peter's First Epistle early enough to allow for this. S. Peter's martyrdom may have taken place A.D. 68, S. Paul's being fixed A.D. 67. Dionysius of Corinth says that they suffered "about the same time," which would cover an interval of two or three years but not longer. According to a very early tradition they suffered on the same day though not in the same year. Bishop Lightfoot has shown that this tradition may have arisen from the fact of their bodies having been transferred on the same day from the cemetery in the Appian Way to a temporary resting-place in the catacombs of S. Sebastian, pending the erection of permanent shrines, for S. Peter at the Vatican,

---

[1] 1 S. Pet. iv. 15, 16; Rev. i. 9, xi. 7.
[2] Eusebius, *H. E.* ii. 25.

and for S. Paul on the Ostian Way. This transference took place 29 June, A.D. 258.

Jerusalem was taken by Titus, A.D. 70, after a siege of appalling fierceness and obstinacy, and its inhabitants were pretty nearly exterminated. It is unlikely that Titus or Vespasian was favourably disposed to Christians after this, as they must have regarded them as having a close connection with the Jews. Sir William Ramsay quotes Sulpicius Severus, the biographer of S. Martin, a writer of the fourth century, as attributing to Titus the advice at a Council of War to destroy the Temple, "in order that the religion of the Jews and the Christians might be more completely exterminated ; for the religions, though opposed to each other, had the same origin. The Christians had arisen from among the Jews ; and when the root was torn up the stem would easily be destroyed." The importance of Sulpicius as a writer is due to his having used Tacitus freely, and here he may be quoting from that writer's lost Histories.

In any case there is good ground for thinking that the persecution begun by Nero did not cease either before or with his death, though it was certainly relaxed. Tacitus, indeed, tells us that the persecution aroused general compassion. So we may assume that the persecution went on spasmodically and fitfully, but never ceasing altogether, until the second great persecution under Domitian, when it broke out with renewed fury. There is no reason to set aside the unanimous tradition that there was such a persecution in this reign. It is supported by the Apocalypse—if we may be allowed to take A.D. 95 as the approximate date of that book—which is plainly written in the white heat of persecution by one who could look back on a considerable period of it, and who saw no hope in reconciliation with the Empire, but only in its destruction. It breathes the very spirit of the persecuted. It is written by one who had been present in the courts when Christians were tried, and in the place of punishment where they were tortured and executed. In this reign, too, the worship of the emperor became specially prominent. Domitian seems to have taken it very seriously, and to have delighted in the title *Dominus et Deus*. His persecution is marked by some names of note. According to Dion Cassius,[1] Flavius Clemens, consul A.D. 95, and his wife Domitilla, niece of the emperor, were tried on a charge of sacrilege and atheism. The word Christian is not mentioned. They were said to have adopted Jewish customs. Clemens was executed and Domitilla banished. Many others were put to death, or punished on the same charge, among them Acilius Glabrio, who had been consul A.D. 91. Clemens and Domitilla were almost certainly Christians,[2] and Domitilla was reverenced as a martyr. Acilius Glabrio was probably a Christian also, and was one of

---

[1] *Hist. Rom.*, xvii. 14.
[2] Ramsay, *C. in R. E.*, p. 261.

many Roman citizens who perished as Christians, A.D. 95. According to Dion, Clemens and Acilius Glabrio were charged with sacrilege or atheism, but according to Suetonius with treason. The explanation may be that the religious charge aroused Domitian's suspicions, and he suspected them of plotting against his life. His motives were most likely political. A Christian who refused to worship the emperor was a traitor and incurred punishment as such.

Domitian was assassinated A.D. 96, and was succeeded by Nerva, under whom there was a lull in the persecution. Dion states that Nerva released those who were waiting their trial for sacrilege.[1] He also allowed the banished to return.

Trajan, A.D. 98–117.

Nerva's short reign came to an end A.D. 98. Trajan, who succeeded, reigned until A.D. 117.

The famous letter of Pliny about the Christians belongs to this reign. Together with Trajan's reply, it throws a flood of light on the relations between the Church and the civil power.

Pliny was the Roman proconsul in Bithynia, A.D. 112, and there came across Christians for the first time, at any rate in an official capacity. He was puzzled as to how they ought to be treated. "I have never been present at the resolutions taken concerning the Christians," he explained, "therefore I know not for what causes or how

[1] *Hist. Rom.*, lxviii. 1.

far they may be objects of punishment, or to what degree our complaints may be carried on against them. . . . Must they be punished for the Name, although otherwise innocent? Or is the Name itself so flagitious as to be punishable?"

Pliny was a distinguished lawyer and public man. He had served in the Army as a military tribune in Syria; he had been quaestor, tribune, and praetor under Domitian, and consul under Trajan. Yet it is possible for him to allege ignorance as to the authorized treatment of the Christians. It may be assumed that the resolutions at the taking of which he had not been present referred to some new orders made by Trajan. But the letter shows that persecution at that date was a very minor matter in the eye of the State. In Rome the Christians had seemed so unimportant that Pliny had not thought it worth while to inform himself as to the right way of dealing with them before he went out to Bithynia to take up his governorship. It was plainly a surprise to him to find how many there were, and that the heathen temples were empty of worshippers in consequence. His procedure, as given in letters to Trajan, was as follows:—

"I have asked them if they were Christians, and to those who have avowed the profession I have put the same question a second and a third time, and have enforced it by threats of punishment. When they have persevered I have ordered them to execution. For I did not doubt that whatever their confession might be, their audacious behaviour and immovable obstinacy required punishment. Some who were infected with the same kind of madness, but were Roman citizens, have been reserved by me to be sent to Rome."

The procedure is plain. Those charged with being Christians were questioned, and, if obdurate, were put to death. Roman citizens were sent to Rome. But matters did not stop there.

"An information without a name was put into my hands containing a list of many persons who deny that they are, or ever were, Christians. Others, also accused by an informer, admitted that they were Christians, or rather had been Christians, but had entirely renounced the error; some three years, some more, some even above twenty. All these worshipped your image and the images of the gods, and they even vented imprecations against Christ; they affirmed that the sum of their fault consisted in assembling upon a stated day before it was light to sing alternately among themselves hymns to Christ as to God; binding themselves by oath not to be guilty of any wickedness; not to steal or to rob; not to commit adultery nor to break their faith when plighted; nor to deny the deposits in their hands when called upon to restore them.

"These ceremonies performed, they usually

departed and came together again to take a repast, the meat of which was innocent and eaten promiscuously; but they had desisted from this custom since my edict wherein, by your commands, I had prohibited all public assemblies.

"From these circumstances I thought it necessary to try to gain the truth, even by torture, from two slave-girls who were called deaconesses. But I could discover only an obstinate kind of superstition carried to great excess."

He goes on:—

"To me an affair of this kind seems worthy of your consideration from the multitude involved in danger. For many persons of all ages, of all degrees, of both sexes, are already and will be constantly brought into danger by these accusations. Nor is this superstitious contagion confined only to the cities; it spreads itself through the villages and the country. As yet, I think it may be stopped and corrected. It is very certain that the temples which were almost deserted now begin to fill again; and the sacred rites which have been a long time neglected are again performed. The victims which hitherto had few purchasers are sold everywhere. From hence we may easily infer also that numbers of people might be reclaimed if there was a proper allowance made for repentance."[1]

[1] *Letters of Pliny*, x. 97.

Certain inferences may legitimately be drawn. There is no specific law against Christianity. Pliny acts under the general police powers given to a Roman governor, among whose most important functions was that of regulating all religious matters, especially those concerned with the worship of the emperor. In doing so he acted as the emperor's deputy, and carried out the general orders issued from head-quarters by his own or a preceding emperor.

It is quite plain that neither Trajan nor Pliny makes any new departure in procedure. Christians were already liable to death "for the Name." Lax administration had left them alone. Pliny revived the persecution, and Trajan approved generally, but somewhat modified his procedure. "If they are brought into your presence and convicted, they must be punished; but with this reservation, that if any one of them has denied himself to be a Christian, and makes his assertion manifest by an invocation of our gods, although he may have been suspected before, his repentance must entitle him to a pardon. But anonymous informations ought not to have the least weight against any crime whatever. They would not only be of dangerous consequence, but are absolutely against the principles of my government." [1]

Christians are not to be hunted out. Anonymous accusations are no more to be received against them than against other people. If they

[1] *Letters of Pliny*, x. 98.

are accused they may recant; but if they obstinately refuse to do so they must die.

The names of two men of note are recorded as having perished under Trajan. One was Simeon, said by Hegesippus to have been the son of the Cleophas who is mentioned in the Gospels, and to have been the second Bishop of Jerusalem. Being accused by heretics, "he was tormented many days, and died a martyr with such firmness that all were amazed, even the president himself, that a man of one hundred and twenty years old should bear such tortures. He was at last ordered to be crucified."[1]

The other was Ignatius, Bishop of Antioch. According to Eusebius[2] he was "the second bishop to carry on the Petrine succession," and was sent from Syria—presumably after being condemned at Antioch—to Rome, and was there cast to the beasts. On his journey through Asia he encouraged the different Churches in the cities where he stayed, and wrote a number of letters. He wrote to the Romans to ask them not to interfere on his behalf, and to desire their prayers. "Only pray for me for strength, both outward and inward, that I may not only speak, but also have the will, that I may not only be called a Christian, but found to be one." Again. "I am writing to all the Churches, and I give injunctions to all men that I am dying willingly for God's sake, if you do not hinder it.

[1] Eusebius, *H. E.* iii. 32.   [2] Ibid., 36.

I beseech you, do me not an unseasonable kindness. Suffer me to be eaten by the beasts, through whom I can attain to God. I am God's wheat, and I am ground by the teeth of wild beasts that I may be found pure bread of Christ. . . . From Syria to Rome I am fighting with wild beasts, by land and sea, by night and day, bound to 'ten leopards,' and they become worse for kind treatment. Now I become the more a disciple for their ill deeds, ' but not by this am I justified.' I long for the beasts that are prepared for me, and I pray that they may be found prompt for me. . . . Grant me this favour. I know what is expedient for me; now I am beginning to be a disciple. May nothing of things seen or unseen envy me my attaining to Jesus Christ. Let there come upon me fire and cross and struggles with wild beasts, cutting and tearing asunder, rackings of bones, mangling of limbs, crushing of my whole body, cruel tortures of the devil if I may but attain to Jesus Christ."

These are the words of an heroic soul, impatient and ambitious to drink the cup his Master drank of, conscious, perhaps, of his own weakness and the natural shrinking of the flesh. It is not that he loves life less, but that he loves Jesus more.

HADRIAN, A.D. 117–138

So far as the Church was concerned, the reign of Hadrian was comparatively uneventful. He seems to have discouraged persecution. That, at least, is the impression made by his rescript to Minucius Fundanus, who was Proconsul of Asia about A.D. 124, twelve years after Trajan dispatched his famous rescript to Pliny. The effect of it was decidedly to restrain the ardour of persecutors. Christians may be accused in the courts, but it must be by a formal accusation made by a prosecutor, not by a popular outcry by a mob. If the accuser proves that the accused has done anything contrary to the law he is to be punished proportionably to his offence. But if the prosecution turns out to be unfounded and malicious the prosecutor is to be punished severely.

We see by this that prosecutions are permitted rather than encouraged. That in any prosecution there has to be a definite prosecutor, who may be punished if his case fails. One clause is ambiguous, perhaps deliberately. If Christians are proved to have done anything contrary to the laws they are to be punished; but it is not clear whether being a Christian is in itself an illegal act or no. Probably it was left intentionally to the discretion of the magistrate.

Antoninus Pius, A.D. 138–161

Antoninus Pius seems to have continued the policy of Hadrian. Eusebius [1] records that he wrote to the Larissaeans, Thessalonians, Athenians, and all the Greeks, forbidding any

[1] Eusebius, *H. E.* iv. 26.

disorderly procedure against the Christians. In spite of the imperial policy outbreaks took place. The martyrdom of Polycarp at Smyrna, A.D. 155, is a conspicuous instance.

Polycarp was born about the year A.D. 70, and was said by Irenaeus, who saw him in his youth, "to have been established as Bishop of Smyrna by the Apostles." Tertullian adds that the Apostle who established him was S. John. Irenaeus is quoted by Eusebius as having put down his own youthful recollection of him in a letter written to the heretic Florinus :—

"I can even describe the place where the blessed Polycarp used to sit and discourse, his general mode of life and personal appearance; his discourses to the multitude, how he would speak of his familiar intercourse with John and with the rest of those who had seen the Lord; and how he would call their words to remembrance." [1]

He visited Rome when Anicetus was bishop to confer with him on the controversy respecting the right day for keeping Easter. Anicetus was the bishop who succeeded Pius, the brother of Hermas. They could not agree about Easter, but he turned many heretics from their error to the true faith, and Anicetus "conceded to Polycarp the Eucharist by way of showing him respect," by which phrase we are to understand that Anicetus permitted Polycarp to celebrate the Eucharist in his presence. His martyrdom

[1] Eusebius, *H. E.* v. 20.

Persecution—From Nero to Marcus Aurelius

was the last act of a persecution which took place in the year A.D. 155 or A.D. 156 at Smyrna. The details of his passion are given in a letter from the Church at Smyrna to the Church at Philomelium, and "to all the Holy Catholic Churches," written immediately after the event from which the account given below is taken, for the most part in a literal translation of the actual words of the Smyrnaeans.

There had been several martyrs who had withstood torments and the wild beasts, including Germanicus, a youth whom the proconsul pitied and tried to save. Only one apostatized— Quintus, a Phrygian, "who had forced himself and some others to come forward of their own accord," but whose heart failed him when he saw the beasts. The crowd then cried out "Away with the atheists! Let Polycarp be searched for!" Polycarp, when he heard it "wished to remain in the city, but the majority persuaded him to go away, and he went out quietly to a farm not far distant and stayed with a few friends, doing nothing but pray night and day for all, and for the Churches throughout the world, as was his custom." The search persisted, so he moved to another farm. A slave under torture betrayed his hiding-place. Late in the evening they came to the house. He might have escaped then, but would not, saying, "The will of God be done." He went down and talked with them, and ordered food to be set before them, and asked them to allow him one hour in which he might pray undisturbed. " To this," in the words of the letter of the Church of Smyrna, " they assented, and he stood and prayed, being so filled with the grace of God that for two hours he could not be silent, and those who heard were astonished, and many repented that they had come against such a venerable old man." "Now when he had at last finished his prayer," the letter goes on, " having remembered all whom he had ever met —small and great, high and low, and the whole Catholic Church throughout the world — the hour arrived for his departure. They set him on an ass, and led him into the city, it being a great Sabbath day. And there met him Herod, the head of the police, and his father Nicetes. They placed him in their carriage, and, sitting by him, began to persuade him, saying 'What harm is there in saying "Lord Caesar," and offering sacrifice and so forth, and saving yourself?' At first he did not answer them, but when they persisted, he said 'I am not going to do what you advise.' So they gave up trying to persuade him, and began to speak fiercely to him, and turned him out with such haste that, in getting out of the carriage, he scraped his shin; and, without turning round, as though unhurt, he walked on at once quickly, and was brought to the arena, where the uproar was so great that nothing could be heard. When Polycarp entered the arena a voice was heard from heaven, saying 'Be strong, Polycarp, and play the man!' No one saw the speaker, but our friends who were present heard the voice. When he was brought forward there was a great uproar from those who heard that Polycarp had been arrested. The proconsul asked him if he were Polycarp, and when he admitted it, he tried to persuade him to deny, saying 'Respect your age,' and suchlike things as they are accustomed to say—'Swear by the genius of Caesar. Think better of it. Say "Away with the atheists."' But Polycarp, with a stern countenance, looked on all the crowd of lawless heathen, and, waving his hand at them, groaned, and, looking up to heaven, said 'Away with the atheists!' The proconsul pressed him and said 'Swear and I release you. Curse Christ.' Polycarp said 'Eighty and six years have I served Him, and He never did me wrong. How can I blaspheme my King Who saved me?'"

The proconsul tried threats. "I have wild beasts at hand, and I will cast you to them unless you change your mind." He answered "Call them." The proconsul: "If you despise the beasts I will have you burnt." Polycarp: "You threaten fire that burns for a moment, but you know nothing of the judgement to come and the fire that burns for ever. Bring what you will."

"And with these and many other words," the account continues, "he was filled with courage and joy, and his face was full of grace so that not only did it not fall in trouble at the things said to him, but that the proconsul, on the other

F

hand, was astounded, and sent his herald into the midst of the arena to announce three times 'Polycarp has confessed that he is a Christian.' When this had been said by the herald all the multitude of heathen and Jews living in Smyrna cried out with uncontrollable wrath and a loud shout 'This is the teacher of Asia, the father of the Christians, the destroyer of our gods, who teaches multitudes neither to offer sacrifice nor to worship!' And when they had said this they cried out and asked Philip the Asiarch to loose a lion on Polycarp. But he said he could not legally do this since he had closed the games. Then they cried out with one voice that he should burn Polycarp alive; for the vision which had appeared to him on his pillow must be fulfilled, when he saw it burning while he was praying; and he turned and said prophetically to those of the faithful who were with him, 'I must be burnt alive.'"

These things happened more quickly than it takes to tell, and the crowd gathered immediately and got ready wood and faggots from the workshops and baths, the Jews being extremely zealous, as is their custom, in assisting at this. When the fire was ready he put off his clothes, loosened his girdle, and tried to take off his shoes, which he had not been accustomed to do before because the faithful vied with one another in doing this for him. So great was the respect he had been treated with, even before his martyrdom, because of his noble life. When about to be nailed to the stake he said "Leave me thus, for He Who gives me power to endure the fire will grant me to remain unmoved in the flames even without the nails." When bound he looked up to heaven and said "O Lord God Almighty, Father of Thy beloved and blessed Child, Jesus Christ, through whom we have received knowledge of Thee, the God of angels and powers and all creation, and of the whole family of the righteous who live in Thy sight; I bless Thee that Thou hast granted me this day and hour that I may share among the number of the martyrs in the cup of Thy Christ for the resurrection to eternal life of soul and body in the immortality of the Holy Spirit. And may I be received among them before Thee as a rich and acceptable sacrifice, as Thou the God Who lies not and art truth hast prepared beforehand and shown forth and fulfilled. Wherefore I praise Thee for all things, I bless Thee, I glorify Thee through the eternal and heavenly High Priest Jesus Christ, Thy beloved Child, through whom be glory to Thee, with Him and the Holy Spirit, now and throughout the ages. Amen."

The fire then blazed up, but did not consume him, and he was dispatched with a dagger. His disciples begged for his body, but were refused; Nicetes, at the request of the Jews, asking the governor not to give the body, "lest they leave the Crucified and begin to worship this man." The letter remarks that this was impossible. "For Him we worship as the Son of God, but

the martyrs we love as disciples and imitators of the Lord."
The body was burned, but the bones were gathered up and hidden where " the Lord will permit us to meet according to our ability in gladness and joy to celebrate the birthday of his martyrdom." [1]

MARCUS AURELIUS, 161–180

Antoninus Pius had adopted, by the desire of Hadrian, a youth of seventeen, already a professed Stoic philosopher, who succeeded him A.D. 161, and is known to fame as Marcus Aurelius. He is the classical instance of a philosopher on a throne. " His virtue," Gibbons says, "was the well-earned harvest of many a learned conference, of many a patient lecture, and many a midnight lucubration." It might indeed seem to have been more congenial to the lecture-room than to the senate or the camp.; and he did, in fact, lecture publicly on philosophy in Greece, in Asia, and in Rome. Nevertheless he was a conscientious and painstaking emperor, and as a general fought several by no means inglorious campaigns on the Danube against the Quadi and Marcommanni.
He wrote a book of meditations, called a *Discourse with himself*, which has become famous

[1] See the letter of the Church of God abiding in Smyrna to the Church of God dwelling in Philomelium.—Bishop Lightfoot, *Apostolic Fathers*, vol. iii, part ii.

and is still widely sold. It is perhaps not beyond the mark to say that hardly any book has enjoyed so great a reputation among those who have not read it.

The austere standard of morals which the writer sets before him in this book he strenuously endeavoured to carry out, and not unsuccessfully. He has been canonized, if the use of the term may be permitted, by the general acclaim of historians, and he may safely be regarded as the fine flower of pagan virtue.

His character is, however, very unlike that of the Christian saint. The difference consists mainly in the fact that the pagan tends more and more to be centred in himself; the Christian makes it his great aim to escape from himself. Both exercise a rigid self-discipline, but Marcus that he may be master in his own house; S. Paul —if S. Paul may be taken as a type of Christian saintliness—that he may render his body an obedient instrument to the Spirit; in other words that not himself, but Christ, may rule there.

The author of the meditations records with complacency a catalogue of his own virtues. S. Paul, though on one occasion controversy led him into the foolishness, as he called it, of doing the same, is careful to explain that he had no pride in these things, but preferred to glory in his infirmities, because the strength of God had its opportunity in his own weakness. One is to be saved by his own unassisted efforts. The other cries out for deliverance and finds it in

Jesus Christ crucified. One finds his life by seeking it with extraordinary diligence and resolution; the other by an almost reckless readiness to cast it away.

Gibbon finds in "the mildness of Marcus" the only defective part of his character. Unfortunately for the Christians, this mildness, though it covered the gallantries of an erring wife, was not extended to them.

Nor is this surprising. He was a devout adherent of the ancient gods, and apparently a serious believer in the worship of the emperors. At his request his erring wife Faustina was declared a goddess by the senate, and it was decreed that newly married couples should pay their vows at her shrine.[1] He was too of an over-conscientious, not to say scrupulous and worrying disposition, to whom the almost easy-going tolerance of his predecessors was impossible. Unlike them he could never have rested on the illogical position that though it was criminal to be a Christian, no steps need be taken to stamp out the crime; that the magistrate was to turn a blind eye unless his attention were called to it.

Celsus speaks of them as being sought out and punished with death.[2]

Melito, Bishop of Sardis, wrote about A.D. 170–171, in a remonstrance to the emperor:—

"What indeed never happened before, the race of the pious is now persecuted, driven

[1] *Hist. Rom.*, lxxi. 31.
[2] Origen, *Against Celsus*, viii. 69.

about in Asia by new and strange decrees. For the shameless, informers, and coveters of other men's goods, taking opportunity from the edicts of the emperor, openly perpetrate robbery."[1]

Athenagoras (A.D. 177–180) also remonstrated with the emperor, "You allow us to be harassed, plundered, persecuted, for our name alone."[2]

No doubt the change was due directly or indirectly to the emperor. At the same time the story of the so-called Thundering Legion seems to point to a change of attitude towards the end of the reign.

The facts seem certain. Marcus Aurelius in one campaign, probably A.D. 174, in his German wars, was surrounded by his enemies and without water when a timely thunderstorm saved him and his troops. The Twelfth Legion, Fulminata (Thunderstruck), was present, and this legion probably contained a large number of Christian soldiers, as it was recruited in Asia Minor, in the Melitene district, where Christians are known to have been numerous. The event was considered miraculous at the time, and by Christians was attributed to the prayers of the Christian soldiers. Dion Cassuis records a rumour that the rain was the work of an Egyptian magician. Marcus Aurelius had a medal struck to commemorate the event, on which it is credited to Jupiter Pluvius. Tertullian[3] insists that Marcus himself (in a letter to the Senate) gave the prayers of his Christian soldiers

[1] Eusebius, *H. E.* iv. 26.
[2] *Plea for the Christians*, i.   [3] *Ap.* 5.

credit for this deliverance, and that in consequence the execution of the persecuting laws was relaxed and unjust accusers were severely punished. Tertullian was, we can hardly doubt, writing in good faith as he was addressing his Apology to the Senate, who must have known what had happened. It would have been a singularly useless lie for him to have called their attention to a letter which Marcus had written to them, if they knew perfectly well that he had done nothing of the kind. He may have been mistaken, though he wrote only twenty-three years after the event. If he is correct there must have been a relaxation of persecution for which we have no other evidence. Meantime, pending further evidence, it is best to suspend judgement.

The best-known victim of the persecution was Justin Martyr, who with six companions perished at Rome early in the reign, when Rusticus was Prefect of Rome, which office he assumed at the end of the year A.D. 163 and held until A.D. 167. To him Rusticus said " What training and education have you had ? "

Justin. " I have endeavoured to acquaint myself with all systems of philosophy and every branch of learning. But at last I attached myself to Christianity."

Rusticus. " Are you pleased with that philosophy ? "

Justin. " Yes."

Rusticus. " What is their teaching ? "

Justin. " The true teaching that all Christians

hold is that we believe there is one God, Maker and Creator of all things, visible and invisible, and the Lord Jesus Christ we confess to be the Son of God—announced beforehand by the prophets—Who is come to judge the human race."

The prefect then asked where they met.

Justin. "We meet wherever we can. The God of the Christians is not confined by place, but being invisible He fills earth and heaven, and He is adored and His glory praised by the faithful everywhere."

Rusticus. "Come, tell me where you and your disciples meet."

Justin. "Up to now I have stayed near the house of one Martin by the Tomotianian baths. To all who have come to me to learn about Christianity I have taught the true doctrine."

Rusticus. "Are you a Christian?"

Justin. "Indeed I am."

The same question was asked of his five companions, Chariton, Charitana, Evelpisto a Cappadocian, Hierax a Phrygian from Iconium, and Paeon, and the same answer given.

Then the prefect turned to Justin and said, "You are reputed to be eloquent, and think you hold the true teaching; if you are beaten to death do you believe you will ascend into heaven?"

Justin. "I hope if I suffer the punishment you speak of that I shall have what they have who keep the commands of Christ."

Rusticus. "Do you think that in the future

you will ascend the sky and receive some reward?"

Justin. " I do not think ; I know. I hold it so certain that I have no doubt."

The prefect then urged them to sacrifice, but they all refused.

Rusticus. " Unless you obey my commands you shall be punished without mercy."

Justin. " For the sake of our Lord Jesus Christ we pray that we may endure punishment and be saved." [1]

They were then led away, scourged, and afterwards dispatched with the axe. Their remains were collected by their friends and buried secretly.

The principal scenes of martyrdom, so far as is known, were Lyons and Vienne in Gaul. There the Christians were first boycotted " so that we should not only be excluded from houses and baths and markets, but everything belonging to us was prohibited from appearing in any place whatever," and then mobbed, when we read that " they nobly bore all the evils that were heaped upon them by the populace, clamours and blows, plundering and robberies, stonings and imprisonments—everything that a savage people could delight to inflict upon enemies." They were then brought before the governor, who asked if they were Christians, and those that confessed were condemned to torture and death.

One of the brethren, Vittias Epagathus, not himself charged, asked to be heard in defence of

[1] From Ruinart, *Acta Martyrum Sincera.*

Persecution—From Nero to Marcus Aurelius 43

the accused. He was asked if he was a Christian; he confessed and was condemned. Of the first martyrs, ten we are told fell away, though most of them afterwards seem to have withdrawn their denial and suffered accordingly. The rest were steadfast throughout.

A reign of terror seems now to have set in, fresh arrests being made daily until all the zealous members of the two Churches were in prison. Popular frenzy was even further aroused by the confessions of some heathen slaves belonging to the brethren, who under fear of torture accused their masters of infanticide, incest, and other horrible crimes. After this, we are told, the martyrs endured tortures beyond description.

One of the martyrs, a slave named Blandina, was conspicuous for her courage and the heroism with which she defied her tormentors and encouraged her brethren. "While we were all trembling, and her earthly mistress, who was herself one of the contending martyrs, was afraid lest through the weakness of her flesh she should not be able to profess her faith with boldness, Blandina was filled with such power that her ingenious tormentors, who relieved and succeeded each other all day, confessed that they were beaten. . . . But this blessed saint, as a noble wrestler, repeated 'I am a Christian; no wickedness is committed by us.'"[1]

Sanctus, a deacon of the Church of Lyons, replied to every question as to his name, city,

[1] Eusebius, *H. E.* v. 1.

nation, and status : "I am a Christian," and when every other torture had been tried, red-hot plates were fixed to the most sensitive parts of his body, but he remained unshaken.

Pothinus, the aged Bishop of Lyons, though over ninety, was brought before the tribunal, and died two days later in prison from the effect of the violence with which he had been treated.

When the games began the Christians were exhibited in place of gladiators. Blandina, bound and suspended to a stake, and exposed as food to the wild beasts, had the appearance of being crucified, and by her example and prayers encouraged greatly the other martyrs. "For as they saw her, their sister, they contemplated Him that was crucified for them to persuade those that believe in Him that every one who suffers for Christ will for ever enjoy communion with the living God." But as none of the beasts would touch her she was taken back to prison.

The governor who had condemned Attalus to the beasts, had respited him on learning that he was a Roman citizen until he could get instructions from Rome, but in response to the clamours of the mob sent him to the arena the next day, together with a Phrygian physician named Alexander, who had declared himself by standing at the tribunal and encouraging the accused. Attalus was roasted on an iron chair. On the last day Blandina was brought forth with Ponticus, a youth of fifteen, who, encouraged by her, bore the worst tortures and gave up his life. "But the blessed Blandina, last of all, as a noble mother that had animated her children and sent them on before her as victors to the great King, herself retracing the ground of all the conflicts her children had endured, hastened at last to them with joy and exultation at the issue as if she were invited to a marriage feast, and not to be cast to wild beasts. And thus, after scourging, after exposure to the beasts, after roasting, she was finally thrown into a net and cast before a bull, and was tossed by him and then dispatched." The sufferings of Blandina as of other martyrs seems almost beyond the possibility of human endurance. A belief seems to have been current in the Early Church that some measure of unconsciousness was permitted them. Eusebius says that Blandina after a certain point had no longer any consciousness of what was done on account of her " pious hope, confidence, faith, and fellowship with Christ."

It is noteworthy that their persecutors took great pains to destroy the bodies. Guard was kept so that the mangled remains should neither be buried nor carried away, and in the end those that were not eaten by the wild beasts were burnt and the ashes cast into the Rhone. "Now we shall see whether they will rise again, and whether their God is able to help them and rescue them out of our hands." Another taunt was "Where is their God, and what good has their religion been to them, which they preferred to their own life?"[1]

[1] Eusebius, *H. E.* v. 1.

III

GNOSTICS, MONTANISTS

The Gnostics

BESIDES persecution the Church had to face other and more insidious dangers. There were perils of the intellect and of the spirit, as well as of the flesh. The first were due principally to those keen and subtle intellects—for the most part outside the Church—who scorned the simplicity of the Gospel, dismissed the statements of the Creed as childish fables to be interpreted in a non-natural sense, and produced elaborate systems of their own, which are meaningless to us but seem to have made a strong appeal to the intellectuals of that day. These were the Gnostics. In contrast to them there arose hot-headed zealots within the fold, who demanded a stricter discipline and more sensible fruits of the Spirit than the Church of their day could show, and threatened disruption if their demands were not granted. They were the followers of Montanus, afterwards known as Montanists.

Gnosticism was not so much a religion as a philosophy which attempted to answer the question "Why does evil exist?" The Gnostics held various opinions, but on one point they all seem to have been agreed, namely, that matter was essentially evil, and that if evil did not originate in matter it was inextricably involved in it. The material world was therefore an evil thing, and the Supreme Being must be disconnected from it as far as possible. This was done by interposing a whole series of emanations or aeons between the Supreme Being and the Creator, Who was generally regarded as a more or less maleficent deity, and frequently identified with the God of the Old Testament.

Simon Magus, the Samaritan sorcerer as he is described in the Acts, who was baptized by S. Philip the deacon, but was afterwards rejected and cursed by S. Peter, was looked upon by Catholic writers as the Father of Gnostics. He figures largely in the ecclesiastical romances of the early Church, but except for this brief appearance in the Acts he remains for us a personage of romance rather than of history. Menander, another Samaritan, his disciple, said that the Supreme Being was unknown and that he himself was the Saviour.

Cerinthus is one of the earliest of whom we have any real knowledge. He lived in Asia, and was a contemporary of S. John. Polycarp used to relate that "John, the disciple of the Lord, went into a bath at Ephesus, and seeing Cerinthus within ran out without bathing, and exclaimed,

'Let us flee, lest the bath should fall in while Cerinthus, that enemy of truth, is within.'"[1] He taught that Jesus was born of Joseph and Mary in the ordinary course of human generation, and that after His baptism the Christ descended upon Him in the form of a dove from the Supreme Ruler, and that He then proclaimed the Father and worked miracles. When Jesus suffered, Christ left Him, being pure spirit and incapable of suffering.[2]

Saturninus was a native of the Syrian Antioch. He taught that the Saviour was without birth, body, or figure, but had the appearance only of a man, and came to destroy the God of the Jews. Some at least of his followers practised an extreme asceticism, abstained from animal food, and taught that marriage and generation are from Satan.

The Nicolaitanes, according to Irenaeus, were the followers of Nicolas, the proselyte of Antioch, who was one of the seven. They were said by Irenaeus to have led lives of unrestrained indulgence, a charge repeated by Tertullian. They appear to have been another early Gnostic sect, and are condemned in the Apocalypse.

Tatian, once the disciple of Justin, seems afterwards to have belonged to the school of the Encratites, and preached against marriage and the use of animal food.

Basilides taught at Alexandria in the reign of

[1] Eusebius, *H. E.* iii. 28.
[2] Irenaeus, *Against Heresies*, i. 26.

Hadrian. Besides the usual categories of aeons he maintained that Christ was a man only in appearance, that Christ did not suffer on the Cross, but Simon of Cyrene in His likeness, while Jesus ascended unseen to the Father.

Carpocrates was another founder of a school. His followers are accused of practising magical arts and leading licentious lives, and so bringing dishonour on the Church. The heathen " seeing the things they practise speak evil of us all, who have in fact no fellowship with them, either in doctrine or morals." [1]

Marcion, perhaps the most formidable of all the Gnostics, is said to have been the son of a Christian bishop and to have been brought up as a Christian. His system is perverted Christianity rather than heathenism with Christian additions. He was a native of Pontus, and Tertullian, who wrote a treatise against him in five books, indulges in many sarcasms at the expense of the climate of Pontus, the manners, the morals, the habits, and the civilization of its inhabitants, and concludes that " nothing in Pontus is so barbarous and sad as the fact that Marcion was born there." He also calls him a ship-master, but that is possibly only a term of abuse. He tells us that Marcion came to Rome in the time of Eleutherus as a Christian, with a large sum of money as a present for the Roman Church ; that with Valentinus he was more than once expelled " on account of their ever restless

[1] Irenaeus, *Against Heresies*, i. 25.

curiosity, with which they infected the brethren," and they were finally permanently excommunicated, Marcion's money being returned.[1] They then spread their doctrines abroad.

Tertullian's dates are possibly wrong, and it is more probable that Marcion taught at Rome under Anicetus. According to Tertullian he taught that the God of the Old Testament, " the author of evils, delighted in war, was infirm of purpose, and contradicted Himself." That Jesus came from the Propator or first aeon, and was manifested in the form of a man, and that the body was incapable of salvation. He mutilated the Scriptures to make them fit his theories. Of the Gospels he only recognized S. Luke's, and that in a mutilated form. Like some later writers, he rejected the first two chapters entirely, beginning thus : " In the fifteenth year of Tiberius Caesar God descended into Capernaum, a city of Galilee." He treated the rest of the books of the New Testament in the same way, his object throughout being to show that his Christ was not only an improved version of the Catholic Christ, but had come from a previously unknown God, having no connection with the Creator, the God of the Old Testament.

Marcion has laid down the position that Christ, Who in the days of Tiberius was revealed for the salvation of all nations by a previously unknown God, is a different Being from Him Who was

[1] Tert., *Against Marcion*, iv. 3.

ordained by God the Creator for the restoration of the Jewish State. To show his critical method one instance may be given. The words "a spirit hath not bones as ye see Me have" are changed into " a spirit, such as ye see Me to be, hath not bones."[1] Marcion also forbade marriage as being impure ; and ordained that no one might be admitted to baptism unless living in a state of celibacy. His followers were very much in earnest, and there were martyrs among them. One of them, Asclepius, was burned alive at Caesarea in the persecution of Diocletian.[2]

Valentinus came from Egypt to Rome, and, according to Tertullian, expected to be made a bishop, " because he was an able man both in genius and eloquence. But being passed over for a confessor he broke with the Church."[3]

Irenaeus[4] has given a pretty full account of the Valentinian tenets which were held in Gaul in his day. They called their deities aeons, and believed in a Pleroma or fullness of thirty aeons, all apparently deriving their descent from one pre-existent and eternal aeon. The last of the aeons, who was called Sophia or Achamoth, fell a prey to passion, and at last gave birth to the Demiurge, who created the visible world, and is the Father and God of everything outside the Pleroma. He is the God of the Old Testament.

---

[1] Tert., *Against Marcion*, iv. 43.
[2] Eusebius, *Martyrs of Palestine*, x.
[3] Tert., *Against the Valentinians*.
[4] Irenaeus, *Against Heresies*, i. 1.

The Pleroma is separated from the rest of the universe by Horus or Stauros. The Demiurge created the material part of man, but his mother infused her spiritual essence into him unknown to the Demiurge.

Men were divided into three classes :—

First, the animal man, who was incapable of salvation; secondly, the natural man, who can be saved by working. "We of the Church are such persons."[1] Thirdly, spiritual men, who cannot be lost. Like gold which, however much submerged in filth, retains its nature uncorrupted, so no conduct can injure their spiritual substance. They must, however, be perfected by knowledge. Irenaeus asserts that "the most perfect" among them made no scruple of taking part in idolatrous festivals, and do not even keep away from gladiatorial shows, "that bloody spectacle hateful both to God and man."[2] That others gave themselves up to the lusts of the flesh, maintaining that carnal things should be allowed to the carnal nature and spiritual things to the spiritual. Christ was the Son of the Demiurge and passed through Mary as water through a tube, but the Saviour, Who was the creation of the united Pleroma, descended on Him at His baptism and left Him when He appeared before Pilate.

This brief and imperfect sketch does not perhaps represent so much the teaching of Valentinus as that of the Valentinians known to Irenaeus in

[1] Irenaeus, *Against Heresies*, i. 6.   [2] Ibid.

Gaul. There were many other sects and schools of Gnostics—Ophites, who paid honour to serpents; Cainites, who venerated Cain; Sethites, who had a devotion for Seth; and others. There is a family likeness among all their beliefs.

The Church, like the Gnostics, had to face the problem of evil. Unlike them, it offered no solution, but held out the hope that evil might be overcome by presenting a new revelation of the character of God as shown in the Incarnation, the Passion, and the Resurrection. Like Celsus and Porphyry and the pagan philosophers, the Gnostics found this way of meeting the difficulty too simple and childish. They were the rationalists and intellectuals of their day, and tried to work out a scheme that would meet all difficulties. Christians were branded by them as the " simple people." They taught salvation by knowledge rather than by the Cross or even by works. Some of them, of whom Marcion was one, perhaps made an honest attempt to restate the Gospel in the light of the intellectual needs and perplexities of their day. But most Gnostics approached the Christian Faith from outside, and were philosophers seeking an explanation of the problems of life, and using as much of the Gospel as would serve their purpose—" heresy which is ever mending the Gospel," as Tertullian put it.

The Church defeated them not so much by argument as by relying on the plain facts of our Lord's life as related in the Gospels, and its doctrine of salvation by the Cross. The Catholic teachers saw that to rob the Incarnation of reality was, for the plain man, to evacuate it of meaning.

" For if He did not truly suffer, no thanks to Him, since there was no suffering at all ; and when we shall begin to suffer He will seem to be leading us astray, by exhorting us to endure buffeting and to turn the other cheek, if He did not Himself in reality suffer the same ; and as He misled those who saw Him by seeming to them to be what He was not, so does He also mislead us by exhorting us to endure what He did not endure Himself. We shall be even above the Master because we suffer and sustain what our Master never bore or endured." [1]

THE MONTANISTS

Montanus was a Phrygian, and the Montanists appear as a sect about the middle of the second century. He began, when a recent convert, by " being wrought up into a certain kind of frenzy and irregular ecstasy, raving and speaking and uttering strange things, and proclaiming what was contrary to the tradition and teaching that had prevailed in the Church." [2] This statement, however, is from a hostile pen, that of Apollinarius, Bishop of Hierapolis. The Phrygian mind was congenial, and Montanus soon

[1] Irenaeus, *Against Heresies*, iii. 18.
[2] Eusebius, *H. E.* v. 16.

found followers, among them two women, Maximilla and Priscilla, who prophesied "in a kind of ecstatic frenzy, out of all reason, in a manner strange and novel."[1] It was in the beginning a movement like many Protestant revivals in the Church. It has much in common both with the early history of the Society of Friends and with the beginnings of Methodism. The following account might almost have been written of Montanism:—

"The new Society was a collective protest against the presbyterian" (substitute episcopal) "system as inefficient for purposes of evangelization. Fox's earliest recorded convert was a middle-aged widow at Nottingham, Elizabeth Horton, who became the first woman preacher of the Society. His adherents were soon numbered by thousands . . . ranters, shakers, seekers, and visionaries of all sorts, who brought with them an exuberant emotional piety . . . and a marvellous unrestraint of speech. The community exhibited the signs, mental and physical, of strong religious enthusiasm."[2]

Readers of Dr. Bigg's *Unity in Diversity* will remember his contrast between Mystical Christianity as exemplified by S. Paul and Disciplinary Christianity as taught and practised by S. Peter. Both elements must exist side by side in the Church if it is to be healthy. Man has to be sober and vigilant as well as making melody in

[1] Eusebius, *H. E.* v. 16.
[2] Art. on George Fox, *D. N. B.*

his heart. There must be the belief in the living power of the Spirit, but its manifestations must be disciplined and kept within the bounds of Catholic order. Excess in either direction is bound to provoke reaction. It is possible that with the disappearance of the early Christian prophets the Church relied too much on its regular ministers, its sacraments, its traditional teaching, and its apostolic Scriptures, and too little on the direct inspiration of the Spirit. Hence the opening for Montanism.

The movement spread in Asia, and from Asia to Thrace and the Rhone valley. In A.D. 177 the confessors of Lyons and Vienne sent Irenaeus with a letter against Montanism to Eleutherus, Bishop of Rome. Montanism probably reached Africa about the same time, as Perpetua and her companions (A.D. 203) were probably Montanists, and Tertullian certainly was by that time. They were difficult people to contend with, as their peculiar tenets were supported by the infallible pronouncements of inspired prophets. Maximilla is quoted by an opponent as exclaiming, " I am chased like a wolf from the flock. I am no wolf. I am utterance, spirit, and power."[1] If this is at all characteristic they must have been extravagant, to say the least. Tertullian, it is true, denies that the prophecies contain anything out of harmony with apostolic tradition, but it is doubtful if this safeguard counted for much in practice.

[1] Eusebius, *H. E.* v. 16.

The three main ways in which they differed from Catholic usage were (1) in adding to the fasts of the Church and inventing a new form of abstinence called zerophagy—an abstinence from all except dry foods; (2) in discountenancing marriage and absolutely forbidding second marriages; and (3) in disallowing absolution for mortal sin after baptism. "It is on this account that the new prophecies are rejected; not that Montanus and Priscilla and Maximilla preach another God, nor that they separate Jesus Christ from God, nor that they overturn any particular rule of faith or hope, but that they plainly teach more frequent fasting than marrying. . . . They charge us with keeping fasts of our own; with prolonging our stations into the evening; with keeping our food unmoistened by any flesh and by any juiciness of any kind of succulent fruit; also with abstinence from the bath, suitable to our dry diet."[1]

Second marriage is a kind of adultery. In any case celibacy is preferable to the married state. "Let us see how different a man feels himself when he chances to be deprived of his wife. He savours of the Spirit. If he is praying he is near heaven. If he is studying the Scriptures he is wholly in them. If he is singing a psalm he rejoices in it. If he is exorcising a demon he is confident in himself."[2] Marriage, however, was not forbidden. "We do not reject marriage, but

---
[1] Tert., *On Fasting*, i.
[2] Tert., *Exhortation to Chastity*, x.

simply refrain from it. Nor do we prescribe celibacy as the rule, but only recommend it, observing it as a good, yea even as the better state."

The most serious point of difference was with regard to discipline. The Church was inclined to adopt the teaching of Hermas and allow one penance, followed by absolution, for post-baptismal sin. The Montanists would admit none. This is not to say that the door of hope was to be shut on the sinner, but that he was to be left to the mercies of God and not to be restored to communion. The Church should not take the responsibility of absolving man "for offences which are to be reserved for God, by whom the offences have been condemned, without discharge, which not even Apostles or martyrs have judged condonable." [1]

Tertullian would apparently confine the powers of absolution to the Montanists. "It is to *spiritual* men that this power will appertain, either to an Apostle or else to a prophet. . . . The *Church* will forgive sins, but it will be the Church of the Spirit by means of a spiritual man, not the Church which consists of a number of bishops." [2] But the Church will not use its power by direction of the Spirit. As Tertullian expresses it : "' But,' you say, ' the Church has the power of forgiving sins.' This I acknowledge, who have the Paraclete Himself in the persons of the new prophets, saying 'The Church has the power

[1] Tert., *On Modesty*, 22.   [2] Ibid. xxi.

to forgive sins; but I will not do it, lest they commit others withal.'"[1]

It did not follow that those who became Montanists broke off communion with the Church. On the contrary, it is plain that Perpetua and her companions are in full communion. They are ministered to by a deacon, and have visions of their bishop, Optatus. There seems to have been no breach of communion when Tertullian wrote his treatise *On the Veiling of Virgins*.

After Tertullian they seem to have disappeared in the West. Cyprian calls Tertullian the Master, which he would hardly have done if he had left behind an abiding schism. In the East Montanist baptisms were disallowed by the Councils of Laodicea, *circa* A.D. 367, and Constantinople, A.D. 381. In Phrygia they seem to have been finally crushed by Justinian, when the last remnants gathered themselves, with their wives and children, into the church, set fire to the buildings, and so perished.

It is difficult to estimate the ultimate influence and effect of the Montanists. Professor Gwatkin[2] would trace the decline of preaching after the fifth century to its being discredited through their failure. This seems to give too long an interval between cause and effect. Montanism had passed its zenith by A.D. 250. As late as A.D. 375, which is the earliest possible date for the Apostolic Constitutions, we find the sermon

[1] Tert., *On Modesty*, xxi.
[2] *Early Church History*, ii. 94.

occupying a recognized and important place in the Sunday Eucharist. There is in fact little, if any, evidence to show what the effect of Montanism was. We may, however, be fairly sure that its tendency was to screw up the ascetic discipline of the Church, and give a great impetus to a movement already begun in the direction of celibacy and more stringent fasting.

IV

SOME CHRISTIAN WRITERS FROM CLEMENT TO TERTULLIAN

OF the Christian writings outside the Canon of the New Testament which belong to the first century we have the *First Epistle of Clement*, a letter addressed to the Church at Corinth probably between A.D. 95 and A.D. 100. There had been trouble in the Corinthian Church, certain presbyters had been deposed, and the Church of Rome sent this letter to protest against " the abominable and unholy sedition." Clement's name is not mentioned, but tradition has imputed the authorship to him. The early episcopal lists make him out to have been Bishop of Rome at the end of the first century, so the ascription of authorship is probably well founded. The letter is Pauline in style and devout in tone.

The *Didaché*, or Teaching of the Twelve Apostles, was only discovered in 1875, though there are several references to it (or some similar work) in early Christian literature.

It consists of two parts :—

1. The "Two Ways": a manual of the principles of Christian behaviour to be taught to catechumens.

2. A series of instructions on worship, Baptism, fasting, the Eucharist, the treatment of prophets, Apostles, and itinerant Christians generally.

Its date is uncertain ; it may very well be a later compilation from earlier documents. The ethical part, the " Two Ways," is found also in the *Epistle of Barnabas* and elsewhere, and is probably derived originally from Jewish sources. The *Didaché* is probably the earliest of the numerous " Church Orders," as they are called, or manuals of worship and morals, which have come down, and of which some account will be given later.

The *Epistle of Barnabas*, as it is called, though like the Epistle of Clement anonymous, may probably be attributed to the end of the first or the beginning of the second century. Its aim is to show that the Old Testament Scriptures are to be understood in an allegorical sense. For instance, the command not to eat pork is really a command not to consort with men who are like swine. Law and prophets alike not only are fulfilled in Christ, but apparently were never meant to have any literal fulfilment, except so far as they are literally fulfilled in Him. The writer evidently wished to combat the argument that the ex-Jewish ceremonial law is literally binding on Christians. The book concludes with the " Two Ways," very much as in the *Didaché*. It had great authority in the early Church and was for some time—at any rate in some circles—accounted canonical. Clement of Alexandria reckoned it so. Origen referred to it as a Catholic Epistle, and it is included in the *Codex Sinaiticus* among the books of the New Testament.

Papias, Bishop of Hierapolis, a contemporary of Ignatius, was reported by Irenaeus to have been the author of a work in five books, of which only a few fragments remain. Eusebius says he was "very limited in his comprehension, as is evident from his discourses," but if not a companion of the Apostles, he took trouble to learn from those who had been.

> "If I met with any one who had been a follower of the elders anywhere, I made it a point to inquire what were the declarations of the elders? What was said by Andrew, Peter, and Philip? What by Thomas, James, John, Matthew, or any other of the disciples of our Lord? What was said by Aristion and the presbyter John, disciples of the Lord?" [1]

What would we not give now for the collections of this unvalued Boswell! Eusebius notes here that there are two Johns mentioned by Papias—the Apostle and the Presbyter. "So that it is proved that the statement of those is true who assert that there were two of the same name in Asia, and that there were two tombs in Ephesus, and that both are called 'John's' even to this day." From which he concludes that the Revelation, if not written by the Apostle, was written by John the Presbyter. He seems to have been a millennarian, believing there would be a

[1] Eusebius, *H. E.* iii. 39.

millennium after the Resurrection, when Christ would reign on earth; and Eusebius says this was "the cause why most of the ecclesiastical writers were carried away by a similar opinion."

Papias records, on the authority of John the Presbyter, that S. Mark was the interpreter of S. Peter, and "whatsoever he recorded he wrote with great accuracy, but not in the order in which it was spoken or done by our Lord, for he neither heard nor followed the Lord; but, as before said, he was in company with Peter, who gave him such instruction as was necessary, but not to give our Lord's discourses arranged systematically." Of S. Matthew's Gospel he wrote: "Matthew wrote his discourses in the Hebrew dialect, and every one translated it as he was able." He quoted the First Epistle of S. John and that of Peter.[1]

Ignatius, the Bishop of Antioch, who was martyred during the reign of Trajan, was the author of several letters, the number and genuineness of which has been much disputed. Eusebius says that he wrote seven while travelling from Antioch to Rome; four from Smyrna to the Ephesians, Magnesians, Trallians, and Romans, and three from Troas to the Philadelphians, Smyrnaeans, and Polycarp. But in the Western Church from the first half of the ninth century, when a Latin version first appeared, the accepted edition contained six additional letters. Archbishop Ussher discovered the Greek manuscripts of an edition containing

[1] Eusebius, H. E. iii. 31.

Some Christian writers from Clement to Tertullian

only the seven mentioned by Eusebius. He was able to prove that the six additional letters were forgeries, and that the forger had also made considerable additions to the seven genuine letters. There the matter rested until 1844, when Canon Cureton published a Syriac edition containing three of the seven letters only, and these in an abbreviated form. Bishop Lightfoot has, however, shown to the satisfaction of the majority of critics that the middle rescension of Archbishop Ussher, and not the abbreviated edition of Canon Cureton, is correct, and that the additions of the long rescension were the work of a fourth-century forger.[1]

Of these letters, those to the Ephesians, the Magnesians, the Trallians, and the Philadelphians were written to acknowledge deputations consisting of the bishop and a deacon from each of those Churches which had visited him and brought him messages of comfort and greeting. The letter to the Church of Smyrna is an acknowledgement of his stay there, and so is the letter to Polycarp.

Through all certain preoccupations run like threads of a pattern.

1. The need of unity. Unity depends on each Church cleaving to its bishop, surrounded by his presbyters and deacons. No other unity is possible.

"Therefore it is necessary that you should do

[1] The question is discussed at length by Bishop Lightfoot, *Apostolic Fathers*, vol. i, pt. 2.

nothing without the bishop, but be also in subjection to the presbytery, as to the Apostles of Jesus Christ our hope. . . . Likewise let all respect the deacons as Jesus Christ, even as the bishop is also a type of the Father, and the presbyters as the council of God and the college of Apostles.

"Without these there is not even the name of Church."[1]

2. Warnings against Docetists. These heretics taught that the sufferings, and in some cases the life of Jesus Christ, were unreal and only an appearance.

"Be deaf, therefore, when any one speaks to you apart from Jesus Christ, Who was of the family of David and of Mary, Who was truly born, both ate and drank, was truly persecuted under Pontius Pilate, was truly crucified and died in the sight of those in heaven and on earth and under the earth; Who also was truly raised from the dead, when His Father raised Him up, as in the same manner His Father shall raise up in Jesus Christ us who believe in Him without whom we have no true life. But if, as some affirm who are without God—that is, are unbelievers—His sufferings were only a semblance (but it is they who are merely a semblance), why am I a prisoner, and why do I long to fight with wild beasts? In that case I am dying in vain. Then, indeed, am I lying concerning the Lord."

[1] *Trallians*, iii. 3.

He also protests against Judaizing tendencies, which he may have associated with the Docetists.

3. He emphasizes throughout our Lord's divinity. For instance, in his letter to the Ephesians he wrote:—

"There is one Physician, of a nature at once human and divine, both born and without birth, God in man, true life in death, both of Mary and of God, first passible and then impassible, Jesus Christ our Lord."[1]

4. He is concerned for the fate of his own Church at Antioch, and asks for the prayers of the Church to whom he writes, requesting that deputations may be sent to encourage and strengthen them.

The outstanding feature of Christian literature, from Trajan to Severus, was the apology. And for an obvious reason. During the first part of the period heresy did not attract very much attention. It may be there had not been much time for it to develop, or perhaps the Church was too fully occupied with dangers from without. On the other hand, the Empire was ruled by a succession of able emperors, who had the appearance at least of relaxing the laws against Christianity. They were men it was worth while to win, and whom there was some hope of winning. It was no use to address apologies to Nero or Domitian.

Later on, at the end of the second century,

[1] Ephesians vii.

68 Church History from Nero to Constantine

the apologies were addressed not so much to the emperor as to the heathen world in general.

Among the earliest apologists of whom we have any knowledge are Aristides and Quadratus. They both wrote in Greek. The Apology of Aristides has only been discovered in comparatively recent times. He is said by Eusebius to have addressed his work to Hadrian. Professor Rendel Harris, who discovered a Syriac version of the Apology, gives reasons for thinking that it was presented to Antoninus Pius during an unrecorded visit of that emperor to Smyrna, and early in his reign, not much after A.D. 138. In the Apology Aristides is called a philosopher. There are said to be four races of men—Barbarians, Greeks, Jews, Christians. The errors of the first three are described, and the usual arguments brought forward against idolatry and against the heathen gods on account of their immorality. He is particularly sarcastic at the expense of the Egyptians. In his statement of the Christian Faith the rudiments of a creed can be discovered :—

" They know and believe in God, the Maker of heaven and earth,

" And in Jesus Christ, Who is named the Son of God, Who came down from heaven and, from a Hebrew Virgin, clad Himself in flesh.

" He was pierced by the Jews.

" He died and was buried.

" After three days He rose and ascended to heaven.

"He is about to come to judge.
"We live in expectation of the world to come."

The Christians are said to reckon the beginning of their religion from Jesus Christ, Who is named the Son of God Most High; the Jews from Abraham.

It is more than possible that Celsus had read this Apology when he made his attack on Christianity.[1]

Quadratus is quoted by Eusebius as having stated that some of those upon whom our Lord worked miracles "remained living a long time, not only whilst our Lord was on earth, but likewise when He had left the earth. So that some of them also lived to our own times."[2] But except the fragment in Eusebius, the work has perished.

Justin Martyr wrote his Apologies about A.D. 150. He was a Platonist philosopher who became a Christian, moved by their fortitude under persecution. "For whilst I, too, was delighted with the doctrines of Plato, and heard the Christians calumniated, but at the same time saw them intrepid at the prospect of death and other terrors, I reflected that it was impossible they should live devoted to vice and voluptuousness. For what lover of pleasure or libertine who reckons the indulgence of the flesh as the supreme good would embrace death in order

[1] See *Texts and Studies*, vol. i. Ed. J. Armitage Robinson.
[2] *H. E.* iv. 3.

to be deprived of the objects of his own desires ?"[1]

His principal extant works are—

The *First Apology* addressed to the Emperor Antoninus.

The *Second Apology* apparently addressed to Antoninus and Marcus Aurelius.

The *Dialogue with Tryphon the Jew*.

According to Eusebius, he was prosecuted after his Second Apology, at the instigation of Crescens, the cynic philosopher whom he had attacked. This attack was anticipated by Justin in his Second Apology: "I also expect to be waylaid by some one of those who I have named, or to be put to the rack, even by Crescens himself, that unphilosophical and vainglorious opponent."[2]

His martyrdom took place in the reign of Marcus Aurelius.

Athenagoras, before his conversion an Athenian philosopher, addressed an apology to Marcus Aurelius in the year A.D. 177. He is said by Philip of Side to have been converted through reading the Scriptures with a view to their refutation. He also wrote a treatise on the Resurrection.

Theophilus, who became Bishop of Antioch in A.D. 168, wrote a Defence of Christianity to a heathen acquaintance named Autolycus, apparently as the result of a conversation in which Theophilus had tried to explain the Christian religion. Afterwards he followed up his oral

[1] *Second Apol.* xii.   [2] Ibid., iii.

Some Christian writers from Clement to Tertullian 71

explanations with the written Apology which has survived. He also wrote anti-heretical and other works which have perished.

Melito, Bishop of Sardis, wrote many works of which only fragments have come down to us, and among them an Apology addressed to Marcus Aurelius. He is described after his death by Polycrates of Ephesus as one of the great lights in Asia, "whose life was altogether under the influence of the Holy Spirit, who now rests at Sardis,[1] awaiting the episcopate from heaven, when he shall rise from the dead."

Among the Apologies the *Octavius* of Minucius Felix must be mentioned. Lactantius makes the following allusion to its author :—

"And if by chance any of the learned have made a special study of Christian truth, they have been unequal to its defence of it. Of those with whose writings I am acquainted, Minucius Felix was a distinguished lawyer. His book, called *Octavius*, shows that he might have been a competent defender of the truth, if he had concentrated himself on the subject."[2] Jerome also alludes to him as an advocate and a man of learning. He was a Latin, possibly an African Latin, who practised at Rome. His Apology takes the form of a dialogue between two friends, one a Christian, the other a heathen, while Minucius himself acts as umpire. It is Ciceronian in style, and full of classical allusions, composed by a scholar for scholars. This may account for the

[1] Eusebius, *H. E.* v. 24.   [2] *Inst. Div.* v.

line the argument takes. It does not mention Christ, hardly quotes from the Scriptures, and leaves on one side the more characteristic Christian doctrines. It meets the educated heathen on his own ground, points out the weakness of his position, and shows that Christianity has on the face of it a claim to the serious consideration of right-thinking men.

Its date is uncertain. It has points of resemblance with the Apology of Tertullian, written A.D. 197, and the question is, Did Tertullian borrow from Minucius, or Minucius from Tertullian? It seems unlikely that Tertullian should have been a borrower in a case like this, and, pending further evidence, it seems best to date it between the accession of Caracalla, A.D. 217 and A.D. 249.

Among writers who were not Apologists Hermas wrote an apocalypse called *The Shepherd* not later than the year A.D. 148. The Muratorian fragment contests its claim to be canonical Scripture, which some had asserted, and states that it was written "quite recently in our time in the city of Rome, while his brother Pius was sitting on the stool of the church of the City of Rome." Pius was Pope A.D. 145, so that presumably *The Shepherd* was written in Rome about that time, though some think it was written at intervals during the twenty or thirty years before. Irenaeus reckons it as Scripture, but Tertullian states that the Church had definitely decided against its canonicity.

The book consists of three parts :—
I. Visions.
II. Mandates.
III. Similitudes or Parables.

The object of the book is to show that, contrary to an opinion commonly held, repentance was possible for sin committed after baptism, though only once. "All the sins which they have formerly committed, and all the sins of the saints which they have committed against the day, shall be forgiven them if they repent whole-heartedly and put aside duplicity from their heart. But if they shall still sin after this day has been fixed they shall find no salvation."[1]

The Mandates are instructions on Christian ethics, and are interesting as showing the ideal of the Christian life as held in the second century. The Similitudes or Parables are sermons given in an allegorical form.

Among other writers whose works have perished, or of which only a few fragments remain preserved by Eusebius,[2] Hegesippus must be mentioned. He wrote five books of *Hypomnemata*, or Notes, containing "the plain tradition of the Apostolic doctrine," apparently directed against the Gnostics. He lived in Palestine, but came to Rome when Anicetus was bishop. His interest is due to the importance he attaches to the succession of bishops in each Church as a guarantee against heresy, for

[1] *The Shepherd*, vis. ii. 2.   [2] *H. E.* iv. 22.

which he first employs the term *diadoché*, or succession. He wrote about A.D. 175.

Irenaeus was a native of Asia, and as a young man was a disciple of Polycarp; he was born, therefore, probably not later than A.D. 135. He left Smyrna at Polycarp's death, and is next heard of at Lyons as a presbyter in the Church there at the time of the great persecution, A.D. 177. Later on he apologizes for the comparative rusticity of his style, on the ground that "I am resident among the Celtae, and accustomed for the most part to use a barbarous dialect." At Lyons he was a presbyter under Pothinus, who died in A.D. 177 at the age of ninety, and was thus linked with the Apostles. Irenaeus succeeded, and seems to have died in peace twenty years later. Jerome says he was martyred, but neither Eusebius nor Tertullian make mention of any martyrdom. His great work was his *Refutation of Knowledge falsely so-called*, commonly cited as *Against Heresies*, which was directed against the Valentinian school of Gnosticism, and is one of the principal sources of our knowledge of their tenets.

One of his arguments has a special interest to-day. The Gnostics maintained that the Apostles had a secret doctrine which was not delivered to the Church of which they—the Gnostics—were the depositaries. Irenaeus retorts with an argument drawn from the succession of the bishops. If the Apostles, he says, had this secret doctrine they would have imparted it to those "whom they were leaving behind as their successors, delivering up their own place of government to those to whom they were committing the care of the Churches, and they in turn would have handed it on to others." He takes "the very great, the very ancient and universally-known Church of Rome" for an example. It had been founded by the Apostles S. Peter and S. Paul, and committed to the care of Linus; after Linus, Anancletus; and so on down to his own day.

TERTULLIAN

The greatest of the ante-Nicene writers was perhaps Quintus Septimius Florens Tertullianus, commonly known as Tertullian, who is thus described by Jerome in his work *De Viris illustribus* :—" Tertullian, a presbyter, the first Latin writer after Victor and Apollonius, was a native of the province of Africa and city of Carthage, the son of a proconsular centurion. He was a man of sharp and vehement temper, flourished under Severus and Antoninus Caracalla (A.D. 113–216), and wrote numerous works. . . . I saw at Concordia, in Italy, an old man named Paulus. He said that when young he had met with an aged amanuensis of the blessed Cyprian, who told him that Cyprian never passed a day without reading some portion of Tertullian's works, and used frequently to say 'Give me my master,' meaning Tertullian.

After remaining a presbyter of the Church until he had attained middle life, Tertullian was driven by the envy and contumelious treatment of the Roman clergy to embrace the opinions of Montanus, which he has mentioned in several of his works under the title of 'The New Prophecy.' . . . He is reported to have lived to a very advanced age, and to have composed many other works which are not extant."[1] He was born probably not later than A.D. 155, and was brought up as a heathen and educated as a lawyer, in which profession he "acquired an accurate knowledge of Roman law noteworthy among the eminent men in Rome."[2] He may have been the great lawyer Tertullianus, mentioned in the *Corpus*, but this is only a guess.

The date of his conversion is unknown, but it was probably about A.D. 195. Afterwards he became a presbyter. Some time before A.D. 207, the date of the latest form of his treatise against Marcion, he became a Montanist, and subsequently seceded from the Church. There is no record that he was ever a martyr.

He had a fiery and passionate temperament, an almost unequalled command of invective and sarcasm, and a wonderful talent of putting his opponent's case with an air of reality and then covering it with opprobrium and ridicule. Whatever made him turn to Christianity sent him over with considerable impetus. He recoiled from

[1] See Introduction to Tertullian, *A. N. C. L.*
[2] Eusebius, *H. E.* ii. 2.

heathenism with a bound. His active mind took in the doctrines of Christianity, but without imbibing very deeply the spirit of Christ. His hot African temperament could not brook half-measures. He had no gentleness, could not make allowance for weakness, and was as hard on the failings of the sinner as on the arguments of an opponent. In private life he may have been the most amiable of men, but in his writings he has no charity. Of this weakness he seems to have been aware himself. In his treatise on Patience he apologizes for having dared to compose a treatise on Patience, for practising which he is quite unfit. "So I most miserable, ever sick with the heats of impatience, must of necessity sigh after and pray and persistently plead for that health of patience which I possess not."[1] In controversy his tone was offensive in more senses than one. He was aggressive and provocative, and did not disdain the coarsest personalities. This is how he begins his polemic against Marcion :—

"The Euxine Sea, as it is called, is self-contradictory in its nature and deceptive in its name. As you would not account it hospitable from its situation, so it has separated itself from our more civilized waters by a certain shame at its own barbarous character. The fiercest nations inhabit it, if it can be called habitation where life is passed in waggons. They have no fixed abode, their life is coarse, their lust promiscuous and

[1] *On Patience*, i.

shameless. They kill and eat their parents at their feasts. Those who have not died so as to become food for others are thought to have died an accursed death. Their women carry battle-axes and prefer warfare to marriage. Their climate is always bad. The day is never clear, the sun never cheerful; the sky is always cloudy; the whole year is wintry, the only wind that blows is the north. All things are torpid and stiff with cold. Nothing has the glow of life. Nothing, however, in Pontus is so barbarous and sad as the fact that Marcion was born there, fouler than any Scythian. . . ."

He addressed a vigorous apology (A.D. 197) to the Roman Senate, protesting against the injustice that, unlike other offenders, Christians were punished not for crimes but for their name. He scoffs at the rule that Christians are not to be hunted out but must be condemned if arrested. " If you do not inquire, why do you not absolve ? Military posts are distributed through all the provinces for tracking robbers. The Christian alone must not be tracked, but may be charged." [1]

His tone throughout is defiant and provocative. Like other apologists he pours scorn on the immoralities of the pagan gods, but goes further, and threatens his persecutors with the fires of the Day of Judgement and hurls at them prophecies of the triumph of the Church. Persecution is useless. " We conquer in dying; we go forth victorious at the moment we are subdued. Call

[1] *Apol.* ii.

us, if you like, Sarmenticii and Semaxii, because bound to a half-axle stake we are burned in a circle of faggots. This is the attitude in which we conquer; it is for us a robe of victory and triumphal car. . . . The oftener we are thrown down by you, the more in number we grow; the blood of the Christian is seed."[1]

In his attitude to Christianity he is a Puritan, if we define a Puritan as the man who carries to extremes the principle of renunciation. Renunciation is an essential principle of Christianity. The Christian has to renounce sin and the occasions of sin, but he has also to live in the body and in a world in which good and evil are almost inextricably mingled. We cannot avoid all possible occasions of sin, as S. Paul saw, unless we go out of the world altogether. The Puritan is the man who at the dictates of logic, or a scrupulous conscience, or a morose temper, carries the renunciation of the occasions of sin to extreme lengths, and sometimes at the expense of charity and humanity. The Puritan of the seventeenth century banned music, dancing, and the most harmless amusements because they sometimes led to sin. Tertullian would separate the Christian as far as possible from all contact with idolatry and from all secular pleasures and amusements, and reduce eating and drinking to the barest minimum necessary to support life. He sometimes reminds us of Macaulay's Puritan, who objected to bear-baiting, not because

[1] *Apol.* ii. 50.

it gave pain to the bear, but because it gave pleasure to the spectators. The ascetic renounces the pleasures of life for himself because he feels God has called him to this kind of life. The Puritan would deprive others as well by making it a rule for all. The attraction Tertullian found in Montanism lay perhaps not so much in its doctrines of the New Prophecy as in its Puritanism. For Tertullian life in the world is at best an evil. In his letter to the confessors in prison he congratulates them on their incarceration. "You have gone out of a prison rather than into one." "You have no occasion to look on strange gods; you do not run against their images; you have no part in heathen holidays even by bodily mingling in them; you are not annoyed by the foul fumes of idolatrous solemnities; you are not pained by the noise of the public shows, nor by the atrocity or madness or immodesty of their celebrants; your eyes do not fall on brothels; you are free from causes of offence, from temptations, from unholy reminiscences."[1]

The ruthlessness of his logic recalls Law's *Serious Call.* Christians may at any moment be called to face the prison and the torture-chamber; therefore their whole life is to be a course of training for martyrdom. This is one of his arguments for fasting:—

"That a Christian may enter prison in like condition as if he had just come out of it; to suffer there not penalty but discipline, and not

[1] *To the Martyres*, ii.

the world's tortures but his own habitual observances ; and to go forth out of custody to the conflict with all the more confidence, having nothing of the flesh about him, so that the tortures may not have even material to work on, since he is cuirassed in a mere dry skin and cased in horn to meet the claws, the succulence of his blood already sent on before him, the advance luggage, so to speak, of his soul—the soul itself now hastening after it, having already by frequent fasting gained a most intimate knowledge of death."[1]

He was very sensitive on the subject of women's dress, and wrote a treatise about it, as he disliked intensely any unnecessary adornment. It was probably to warn the frivolous of the awful realities they might have to face at any moment that he argued against such adornment, on the ground that it unfitted the wearer for martyrdom. Whether that be so or not, it helps us to understand the grim background of the stage on which the Christian life was set, and to sympathize with the impatience of so fiery a writer. This is what he says :—

"I know not whether the wrist that has been wont to be surrounded with the palm-leaf, like a bracelet, will endure till it grow into the numb hardness of its own chain. I know not whether the leg that has rejoiced in the anklet will suffer itself to be squeezed into the gyve. I fear the neck beset with ropes of pearl and emerald will

[1] *On Fasting*, xii.

give no room to the broadsword. Wherefore, blessed sisters, let us meditate on hardships, and we shall not feel them. Let us abandon pleasures, and we shall not regret them. Let us stand ready to endure every violence, having nothing which we may fear to lose. These are the drags on our hope. Let us cast away earthly ornament; we desire heavenly. Love not gold. But Christians always, and now more than ever, pass their time not in gold but in iron; the stoles of martyrdom are now preparing; the angels who are to carry us on high are ready. Do you go forth to meet them already arrayed in the cosmetics and ornaments of prophets and Apostles, drawing your whiteness from simplicity, your ruddy hue from modesty, painting your eyes with bashfulness, and your mouth with silence, implanting in your ears the Word of God, fitting on your neck the yoke of Christ? Submit your head to your husband, and you will be enough adorned. Busy your hands with spinning, keep your feet at home, and you will please better than by carrying your silver and gold. Clothe yourselves with the silk of uprightness, the fine linen of holiness, the purple of modesty. Thus painted you will have God as your lover."[1]

Though himself married, he disliked marriage as a state for Christians, and second marriages were to him anathema.

His attitude to military service and public office has been dealt with elsewhere. He wrote a tract

[1] *On Women's Dress*, xiii.

to prove that flight in time of persecution was unlawful for a Christian. Persecution is the sifting and judging of God. Therefore we must abide it. With the Montanists he would allow no reconciliation for those who committed mortal sin after baptism. On one point he is illogical. Laymen may baptize, "for what is equally received may be equally given." But women may not.

Tertullian is, perhaps, the only ante-Nicene Christian writer who can be read with pleasure for his own sake, waiving all questions of edification or historic interest. He is the first great Puritan writer, and is the precursor of Milton, John Bunyan, and William Law, if the great nonjuror may be called a Puritan. His Latinity is anything but classical, but he is a great writer of prose, though not perhaps of Latin prose.

V

THE CHURCH AND THE WORLD

"THEY (the early Christians) are regarded rightly as enemies of the human race. If it is possible to endorse any judgement of the past we may endorse this one of the authorities of the Roman Empire."[1]

This is a strong statement. It is worth while to examine its truth. Were the Christians of the first days really the enemies of society, so that society was justified in trying to rid itself of them, or are we rather to blame a corrupt society which refused to admit the regenerating influence as long as it could?

To many of the usages of society the Church was undoubtedly hostile. Its attitude towards marriage, towards entertainments and most social and convivial customs, was bound to bring it into conflict with society, as has already been explained. But that was to break down in order to rebuild on surer foundations. It objected to marriage with a pagan because it felt that in such union the ideals of a Christian marriage would be unobtainable. Husband and wife would not devote themselves to the Christian training of

[1] F. C. Conybeare, *Monuments of Early Christianity*, p. 287.

their children, or the organizing of their household on Christian lines. There could be no true happiness. So with entertainments and convivialities, which were intermixed with idolatry.

What we want to know is not, Did the Church encourage Christian young women to break their engagements with young pagans, and Christians in general to stop away from heathen festivities? but, Did the Church forbid Christians to marry, to take part in social festivities as such, to earn their daily bread, to obey the laws, and if necessary help execute them, to serve when required as soldiers or magistrates, to be good affectionate fathers, mothers, husbands, wives, sisters, brothers? Were they, in a word, anti-social?

Family Life

What was their attitude towards marriage and family ties? To quote again from Mr. Conybeare: "There was first that rejection of family ties and relationships which accompanied the belief that the world was speedily and any day coming to an end. Young men and maidens were taught not to marry, husbands, wives not to cohabit and beget any more children. Eunuchism, because of the kingdom of heaven, was even tolerated by the very founder of the religion."

We find little support for this view in the New Testament. Divorce is forbidden, marriage is regarded as a God-made union. Celibacy *for those who can receive it* is regarded as the ideal if pursued for the sake of the kingdom of our Lord. But S. Paul wrote, " If you marry you have not sinned." The Apostles have power to lead about wives. The presbyter-bishops,[1] and the deacons are each to be the husband of one wife. The younger women are ordered to marry, and bear children. And, at the end of the Apostolic period, as though fearing that certain passages in the Gospels might be interpreted as unduly exalting celibacy, the author of the fourth Gospel makes the miracle at the wedding in Cana of Galilee our Lord's *beginning of signs*, which could hardly have been unintentional on the part of the writer.

Polycarp tells the Philippians to teach their wives to walk in the faith given to them, and in love and purity, and tenderly to love their own husbands.

Again, Ignatius in his letter to Polycarp has a passage on the duties of husbands and wives :—

" Speak to my sisters that they love the Lord, and be content with their husbands both in the flesh and in the spirit. In like manner also exhort my brethren, in the Name of Jesus Christ, that they love their wives, even as the Lord the Church. If any one can continue in a state of purity to the honour of Him Who is Lord of the flesh, let him so remain without boasting. If he boast he is lost." [2]

[1] It is assumed that S. Paul uses presbyter and bishop as synonymous terms, and the name presbyter-bishop refers to these officials.
[2] *Ep. to Polycarp*, iv.

The Pastor of Hermas, perhaps the most popular homiletic work in the Church during the second and third centuries, has a disquisition on the Commandments. As elsewhere, there are strict warnings against adultery and impurity of all kinds, and the remarriage of divorced persons is forbidden. A second marriage after the death of husband or wife is allowed. "There is no sin in marrying again, but if they remain unmarried they gain greater honour and glory with the Lord; but if they marry they do not sin." [1]

Justin Martyr condemned the heathen practice of exposing infants, and though he extols the virtue of complete chastity has not a word to say against marriage. "But if we marry it is only that we may bring up children; or if we decline marriage we live continently." [2]

Athenagoras wrote to the same effect:—

"Each of us reckons her his wife whom he has married according to the laws laid down by us, and that only for the purpose of having children. Nay, you would find many among us, both men and women, growing old unmarried in the hope of living in closer communion with God." [3]

Like Justin, he regarded the remarriage of divorced persons as adultery, and goes so far as to condemn all second marriages, regarding a widower who marries again as a "cloaked adulterer."

[1] Bk. ii.   [2] *First Apol.* xxix.   [3] *Apol.* xxxiii.

It may be objected that the early Church was mistaken in its ideal, or at least over-emphasized it, and was thus a weakness to the State when the State badly needed children.

But it must be remembered that in such a time of license the moral force of the example of the men and women living absolutely chaste lives was needed more than anything else. Licentiousness and self-indulgence deprived the State of children, not the celibacy of a few men. Tertullian laid down the lawfulness of marriage. It is good, though celibacy is better. It is true that he says, " Why should we be eager to bear children?" but he is writing a treatise to persuade his wife not to marry again on his death, and he is probably biassed.

The Church from the first took the strongest line against the existing practices of exposing infants and of procuring abortion.

The most touching proof that the martyrs were not fierce fanatics who hated their own flesh and despised human ties is found in the record of the martyrdom of S. Perpetua. S. Perpetua was the mother of a babe, from which she was separated when put in prison. When the babe was restored, she says " the prison became a palace to me."

Mixed marriages were discouraged by S. Paul, and afterwards Tertullian has shown in what a difficult position such marriages placed the wife.

" If a station is to be kept, the husband makes

an appointment with his wife to meet him at the baths; if there are fasts to be observed, the husband that same day gives a dinner; if a procession has to be made, never is family business more urgent. For who would suffer his wife, for the sake of resisting the heathen, to go round from street to street to other men's houses, and, indeed, to all the poorer cottages? Who will, without suspicion, dismiss her to attend the Lord's Supper, which they all defame? Who will suffer her to creep into prison to kiss the martyrs' bonds? . . . To bring water to wash the feet of the holy ones? To save something for them from her food or her cup? If a brother arrives from abroad, what hospitality is there for him? If bounty is to be distributed, the store-rooms are closed. Shall you escape notice when you sign your bed or your body? When every night you rise to pray, will he not think you are working some magic? Will not your husband know what it is which you secretly taste before taking any food? and if he knows it to be bread will he not believe it is that which it is said to be?

"The handmaid of God dwells in an alien atmosphere, and on all the festivals of demons, of kings at the beginning of the year and month, she will be disturbed by the smell of incense. She will have to leave her house by a gate wreathed with laurel, and hung with lanterns, in order to sit with her husband at club meetings and taverns, and she who was once accustomed to minister to her husband in good things will now do so in evil things."[1]

BUSINESS

Again, what was the attitude of Christians towards the work of the world? Is there any foundation for the picture that is sometimes painted of the Church as a communistic society, and those who joined it handed over to the control of its officers, whatever private means they possessed?[2] It seems to have been so at Jerusalem, but even there only partially. Ananias was plainly a free agent. But the example of Jerusalem was not apparently encouraging. S. Paul is urgent against the sin of covetousness. The rich are urged to distribute alms, and the idle to work. "If a man will not work, neither let him eat."

Every sentence in the patristic writings to the effect that Christians have no private property need not be taken literally. They are rather rhetorical expressions, showing the extreme claims which the love of neighbours created. Tertullian wrote in his Apology, "All things are common among us except our wives"; but in his letter to his wife alludes to the making of wills as common among Christians, and implied that he had made one himself. "We who formerly valued above all things our wealth and possessions, now bring what we have into a common stock, and com-

[1] *Tertullian to his Wife*, ii. 4–6.
[2] F. C. Conybeare, *Monuments of Early Christianity*, p. 285.

municate to every one in need." [1] Similar expressions abound in Justin's works, but they do not prevent him from praising the honesty with which Christians transacted business. Indeed, he claims that many pagans were won over to Christianity " by the extraordinary forbearance they have observed in their fellow travellers when defrauded, and by the honesty of those with whom they have transacted business." [2] This certainly points to the fact that Christians carried on business like other folk, even though more honestly. " The wealthy among us help the needy." The frequent exhortations to almsgiving we meet with, and the warnings against covetousness, are proof enough, if proof were needed, that Christians held property and engaged in business like other people. In *The Pastor of Hermas* the rich and the poor are said to be necessary for one another. " The rich man has much wealth, but is poor in matters relating to the Lord, because he is distracted about his riches ; and he offers very few confessions and intercessions to the Lord, and those which he does offer are small and weak. But when the rich man refreshes the poor, and assists him in his necessities, then the rich man helps the poor, and the poor man being helped of the rich intercedes for him, giving thanks to God for him who has bestowed gifts upon him. Both accordingly accomplish their work. The poor man makes intercession, and the rich man bestows

[1] Justin, *First Apol.* xiv.   [2] Ibid., 16.

upon the poor man the riches which he has received from the Lord. . . . Blessed are they who have riches, and who understand that they are from the Lord."

It is true that part of the business of life was forbidden to the Christians as being concerned with idols. Many converts to the Faith were makers of idols or their adjuncts. It was apparently claimed that such might be admitted. " I make but I worship not." The claim is utterly rejected by Tertullian. He will not admit the plea " We must live." He argues first of all that " faith fears not famine." Further, that those who make idols, or paint and gild them, or furnish paint or gold-leaf, or build temples, can divert their labour to similar arts harmlessly employed. "How much more easily does he who delineates a statue overlay a sideboard? How much sooner does he who carves a Mars out of a lime-tree fasten together a chest ! " Indeed, Tertullian labours at some length to show the many ways in which Christians might earn a living.[1] The only trades absolutely forbidden to Christian converts are those definitely bound up with immorality, idolatry, the games and shows of the circus and the theatre, and necromancy. Tertullian, in a well-known passage, claimed that Christians share the business of life.

" We are not Indian Brahmins or Gymnosophists who dwell in woods and exile themselves from ordinary human life ; we are careful to give

[1] *On Idolatry.*

thanks to God our Creator, and we reject no creation of His hands, though we exercise a restraint upon ourselves, lest of any gift of His we make an immoderate or sinful use. So we live with you in the world, abjuring neither forum nor shambles nor bath nor booth nor workshop nor inn nor weekly market nor any other places of commerce. We sail with you or fight with you and till the ground with you, trade with you. How it is we seem useless in your ordinary business, living with you and by you, I am not able to understand." [1]

Amusements

The attitude of the Church to the stage, the games, and the gladiatorial shows was at once its glory and a cause of offence to the heathen. Tertullian, who was a Puritan, it is true, objects to all secular pleasures. "Thou art too dainty, Christian, if thou wouldst have pleasure in this life as well as in the next. . . . Can we not live without pleasure who with pleasure die?" But Tertullian would not be so vehement if the natural human and innocent love of pleasure had not remained even in the converted heart, and if for want of innocent pleasures some were not in danger of being drawn away to the corrupt enjoyments of the heathen. The official attitude of the Church was unyielding in its detestation of the Games. "But we, deeming

[1] *Apol.* xlii.

that to see a man put to death is much the same as killing him, have abjured such spectacles."[1] Tertullian condescends to argue: "For the faith of some either too simple or too scrupulous demands direct authority from Scripture for giving up the Games, and holds that the matter is a doubtful one because such abstinence is not clearly and in words imposed on God's servants." He makes the general objection that Christians should not mingle in heathen assemblies. "Blessed is the man who has not gone into the assembly of the impious nor stood in the way of sinners nor sat in the seat of the scorner." Here speaks the Puritan, and perhaps he was right. He also shows the intimate connection between the stage and idolatry. " The sin of idolatry clings to the shows in respect of their origins, their trifles, their equipments, their place of celebration, their arts." In particular he insists that the stage is hopelessly lewd and immoral and the shows cruel and bloodstained. "He who looks with horror on the corpse of one who has died under the common law of nature, in the theatre gazes down with most patient eyes on bodies mangled and torn and smeared with blood." Finally, he insists on abstention from the Games as a part of the Christian witness. "Apply to the heathen themselves. Let them tell us whether it is right in Christians to frequent the shows. Why, the rejection of these shows is the chief sign to them that a man has adopted the Christian Faith."[2]

[1] Athenagoras, *Plea for the Christians*, 35. [2] Tert., *de Spec.* i.

The dress of Christians did not differ from that of pagans except that luxury or display was from the first discouraged by the bishops. In spite of persecution and the fact that every Christian carried his life—or her life—in his hands, the invectives of Clement of Alexandria, Tertullian, and Cyprian seem to show that the Christian young women of their day took an interest in their appearance. Tertullian did not advocate squalor or slovenliness, or "an entirely uncouth and wild appearance," but inveighs against those "who rub their skin with lotions, rouge their cheeks, dye their hair with saffron, and spend time curling it and dressing it, or adding false hair."

CITIZENSHIP

Celsus appealed to Christians to support the State by undertaking civil office and serving in the Army, and implied that they were backward in fulfilling the duties of citizenship. He urges them "to help the king with all our might, to labour for him in the maintenance of justice, to fight for him; and, if he requires it, to fight under him and to lead an army along with him. To take office in the government of the country, if that is required for the maintenance of the laws and the support of religion." [1]

Were Christians, then, bad citizens?

The Church enjoined the duty of civil obedience except when it conflicted with the divine

[1] Origen, *Against Celsus*, viii. 75.

command. " Render unto Caesar the things that are Caesar's." " The powers that be are ordained of God." " Honour the king." The ruler is God's instrument. These ideas are familiar to us from the New Testament, and the Fathers carry on the tradition. "Thou shalt be subject to the Lord and to masters as the image of God." [1] Justin Martyr claims that, taught of Christ, Christians were more ready to pay taxes than heathen.[2] Tertullian claims that Christians were better subjects than the heathen and insists on the reverence with which the Church regards his office. " But why dwell on the reverence and respect of Christians to the emperor, whom we cannot but look upon as called by our Lord to his office ? So that I might have good grounds for saying that Caesar is more ours than yours, for our God has appointed him." [3]

Christians are charged with having contributed to the downfall of the Roman Empire by refusing to serve in the administration of the Empire. It would be fairer to say that it was the State which refused to avail itself of the services of Christians, for it would have been difficult, if not impossible, for Christians to have been high Roman officials on account of the close connection of State ceremonial with idolatrous observances. No doubt the Puritan type of Christian like Tertullian, who laid special stress on the renunciation involved in the Christian profession, would in any case have

[1] *Ep. of Barnabas*, 19. [2] See also Tertullian, *Apol.* 42.
[3] *Apol.* 33.

advised abstention from any high place. In maintaining the superior modesty of Christians he asserts: "The Christian does not aspire to the aedileship."[1] In this he is probably correct, or we should have had a fiery exhortation warning against such ambitions. He allowed the lawfulness in principle of office for a Christian, but insists that in practice it is too much involved in idolatry, the games, and the shedding of blood to be permitted.

"But what shall believing slaves or children do? Officials likewise, when attending on the lords or patrons or superiors when sacrificing? ... If any man hands wine to a sacrificer or shall help him by any word necessary to the sacrifice, he will be held to be a minister of idolatry. But mindful of the rule we can render service even to magistrates and powers, after the example of the patriarchs and the fathers who obeyed idolatrous kings to the verge of idolatry. There arose lately a dispute whether a servant of God should take the administration of any dignity or power, if he be able to keep himself untouched by any taint of idolatry. "Well, is it possible for any one to hold an office if he can do so without either sacrificing or lending his authority to sacrifice; without farming out victims or assigning to others the care of temples; without looking after their tributes; and without giving spectacles at his own or the public charge and presiding over them; without making proclamations of any idolatrous solemnity; without

[1] *Apol.* 130.

sitting in judgement on any one's life or character, you might bear his judging about money, binding no one, imprisoning no one, torturing no one ? ... If it is credible that this is possible, then it may be done."[1] Tertullian, we must again remind ourselves, was an extremist, but the only point here where he would come directly into conflict with the modern conscience is his refusal to permit the magistrates to judge life. It must, however, be remembered that torture was part of the normal procedure of criminal law. A magistrate had to torture ; it was part of the normal procedure.

The author of the so-called *Egyptian Church Order*, probably Hippolytus, included among those who must not be baptized, unless they renounce their profession, " a magistrate with the sword or a chief of prefects, and him who is clad in purple." But Hippolytus, like Tertullian, was a rigorist. At any rate this rule was not strictly observed. We certainly find that by the time of the persecution of Diocletian a considerable number of Christians were holding office—high and low. As early as the persecution of Decius (A.D. 249) a special clause was directed against the Caesariani, an inferior order of imperial officials. By A.D. 303 Eusebius is able to refer to " the clemency of the emperors towards our brethren, to whom they even entrusted the government of provinces, relieving them from all anxiety about sacrificing. . . ."[2] The man who tore down Diocletian's edict of persecution is described by Eusebius as " highly

[1] *De Idol.* 17.   [2] *H. E.* viii. 1.

esteemed for his temporal dignities." Among the Egyptian martyrs was Philoromus, "who held high office in the imperial district of Alexandria, and who according to his rank and Roman dignity was attended by a military guard when administering justice every day."[1] Adanetus, who was martyred in Phrygia about A.D. 305, is described as being of Roman dignity, of a noble Italian family, a man that had been advanced through every grade of dignity by the emperors, and had filled with credit the offices of chief revenue official and prime minister, which office he held at the time of his martyrdom. It is plain that the numbers of Christians in the higher ranks of the imperial service was increasing, due partly to the growing number of Christians and partly to the fact that the conditions of office were made less intolerable to a believing Christian. On the evidence the Christians can hardly be found guilty of shirking their duties as citizens of this world, however incomparably more important they regarded the duties incumbent on them as citizens of another.

Military Service

Concerning military service there was some difference of opinion, as there is to-day. There were, no doubt, some who were frankly pacificist, and reluctance to serve in the Army was a charge against Christians. Tertullian wrote a treatise—

[1] *H.E.* viii. 9.

De Corona—to commend a soldier who had, through religious scruples, refused to wear a chaplet of flowers, and was denounced as a Christian and thrown into prison. "One of them was conspicuous, more a soldier of God, more steadfast than the rest of his brethren, who imagined they could serve two masters, his head alone uncovered, his crown in his hand, and already by that peculiarity revealed as a Christian."[1] His arguments against military service are partly based on its connection with idolatry. He regarded the crowns as idolatrous, and a Christian soldier might have to guard temples or venerate idolatrous emblems on the standards; but mainly because contrary to the Scriptures. "Christ, in disarming Peter, had unbelted every soldier."

"Shall it be held lawful to make an occupation of the sword, when the Lord proclaims that he who uses the sword shall perish by the sword?"[2] He also argues that a man cannot be a soldier of Christ and a soldier of the emperor.

Origen held the view that, as heathen priests were exempted from military service in order that they might offer sacrifice, Christians should be exempted in order to pray for those who were fighting. "None fight better for the king than we do. We do not fight under him, though he require it; but we fight on his behalf, forming a special army—an army of piety—by offering our prayers to God."[3]

[1] *De Cor.* 1.   [2] Ibid., 10.   [3] *Against Celsus*, viii. 73.

Lactantius took the ground that killing was always unlawful. "It will be neither lawful for a just man to engage in warfare, nor to accuse any one of a capital charge, because it makes no difference whether you put a man to death by word or by the sword, since it is the act of putting to death which is prohibited. It is always unlawful to put to death a man, whom God willed to be a sacred animal." [1]

In the *Church Orders* there is reflected the uncertainty and disagreement that existed in the Church. The Ethiopian text of the Egyptian *Church Order* lays down, "A catechumen or believer, if they wish to be soldiers, shall be rejected because they are far from God." But in the Arabic text the soldier is accepted. He "must be taught not to oppress or accuse falsely, and he shall be content with his pay. If he is pleased to be so let him be brought in." In the Saidic text in one place soldiers are to be rejected; in another we read "A soldier who is in authority cause him not to kill men; if he should be commanded to do it cause him not to hasten to the work." The same contradiction is to be found in the so-called Canons of Hippolytus.

Whatever may have been the attitude of men like Tertullian and Origen, it does not seem to have prevented large numbers of Christians from serving in the ranks. They crop up continually. Tertullian would hardly have written his treatise *De Corona* for the benefit of non-existent

[1] *Instit.* vi. 20.

Christian soldiers. The sentence "One, more a soldier of God, more steadfast than the rest of his brethren," implies that there were many others. Basilides, an officer in the Army, who was in charge of the soldiers on duty at the martyrdom of Potamiaena at Alexandria, afterwards became a Christian but did not renounce his profession on that account. It was only when afterwards urged to swear that he refused, saying "I am a Christian."[1] Dionysius records that in the persecution at Alexandria under Decius "there was a dense body of soldiers standing before the tribunal" who encouraged a wavering Christian to stand firm.[2] In Justin Martyr's supposed letter of Marcus Aurelius to the Senate about the Thundering Legion we read, "I summoned those who go by the name of Christians, and discovered a great number and vast host of them." Even if Marcus Aurelius is innocent of the letter it is unlikely that the writer who fathered it on him would have invented "the great number and vast host" of Christian soldiers if there were no Christian soldiers.

In the reign of Gallienus Marinus a Christian soldier was to have been promoted to the rank of centurion. Another soldier challenged his promotion on the ground that he was a Christian and would not sacrifice to the emperor. Admitting this, he was given three hours in which to make up his mind whether he would sacrifice or not. On

[1] Eusebius, H. E. vi. 5.   [2] Ibid. 41.

The Church and the World

refusing he was beheaded. This incident points to the presence of Christian officers as well as privates in the Army, and that their religion was connived at as long as it did not attract official notice. Eusebius delared that the persecution of Diocletian " began with those brethren that were in the Army."[1] He adds that "great numbers of soldiers" left the Army in consequence and returned to civilian life, rather than renounce their religion. The martyrdom of the forty soldiers of Sebaste is another proof that the Christian soldier was no isolated phenomenon.

The evidence shows that though individual Christians then, as since, regarded the profession of a Christian as inconsistent with military service, the Church did not commit itself to this view, and large numbers of Christians were to be found in the Army. That there were not more was due not so much to the pacificist views of Churchmen as to the difficulties put in the way of Christian soldiers by the Army itself, which at best connived at their presence and at worst carried on an active persecution against them. Our Army in India would be badly off for recruits if Mohammedans and Hindoos were treated as were Christians in the Roman Army.

SLAVERY

As to slavery, the Church accepted it as a matter of course. It introduced no new system

[1] *H. E.* viii.

of economics or social order as such ; but its doctrine of brotherhood and of love to neighbours, of the equality of all in the sight of God, were bound in time to destroy the whole system of slavery. During the period under review it contented itself with directing masters to be humane in their treatment of their slaves. " Thou shalt not issue orders with bitterness to thy maid-servant or thy man-servant who trust in the same God, lest thou shouldst not reverence that God Who is above both ; for He came to call men not according to their outward appearance, but according as the Spirit had prepared them."[1] Christian slaves were regarded as brethren and shared in all the privileges and rights of the Church. They could be ordained. Callistus, the Bishop of Rome, had been a slave. Martyred slaves were honoured in the same way as though free. Blandina, a slave girl, is a notable example. Slaves apparently, according to the *Church Orders*, were not to be received as catechumens without the consent of their masters.

Conclusion

The *Epistle to Diognetus* affords an interesting glimpse of the Church in its relation to society, as it appeared to one of its members, perhaps about A.D. 150 :—

"For the Christians are distinguished from

[1] "The Two Ways," see below p. 107.

other men neither by country nor language nor the customs which they observe. For they neither inhabit cities of their own, nor employ a peculiar form of speech, nor lead a life which is marked by any singularity. . . . But, inhabiting Greek as well as barbarian cities, and following the customs of the natives in respect of food, clothing, and the rest of their ordinary conduct, they display to us their wonderful and confessedly paradoxical method of life. They dwell in their own countries, but simply as sojourners. As citizens they share in all things with others, and yet endure all things as foreigners. . . . They marry, they beget children; but they do not destroy their offspring. . . . They obey the prescribed laws, and at the same time surpass the laws by their lives. They love all men, and are persecuted by all." [1]

We are not to suppose that Christians always lived up to their profession, but in times of persecution it is unlikely that many joined the Church without intending to carry out its way of life; and the apologists would hardly lay claim so hastily to a particular kind of life as exhibited by Christians if their description would be unrecognized by those who knew the facts.

"But among us you will find uneducated persons, working men and old women, if they are unable in words to prove the truth of their doctrines, yet by their deeds they show the good of their belief; they do not rehearse speeches,

[1] v.

but exhibit good works ; when struck they do not strike again ; when robbed they do not go to law ; they give to those who ask of them, love their neighbours as themselves."[1]

There does not seem much justification for the official view that Christians were the enemies of mankind; but no doubt they were sometimes aggressive. The martyrs were not all as meek as their Master. " With what face," asks Tertullian, "will a Christian incense-seller, if he shall pass through temples, with what face will he spit upon the smoking altars, for which he himself made provision?"[2] But the aggressiveness of Tertullian was alien from the Christian spirit, and there is no evidence to show that Christians, as a whole, were intentionally provocative. The truth was that their very existence, their doctrine, their words, their attitude to the business affairs, the everyday life—and amusements—were a challenge and a provocation to heathen men and women.

The ideal of the Christian life as it was commonly held in the first three centuries is to be found in the teaching on the " Two Ways "—the Way of Light and the Way of Darkness. This teaching, originally derived from Jewish sources, is found in the *Didaché*, the *Epistle of Barnabas*, and elsewhere ; it was used for the instruction of catechumens, and was no doubt a popular guide or handbook to right Christian living, and a manual of ethics for the young in the Faith.

[1] Athenagoras xi. [2] *On Idolatry*.

The Way of Light[1]

The Way of Light is as follows: "Thou shalt love Him that created thee: thou shalt glorify Him that redeemed thee from death. Thou shalt be simple in heart and rich in spirit. Thou shalt not join thyself to those who walk in the way of death. Thou shalt hate doing what is unpleasing to God, thou shalt hate all hypocrisy. Thou shalt not forsake the commandments of the Lord. Thou shalt not exalt thyself, but shalt be of a lowly mind. Thou shalt not take glory to thyself. Thou shalt not take evil counsel against thy neighbour. Thou shalt not allow over-boldness to enter thy soul. Thou shalt not commit fornication; thou shalt not commit adultery; thou shalt not be a corrupter of youth. Thou shalt not let the Word of God issue from thy lips if they are defiled with any kind of impurity. Thou shalt not accept praises when thou reprovest any one for transgressions. Thou shalt be meek; thou shalt be peaceable. Thou shalt not be mindful of evil against thy brother. Thou shalt not take the Name of the Lord in vain. Thou shalt love thy neighbour as thine own soul. Thou shalt not slay the child by procuring abortion; nor again shalt thou destroy it after it is born. Thou shalt not withdraw thy hand from thy son or thy daughter, but from their infancy thou shalt teach them the fear of the

[1] From the *Epistle of Barnabas*.

Lord. Thou shalt not covet what is thy neighbour's, nor shalt thou be avaricious. Thou shalt not be joined in soul with the haughty, but thou shalt be reckoned with the righteous hourly. Receive thou as good things the trials that come upon you. Thou shalt not be of a double mind or of a double tongue. Thou shalt be subject to the Lord, or to masters in the image of God with modesty and fear. Thou shalt not issue orders with bitterness to thy maid-servant or thy man-servant who trust in the same God, lest thou shouldst not reverence that God Who is above both; for He came to call men not according to their outward appearance, but according as the Spirit had prepared them. Thou shalt communicate in all things with thy neighbour; thou shalt not call things thine own, for if you are partakers in common of things incorruptible how much more of things corruptible. Thou shalt not be hasty with thy tongue, for the mouth is a snare of death. As far as possible thou shalt be pure in thy soul. Do not be ready to stretch forth thy hands to take, while thou shuttest them when thou shouldst give. Thou shalt love as the apple of thine eye every one that speaketh to thee the Word of the Lord. Thou shalt remember the day of judgement night and day. Thou shalt not hesitate to give or murmur when thou givest. 'Give to every one that asketh thee.' Thou shalt learn who is the good recompenser of the reward. Thou shalt preserve what thou hast received in trust, neither adding to it nor taking from it. Thou shalt judge righteously. Thou shalt not make a schism, but thou shalt pacify them that contend by bringing them together. Thou shalt confess thy sins. Thou shalt not go to prayer with an evil conscience. This is the Way of Life."

The Way of Darkness

"But the way of darkness is crooked and full of cunning, for it is the way of eternal death with punishment, in which way are the things that destroy the soul; that is idolatry, over-confidence, the arrogance of power, hypocrisy, double-heartedness, adultery, murder, rapine, haughtiness, deceit, malice, self-sufficiency, poisoning, magic, avarice, want of the fear of God. In this way are those who persecute the good, those who hate truth, those who love falsehood, those who know not the reward of righteousness, those who cleave not to that which is good, those who attend not with just judgement to the widow and orphan, those who watch not the fear of God, from whom meekness and patience are far off; persons who love vanity, follow after reward, pity not the needy, labour not in aid of him who is overcome with toil; who are prone to evil-speaking, who are murderers of children, destroyers of the workmanship of God; who turn away him that is in want, who oppress the afflicted, who are advocates of the rich, who are unjust judges of the poor, and who are in every respect transgressors."

The Way of Light, far from being offensive, seems winning and attractive. Indeed, it not only seems so now, but did even then, or why did Christians increase so rapidly during the ages of persecution? It seems certain that, as Christians became more numerous and better known, they were hated less, and the persecution became more political and less popular.

The following passage from the Book of Wisdom may perhaps explain the real motives indulging such hatred as there was:—

"Let us lie in wait for the righteous; because he is not for our turn, and is clean contrary to our doings: he upbraideth us with our offending the law. . . . He professeth to have the knowledge of God: and he calleth himself the child of the Lord. He was made to reprove our thoughts. He is grievous unto us even to behold: for his life is not like other men's, his ways are of another fashion. We are esteemed of him as counterfeits. . . . He pronounceth the end of the just to be blessed, and maketh his boast that God is his Father. Let us see if his words be true: and let us prove what shall happen in the end of him. . . . Let us examine him with despitefulness and torture, that we may know his meekness, and prove his patience. Let us condemn him with a shameful death: for by his own saying he shall be respected."

VI

THE CHURCH UNDER FOREIGN EMPERORS

Slackening of Persecution

THE death of Marcus Aurelius marked the close of a definite era in the history of persecution. Under Nero and Domitian persecution had been instinctive and spontaneous. Christianity was new and unpopular. Moreover, Nero wanted a scapegoat, while Domitian was a bloodthirsty and suspicious tyrant. But the four great emperors from Trajan to Marcus Aurelius were men of a different stamp. We may not go as far as Gibbon when he declares that during their reigns "the vast extent of the Roman Empire was governed by absolute power under the guidance of wisdom and virtue,"[1] or agree that "if a man were called to fix the period in the history of the world during which the condition of the human race was most happy and prosperous, he would without hesitation name that which elapsed from the death of Domitian to the accession of Commodus"[2]; but whatever we think of their general policy we feel sure that

[1] *Decline and Fall*, ch. iii.   [2] Ibid.

each of them had a policy towards the Church, and was strong enough to carry that policy into effect. That policy was in general one of persecution, though from Trajan to Pius the rigour of persecution was mitigated by the dislike of these emperors to anonymous and tumultuary accusations—and Christians generally were accused anonymously or by a mob—and further by their naturally tolerant dispositions. They started with a prejudice in favour of toleration, less marked, however, in Trajan than in his two immediate successors. They had three principal motives for persecution.

First, from the side of the law. The Roman Empire always refused, very jealously, to admit the right of any corporation to exist except by its own sanction. But the Church based its right to exist on divine sanction, and regarded itself as independent of the State, and even refused to take part in the State religion. It came in the end to be regarded much as a gigantic Sinn Fein or Trade Union organization might be, as an independent and possibly hostile state within the State, an *imperium in imperio*. Secondly, it was the policy of the State to press the worship of the emperor as the universal religion. Other religions were as far as possible tolerated, but this was to be practised everywhere. It was to be the strong religious bond between the scattered provinces of the Empire. This worship the Church regarded as blasphemous and idolatrous, and did not hesitate to say so. Thirdly, the new religion was unsettling. No prudent emperor, with an eye to the endless possibilities of trouble in his vast dominions, could fail to be apprehensive of anything which seemed likely to cause unsettlement and unrest. And the more the emperor belonged to the old Roman conservative type the more would he resent changes and innovations in religion.

Commodus and the foreign emperors who succeeded were men of another type. Commodus, though not himself a foreigner, was a dissolute boy when he became emperor, given over to the grossest forms of dissipation, not sufficiently interested in public affairs to have a policy, or strong enough, if he did have one, to carry it into effect. His foreign successors had no feeling against Christianity, any more than they had any devotion to the gods of ancient Rome. Christianity was to them one among many religions, and the arrogance of Christians in refusing to worship the ancient gods was not offensive to them as it was to Romans. Their one quarrel with the Church on the ground of religion was its refusal to allow the worship of the emperor. Further they were foreigners and would not have had the Roman legal sensitiveness to the status of the Church as an unlicensed corporation. While except for Severus and possibly Maximinus—and Severus and Maximinus were both persecutors—they were not strong men, and it was beginning to need a strong man to withstand the flowing tide of Christian numbers and influence. Nor had they the Roman sense of responsibility. They were not likely to persecute out of anxiety for the supposed interests of the State.

COMMODUS, A.D. 180–193

Under Commodus at first things took their course and the persecutions was continued. We hear for the first time of martyrs in Africa, when six Christians from Scili were tried and condemned at Carthage, A.D. 180. The proconsul Saturninus, however, behaved with great humanity, tried to persuade them to swear by "our Lords the Emperors," and when they refused urged them to take a month in which to think things over. It was only after this offer was refused that they were condemned to the comparatively lenient punishment of decapitation.[1]

The victims, however, showed no desire to escape their doom. They rather gloried in their religion, and openly exulted in the prospect of death. It is possible that they were Montanists. Their leader, Speratus, in reply to an exhortation to swear by the emperor, replied with an offer to explain the mystery of the Christian religion. Cythius protested in answer to a threat of punishment, " Know, proconsul, that we fear no other except one God, our Lord Who is in

[1] Ruinart, *Acta Martyrum Sincera*.

heaven." Another, Donata, "We give honour to Caesar, but fear and worship we accord to Christ, the true God." Vestia, an aged woman apparently, "This shall my heart always meditate and my life pronounce, 'that I am a Christian.'"[1]

We also read of martyrs in Madaura, A.D. 180.

There was also a persecution in Asia, A.D. 182, under Arrius Antoninus, when Tertullian relates that "all the Christians of the province presented themselves before his judgement-seat, on which, ordering a few to be executed, he said to the rest, 'Unhappy men, if you wish to die you have precipices and halters.'"[2]

Obscure provincials were not, however, the only Christians to suffer. In the year 185 Apollonius, described by Eusebius[3] as a man renowned for his culture and philosophy, was summoned by Perennis, Prefect of the Praetorian Guard, to give an account of himself before the Senate, a procedure which could hardly have been followed unless Apollonius were a senator or a man of distinction. From the Armenian acts of this martyrdom, which have been translated by by Mr. F. C. Conybeare,[4] we learn that when brought before the Senate he was questioned by Perennis in the following manner.

Asked why he would not sacrifice, he replied "Because I am a Christian therefore I fear God, Who made heaven and earth, and sacrifice not to empty idols." Urged to swear by the good for-

[1] Ruinart, *Acta Martyrum Sincera*. [2] *To Scapula*, 5.
[3] *H. E.* v. 21. [4] *Monuments of Early Christianity*.

tune of the autocrat Commodus, he said "I am willing to swear in truth by the true God that we too love the emperor, and offer up prayers for his majesty."

The prefect said "Come, then, and sacrifice to Apollo and to the other gods and to the emperor's images." Apollonius refused, saying, among other things, "But as to sacrifices, I and all Christians offer a bloodless sacrifice to God."

He was remanded for a day in the hope that he would change his mind, but he remained firm and was condemned. The magistrate said "I would fain let thee go, but I cannot because of the decree of the Senate. Yet with benevolence I pronounce sentence upon thee," and he ordered him to be beheaded with a sword. Apollonius said "I thank God for thy sentence." Then in the words of the Acts, "The executioners straightway led him away and beheaded him, while he continued to glorify the Father, Son, and Holy Spirit, to whom be glory for ever. Amen."

After A.D. 185 persecutions seem to have ceased in this reign, which may have been due to the influence of Marcia, the consort or morganatic wife of Commodus, who was herself a sympathizer, if no more, with Christianity. She was instrumental in securing the release of the Christians working in the lead mines of Sardinia, and is likely to have used her influence in favour of toleration. At any rate from this date the persecution was appreciably relaxed.

Severus, A.D. 193–205

In the year A.D. 193 Marcia, the consort of Commodus, found her own name on a list of persons marked for execution. She thereupon arranged successfully for her husband's assassination instead. His successor, Pertinax, was soon murdered by the Praetorians, who put the Empire up to auction, and knocked it down to Didius Julianus as the highest bidder. Septimius Severus, a general of the army of the Danube, at once invaded Italy, and was accepted as emperor by the Senate. Didius was deposed and sentenced to death, and thus ended his dearly-bought reign of sixty-six days.

Severus was an African whose native speech was Phoenician; after consulting the stars he married a Syrian, Julia Domna, and was without the old Roman conservative prejudice against Christianity. According to Tertullian he was once healed by the anointing of a Christian, and a Christian nurse was foster-mother to his son. "Both men and women of highest rank, whom Severus knew well to be Christians, he not only did not injure, but even distinguished them by his testimony, and gave them publicly back to us, in spite of the rage of the mob."[1] Nevertheless, the law was not altered, and persecutions took place, notably in Africa. Tertullian's Apology (A.D. 197) was provoked by one of them.

[1] *To Scapula*, 4.

Severus had trouble with the Jews, and renewed a law of Antoninus Pius forbidding the circumcision of proselytes. He also forbade conversion to Christianity. This was in A.D. 202. It is noteworthy as the first law enacted against Christians. Hitherto they had been prosecuted under the old laws. It was followed by new outbreaks of persecution, principally in Alexandria and Africa.

In Alexandria, Leonides, the father of Origen, was one of the victims.[1] Basilides, one of Origen's disciples, was an officer in the army, and was in charge of the soldiers who led away one Potamiaena to execution, and defended her from the violence of the mob. Noticing his act she bade him be of good cheer, for she would intercede for him with the Lord. She herself was killed by having boiling pitch poured over her body. Not long after Basilides declared himself a Christian,[2] and was condemned to suffer. When questioned by one of the brethren he declared that Potamiaena had appeared to him on three nights after her martyrdom, and had placed a crown on his head, saying that she had entreated the Lord for him, and had obtained her prayer, and that soon she would take him with her. Whereupon he was baptized and soon afterwards beheaded.

The persecution reached Carthage, where Perpetua and her companions suffered in March, A.D. 203.

[1] For Origen, see below, p. 142.
[2] Eusebius, *H. E.* vi. 1.

Perpetua, who was twenty-two years old, was married, and nursing an infant son. She was a lady of some birth and position. Her father, mother, and two brothers were living. One brother was a catechumen, as was Perpetua herself. Her companions who were arrested at the same time were Revocatus and Felicitas, his fellow slave and consort,[1] who was expecting her confinement, Saturninus, and Secundulus. They were all catechumens. The following account of their sufferings is an authentic narrative by Perpetua herself down to the point where it is taken up by another hand, probably Tertullian's.

"When I was in the hands of our persecutors, my father, for the affection he bore me, made new efforts to shake my resolution. 'Father,' I said, 'do you see this vessel lying here?' He said 'I see it.' And I said to him 'Can it be called by any other name than its own?' And he said 'No.' 'Nor can I call myself by anything else than what I am, a Christian.'" Her father then left her for a time, and all the accused were baptized. Though under arrest they had not been taken to prison.

"After a few days we were put in prison, and I was terrified because I had never known such darkness. It was a dreadful day. The heat was terrible, thanks to the crowds there through the extortions of the soldiers. Besides which I was distracted with anxiety for my baby. Then Tertius and Pomponius, the holy deacons, who were

[1] Slaves could not contract a legal marriage.

ministering to us, arranged by payment that for a few hours we should be refreshed by being let out into a better part of the prison. My baby was brought to me almost famished, and I nursed him. Being anxious for him I spoke to my mother about him, and encouraged my brother. I was distressed because I saw that they were distressed on my account. Such were the anxieties I suffered for many days; and I arranged that my baby should stay in the prison with me; and at once I grew strong, and was relieved of worry and anxiety about the child; my prison suddenly became a palace, so that I preferred being there to being anywhere else."

While waiting for her trial she had a vision. She saw a ladder reaching up to heaven, very narrow, and the sides garnished with every kind of cutting and stabbing weapon. Underneath it lay a dragon, in wait to catch any who fell, and to deter others from making the attempt.

Saturus, who was not arrested with the rest, was the first to climb. When he got to the top he said " Perpetua, I am supporting you." Perpetua came next, stepping on the dragon's head. When she reached the top she saw an immense garden, and seated in the midst one like a shepherd milking his sheep, surrounded by many thousands in white robes. He called her and offered her curds from the milk which he had drawn; this she ate; the multitude exclaimed " Amen." Then she awoke. " And I told my brother, and we understood that our passion was imminent, and we ceased to have any more hope in this world. After some days a rumour got about that we were to be examined, and my father came from the city to the prison, overwhelmed with grief. 'Daughter, have pity on my grey hairs; have pity on your father, if I am worthy to be called your father; if I have brought you up; if I have preferred you to your brothers. Think of your brothers; think of your mother; think of your son who cannot survive you. Lay aside this obstinacy; do not destroy us all.'

"As he said this he kissed my hands and threw himself at my feet, and called me not daughter but mistress. I was distressed on my father's account because he alone out of all my family would not rejoice in my passion. I comforted him saying 'What God wills will be done. Know that we are not in our own power, but in God's.' And he went away from me sorrowful.

"The next day when we were at dinner we were carried off suddenly for our examination, and we came to the forum. The rumour ran through all places near the forum, and an immense crowd collected. We went up into the dock. The others were-questioned and confessed. Then it was my turn. And my father immediately appeared with my son and drew me a little aside, beseeching me 'Have pity on thy babe.' And Hilarianus, the procurator, who then acted as judge in place of the deceased proconsul Minucius, said 'Spare your father's grey hair; spare the infancy of your son. Sacrifice for the health of the emperor.' I replied 'I will not.' Hilarianus said 'Are you a Christian?' I replied 'I am.' And when my father attempted to draw me away he was ordered by Hilarianus to be pulled down, and he struck him with a rod. And I was distressed for my father as though I had been beaten myself; so unhappy was I for him in his old age. Then he sentenced us all to the beasts. And we returned joyfully to the prison.

"Then because I had been used to nurse my baby, and had had him with me in prison, I sent at once Pomponius the deacon to ask my father for the child. But he would not give him to me. . . ."

After her return to prison she had another vision, in which she saw her brother Dinocrates, who died when seven years old. "A few days after, while we were all praying, suddenly a voice reached me, and I said 'Dinocrates'; and I was astonished because he had not come into my mind until then. And I began to pray fervently for him. On that night I had the following vision:—I saw Dinocrates coming out of a dark place where there were many others, very hot and thirsty, his face dirty and pale. . . . Between him and me there was a great space, so that we could not get near to each other. Near him was a vessel of water, just out of his reach, up to which he was stretching in order to drink. I awoke and knew my brother was in trouble. But I trusted I could relieve him by prayer. And I prayed for him every day and night with tears. On the day we spent in the stocks I saw the same place which I had seen dark to be full of light, and Dinocrates clean, well-dressed, and refreshed, and where there had been a wound there was a scar. I saw the same vessel of water, now lowered to his middle, with a cup attached to it, out of which he was drinking. And when his thirst was quenched he began to play happily like a child."

We are, no doubt, to understand from this vision that Dinocrates had died unbaptized.

"Soon after, Pudens, the officer in charge of the prison guards, began to make much of us, perceiving that there was great virtue in us, and allowed us to receive visits from the brethren for our mutual refreshment. When the day of the spectacle was near, my father came to me overcome with grief, and began to tear his beard and threw himself on his face on the ground, and cursed his years and said enough to move any created being. I grieved for his unhappy old age."

Perpetua recorded another vision, from which she knew she would have to contend not with beasts but the devil. She ends her narrative :—

"I have told this story up to the day before the Games. Of what takes place at the Games let him write who wills."

Felicitas was confined prematurely, in answer to the prayers of her companions, as she feared that otherwise her execution would be postponed.

When she cried out in her pains, her guards said, " If you cry out now, what will you do when exposed to the beasts ? " She replied, " Now I bear my sufferings alone. Then there will be another in me Who will suffer for me because I shall be suffering for Him."

The child lived and was given to a sister to be brought up as her daughter.

It was the custom for condemned criminals to have what was called "a free supper" on their last night, a supper which seems to have been public as well as free. Perpetua and her companions turned it into an agape, and tried to convert the onlookers, reminding them of the judgement of God, and alleging their own joy in suffering. Saturus said, "Look at our faces carefully that you may recognize us at the Day of Judgement."

They proceeded from prison to the amphitheatre, joyful and firm in demeanour. The men were in front, followed by Perpetua, with Felicitas last of all. When they passed Hilarianus, they cried out, " You are our judge ; God is yours." For this they were scourged.

The narrative continues :—

" He Who had said, 'Ask, and ye shall receive,' gave them the death they desired. For when they talked about the kind of martyrdom they would prefer, Secundulus used to dèclare that he would like to be exposed to all the beasts hat he might wear a more glorious crown. Accordingly, he and Revocatus were attacked first by a leopard and then by a bear. Saturus dreaded a bear more than anything else, and therefore hoped he would be dispatched by one bite from a leopard. He was exposed to a wild boar, which turned on his keeper and inflicted such a wound that he died a few days later, while Saturus was only dragged along the ground; and when he was fastened near a bear the animal would not leave his cage. So that Saturus, being unhurt, was called upon to face a second encounter."

Perpetua and Felicitas were exposed to a savage cow. "First Perpetua was tossed, and she fell on her back. Then sitting up, and perceiving that her clothes were torn, she covered herself as well as she could, thinking more of modesty than pain. Then she did up her hair, for it was not seemly for a martyr to suffer with hair loose, or she would have looked like a mourner. Then she got up, and seeing that Felicitas was hurt, she took her hand and supported her. Both stood up together, and the crowd being moved to pity cried out that they should be led to the Gate of Life (Sanavivaria). There Perpetua was received by a certain catechumen called Rusticus, and appeared as though just woke up—so far was she gone in ecstasy and in the spirit — and began to look round, and say to the wondering bystanders, 'When are we to be exposed to the cow?' When she heard what had happened, she did not believe it until she saw the marks on her body and her clothes. Then she called for her brother and the catechumen and said to them, 'Stand fast in the Faith, and love one another, and do not be offended by our sufferings.'

"Meanwhile, Saturus was talking to the soldier Pudens at another gate, 'As I anticipated and foretold, I have not yet been hurt by any beast. May you believe with your whole heart. Behold, I go forth and with one bite a leopard will take away my life.' Almost immediately, just at the end of the Games, a leopard was let loose, and with one bite covered him with blood, so that the mob shouted in derision at this second baptism, 'Well bathed! Well bathed!' And saved indeed he was who had a bath like that.[1] To Pudens he said, 'Farewell, remember my faith, and do not let these things disturb, but rather let them reassure you.' He also asked for the ring on his finger, and dipping it in his blood returned it, leaving it as a pledge and a memorial of his death. His lifeless body was then thrown down at the place where the throats of the wounded were cut.

"The people shouted for them to be brought into the middle of the theatre that their eyes might be accomplices of the sword in their murder. And they got up at once and moved to where the people wanted them. They kissed one another that they might consummate their martyrdom with the solemn rites of the kiss of

[1] "*Salvum lotum, salvum lotum.*" *Plane utique salvas evat, qui hoc modo laverat.*

peace. Then the others received the death-blow silently, without a movement and without a word, especially Saturus, who had already given up his soul, as he had been the first to climb the ladder. For in the vision he was supporting Perpetua. But Perpetua, that she might leave no woe untasted, was left to a raw gladiator's apprentice, and cried out when she felt the prick of the steel in her bones, and guided his unskilful weapon to her throat. Perhaps so great a woman, who was feared by the unclean spirit, could not have been killed had she not herself been willing." [1]

The story has been given at some length because it is an authentic and contemporary account and enables us to understand much of what was taking place. There was no attempt at a general proscription of all Christians. Rusticus was apparently unmolested. So was Perpetua's brother. The governor tries to secure the release of the accused, but when he fails to persuade them to recant, justice has to take its course. We see the enthusiasm of the martyrs, their sufferings in prison, alleviated in some measure by visits from their friends, permitted by the gaoler whose heart was touched. Finally their joy in suffering, their going out to the beasts as to victory, their treating death as life.

Severus was called to Britain, A.D. 208, on

[1] For the original text with a critical introduction, see *Cambridge Texts and Studies*, vol. I. Ed. J. Armitage Robinson.

account of an invasion of that province by the barbarians of the north. He led his army to the northern extremity of the island, and compelled his enemies to submit, at least in appearance. On his return he fell sick and died at York, February, A.D. 211.

CARACALLA, A.D. 211–217

Severus was succeeded by his sons Caracalla and Geta who began negotiations for dividing the Empire, but before they were completed Caracalla had his brother murdered and became undisputed lord of the whole. Under him an era of toleration for the Church may be said to have begun. Nevertheless, there was a persecution at Carthage at the beginning of the reign, which provoked Tertullian's protest, addressed to Scapula the proconsul. There is no reason to suppose that persecution ceased altogether, but the emperors were uninterested, many provincial governors disliked it, and Christians were probably sufficiently numerous to make it not altogether wise or prudent for private citizens to act as prosecutors.

Caracalla was murdered and succeeded by Macrinus. Julia Domna, the widow of Severus, had been the real ruler of the Empire in the reign of Caracalla. When he died she committed suicide, but her sister Julia Moesa had two daughters, Soaemias and Mammaea, each of whom was a widow, and each had an only son.

Bassianus, afterwards known as the Emperor Elagabalus, was the son of Soaemias. He was at the time high priest of the Sun, and during the reign of Macrinus ministered at the Temple of the Sun in Emesa. Through the machinations of his grandmother Moesa, sister of Julia Domna, he raised the troops in Syria against Macrinus, and succeeded him as emperor.

Apart from his vices, his main interests seem to have lain in the ritual of the worship of the sun. He was murdered by the Praetorians and was succeeded by his cousin, Alexander Severus, the son of Mammaea. Alexander Severus left to his mother the principal cares of State. His own character was amiable enough, and he had none of the qualities of the persecutor. He is said to have placed a statue of Jesus in his oratory by the side of statues of Abraham, Orpheus, and Apollonius of Tyana. In a lawsuit between Christians and a company of victuallers for the possession of a piece of ground, he awarded the site to the Christians. " Better that the land should be devoted to the service of God in any form than that it should be handed over for the use of cook-shops."

His mother, the Empress Julia Mammaea, having heard of the fame of Origen, sent for him when she was staying in Antioch. "With her he stayed some time explaining innumerable matters calculated to promote the glory of the Lord, and to show the excellence of divine instruction." [1]

[1] Eusebius, *H. E.* vi. 21.

Maximinus, a Thracian, who had attracted the attention of Severus thirty-two years before by his gigantic stature and remarkable strength and agility, became emperor when Alexander was killed by the troops near Mainz in A.D. 235. He was a rude and unlettered barbarian, without knowledge of Greek, of a fierce and sanguinary temper, and, according to Eusebius, was instigated to persecute the Church because of the number of Christians in the government services. "Inflamed with hatred against the officials of Alexander, consisting of many believers, he raised a persecution and commanded at first only the heads of the Churches to be slain."[1] The heads of the Churches probably included presbyters as well as bishops. Maximinus is the first persecutor to single out bishops and clergy for destruction. Nevertheless, the persecution was not severe except in Pontus and Cappadocia, where an earthquake had caused ill-feeling, and Serenianus the governor was hostile. Maximinus was killed by his soldiers A.D. 238.

After a rapid succession of emperors Gordian III was placed on the throne, and was succeeded by Philip the Arabian (A.D. 244–249), who not only tolerated, but even favoured the Church, and in later days was, with Alexander, counted among those emperors "who were openly said to be Christian." Eusebius even asserts that at Antioch he wished to attend a public service at Easter, but "was not permitted

[1] *H. E.* vi. 28.

by Babylas the bishop to enter before he had confessed his sins and numbered himself in the ranks of the penitents. For otherwise he never should be received by him unless he first did this . . . on account of the many crimes which he had committed. The emperor is said to have obeyed willingly, and exhibited a genuine and religious disposition and fear of God."[1] Eusebius also states that Origen wrote letters to him and his wife Severa.[2] However, this evidence does no more than show his friendly interest in the Church. The incident at Antioch need only mean that he wished to be present at the Easter Eucharist and was permitted to do so only if placed among the catechumens, who were probably seated close to the penitents. If he had been a Christian, we should have much more definite assurances on the point.

Philip was defeated by rebel legions under Decius, and killed A.D. 249. Since the accession of Severus in A.D. 193 there had for practical purposes been no *Roman* emperors. Severus was an African and a persecutor, but not a systematic one. Caracalla was half Eastern by his Syrian mother Julia Domna. Cruel and brutal as he was he had no particular animus against Christianity. His successors, with the brief interlude of Maximinus until the death of Philip (A.D. 249), were, for the most part, inclined to favour Christianity and showed a friendly interest in it.

[1] *H. E.* vi. 34.   [2] Ibid., 36.

The Church had enjoyed something like toleration over the greater part of a period which began A.D. 185, and as a result made an enormous advance in numbers and influence. Christians began to buy sites and build churches, instead of worhipping in private houses, and gained some measure of popularity and fashion. It is impossible to estimate numbers with any approach to precision, but it seems a not unreasonable guess that the number of Christians was more than doubled between A.D. 185 and 249.

VII

THE CATECHETICAL SCHOOL OF ALEXANDRIA

Clement of Alexandria

ALEXANDRIA was one of the greatest cities of the Empire. It had been founded by Alexander the Great, and after his death became the residence of his companion Ptolemy and his descendants. Under this Macedonian influence it became a centre of Hellenistic thought and culture, the head-quarters of philosophers, poets, and mathematicians from all over the world. It possessed a world-famous and well-endowed University, three libraries, and a staff of professors. It fell to the Romans in the year 30 B.C., when Octavius, afterwards the Emperor Augustus, took possession. Egypt did not become a Roman province, but remained the private property of the emperor. It was the main source of the Roman corn supply, which was shipped on board huge corn-ships at Alexandria. It was also the half-way house between Rome and India. " Merchants have learned the shortest way, and commerce has brought India near to us." The route[1] was up the Nile to Coptos, or some intermediate stopping-place, then by caravan to Myoshormos or Berenice, wells and cisterns being laid along the track. From Myoshormos or Berenice they could go to Arabia, India, Ethiopia, and China. And much trade did go.

Alexandria became also a favourite resort of Jews. According to Philo, there were not less than a million in Egypt, and these were mostly concentrated in Alexandria. Two out of the five districts into which the town was divided were given over to them. There was something like a *rapprochement* between the Jewish intellectuals and the Hellenic philosophers, which was helped considerably by the translation of the Hebrew Bible into Greek in the well-known Septuagint version. Already, as early as Philo in the first century of our era, Plato was claimed as an Attic Moses, and the law was found in Plato, and Plato in the law. It was the business of Philo to provide a Platonist interpretation of the Old Testament. It was, therefore, only in the nature of things that the Christian philosopher should continue in the same path and show that Christianity was not irreconcilable with the nobler conceptions of Plato and the Greek philosophers.

The origin of Christianity in Alexandria is obscure. It is not mentioned in the New Testament, though pilgrims from Alexandria must have been in Jerusalem on the Day of Pentecost,

[1] Friedlander, *Roman Life and Manners*, i. 306.

The Catechetical School of Alexandria 135

and the four thousand converts must have included, one would think, some from Alexandria. Apollos is the only Alexandrian Christian mentioned by S. Paul. According to a tradition mentioned by Eusebius, S. Mark was the founder of the Alexandrian Church, but this tradition is not corroborated. Eusebius gives a list of eighteen bishops, beginning with Annianus, who succeeded S. Mark in the eighth year of Nero. The fame of the Alexandrian Church rests on its catechetical school, which Eusebius, writing in the fourth century, tells us had been established as a school of learning from ancient times. All Churches gave instructions to catechists, and in any Church where numbers were as large something like a regular catechetical school must have arisen. But in Alexandria there was a demand not only for this elementary instruction, corresponding to the ordinary Confirmation or first Communion class, but for something to meet the needs of more sophisticated inquirers. Young Christians studied philosophy, and some fell away; Ammonius Saccas became a heathen, and Ambrose a Gnostic. On the other hand, pagans like Celsus and Porphyry studied Christianity. There was an obvious need for that kind of teaching which the Oxford Mission has been giving in Calcutta to much the same kind of inquirers. The first head whose name has come down is Pantaenus, a native of Sicily and a Stoic philosopher, who became a convert to Christianity and a missionary to the nations of the East ; he had penetrated to India, where he is said to have found the Gospel of S. Matthew in Hebrew, which S. Bartholomew left behind after he had preached there. Pantaenus afterwards settled down as the head of the school. None of his writings have come down.

Clement also began life as a heathen. He was a Greek, and possibly an Athenian, born about A.D. 150. After wandering in many lands he became a disciple of Pantaenus at Alexandria, where he settled down as a teacher, became a presbyter, and eventually succeeded his master. When the persecution broke out, A.D. 202, the school was broken up ; he left Alexandria, and little more is known of him except that he was alive in A.D. 211, and at that date assisting Alexander (who was in prison) in the work of the Church of Jerusalem, of which Alexander was bishop. He was a bearer of a letter from Alexander to the Church at Antioch, in which he is described as " the blessed presbyter, a man endued with all virtue and well approved, whom you already know and will learn still more to know ; who also, being here by the foreknowledge and oversight of the Master, has established and increased the Church of God." [1] His works that survive are the *Protrepticus*, addressed to the heathen ; the *Paedagogus* or *Tutor*, a book of instruction for the ordinary Christian ; the *Stromata* or *Miscellanies*, for the Gnostic or advanced disciple, and a practical treatise entitled,

[1] Eusebius, *H. E.* vi. 11.

What Rich Man can be saved? in which Clement maintained that the right disposition of the soul and not the renunciation of worldly goods was the condition of salvation.

Though Justin claimed philosophy as the handmaid of religion and continued to wear his philosopher's cloak after his conversion, to Clement belongs the credit of being the first to emphasize the importance of profane learning in God's plan for the world, or in other words, to claim all learning as in a sense sacred.

It is not fair to say that the leaders of the Church condemned learning, but some of them were certainly shy of it. Irenaeus has nothing to say against it, but thought it better to be simple and unlettered than puffed up, and he quotes with approval the words of S. Paul, "Knowledge puffeth up, but love edifieth." But they did not condemn learning as such. Tatian did, but Tatian became a heretic, and died a Gnostic. S. Paul and the Christians of the next two centuries had to deal with Gnostics and Greek philosophers, who both tended to over-value knowledge. Man was to be saved by knowledge. They had to warn their disciples that knowledge was good but might be dangerous, that knowledge by itself could not save. Some, no doubt, exaggerated this cautious attitude, and it is quite possible that Celsus had met Christians who scoffed at human learning, and adopted the attitude " Do not inquire; only believe."

T

Tertullian was a man of immense learning, which he used freely enough for controversial purposes, though he has not much to say of its place in the Christian scheme. Clement has no misgivings. He was a learned man himself, though his erudition was not quite so profound as appears at the first reading of his works, as he seems to have been indebted to a dictionary for many of his quotations. He claims with enthusiasm all learning for God. " God is the cause of all good things ; of some primarily as the Old and New Testament ; others by consequence as philosophy." [1] All good things come from God, including philosophy, which is therefore the handmaid of God, and the schoolmaster to bring the Greeks to Christ, as the law was to bring the Jews. " Philosophy is conducive to piety, being a kind of preparatory training to those who attain to faith through demonstration."

Clement, in fact, carries the war into the enemies' camp, and claims the title of Gnostic, the one who knows, for the Christian. S. Paul said of the Christians of his day to the Jews, " We are the circumcision." So Clement says " We are the Gnostics." As though a believer to-day were to say, " We are the Rationalists," and make good his claim to the title. The instructed Christian is the true Gnostic, and brings all his knowledge to bear on the Faith, " so that from geometry and music and grammar and philosophy itself, culling what is useful, he

[1] *Strom.* i. 5.

The Catechetical School of Alexandria 139

guards the Faith against assault."[1] All schools of philosophy were illuminated by rays from the true Light. The Greeks he considered borrowed from Moses. Plato was Moses in an Attic dress. "There is, then, in philosophy, though stolen as the fire of Prometheus, a slender spark capable of being fanned into flame, a trace of wisdom, and an impulse from God."[2]

He thought that women ought to philosophize as well as men,[3] and held the modern view that good is to be done without the prospect of reward or punishment. No twentieth century teacher could be more emphatic. "The true Gnostic is not to abstain from evil out of fear."[4] If he had to choose between the knowledge of God and eternal salvation, he would choose without the least hesitation the knowledge of God. "He does not consider whether any profitable reward or enjoyment comes to him; but drawn by the love of Him Who is the true object of life, and led to what is requisite, practises piety."

"The soul of the wise man and Gnostic, as sojourning in the body, conducts itself towards it gravely and respectfully," he says in one place; but on the whole he seems inclined to carry asceticism further than this maxim would warrant, as the advanced Christian is to aim at complete "apathy" towards external things—detachment as we should call it now.

Clement is a mystic, and his aim is to enter into immediate and realized communion with

[1] *Strom.* i. 9. [2] Ibid., 17. [3] Ibid., iv. 8. [4] Ibid., 22.

God, while external rules sink into relative insignificance. He leans towards the immediate apprehension of God, and away from rules and externals. Clement follows S. John and S. Paul rather than S. Peter. Like all mystics he believed in the prayer of silence, and, like Brother Laurence, did not need any set times or places for the practice of the presence of God. " If some assign definite hours for prayer—as for example, the third, sixth, and ninth—yet the Gnostic prays throughout his whole life, endeavouring by prayer to have fellowship with God." [1]

Clement was right in emphasizing the need and possibility of communion with God, and a life lived on a high spiritual plane. He fell into error when he distinguished too sharply between the different sorts of Christian lives. It is safer for us not to judge, or say which is higher or lower, but to go wherever we are led. The Gnostic in practice must have found it hard not to be a Pharisee, as he is taught not only that "there are degrees of glory in heaven, and the Gnostic who has become perfect on earth will share the highest rank with the Apostles,"[2] but that "to know is more than to believe, as to be dignified with the highest honour after being saved is a greater thing than being saved." In other words, there was more difference between a Gnostic and the lowest category of the saved than between the just saved and the lost. Moreover, the prayers of the Gnostic are received

[1] *Strom.* vii. 7.   [2] Ibid., 14.

with special favour. "The Gnostic receives all that he asks," on account of his worthiness, for "God knows those who are and those who are not worthy."

The danger of this spirit is accentuated by the un-Pauline stress laid on a man's own power of achievement. "But him who from this has trained himself to the summit of knowledge, the elevated height of the perfect man, all things relating to time and space help on."[1]

According to Clement it was only possible to become a true Gnostic after years of arduous preparation.[2] There appear to be three stages of preparation :—

1. The stage of faith, implying a comprehensive knowledge of the essentials.

2. Knowledge, conveying the soul to infallibility, science, and comprehension.

3. Love, which gives the loving to the loved, that which knows to that which is known.

There are two conversions—the first from heathenism to faith, and the second from faith to knowledge.

We are reminded of the three stages in the progress of the mystic — the purgative, the illuminative, and the unitive.

Finally, the perfected Gnostic "is equal to the angels, and urges his flight to the ancestral hall through the holy septennial of heavenly abodes to the Lord's own mansion."

Clement did a service to the Church by claim-

[1] *Strom.* vii. 7.   [2] Ibid., 10.

ing the support of philosophy, and by laying down the principle that all good things are from God, including art and learning. The devil is not to have all the best tunes. But his zeal carried him too far. In his eyes philosophy, instead of being a responsibility to its possessor, puts him into a superior class. There is a touch of the Pharisee in his Gnosticism. He is here rather Platonist than Pauline.

Of his other works the *Tutor* contains much interesting information on the life and manners of both Christians and heathens in Alexandria in that day. The year of his death is uncertain, but it must have occurred before A.D. 215, when Alexander alludes to him, in a letter to Origen, as " having gone before."[1]

Origen

One of Clement's pupils was a boy named Origen, a native of Egypt, a Copt, born A.D. 185. His first teacher had been his father, who had trained him in both Christian and Greek literature. From the beginning he had shown great zeal and ability in his studies and knew most of the Scriptures by heart. Zeal was indeed the key-note of his life. During the persecution at Alexandria he would have given himself up, and was only deterred by the persuasion of his mother, who went to the length of hiding his clothes. When his father was seized he

[1] Eusebius, *H. E.* vi. 14.

The Catechetical School of Alexandria

wrote him a letter in which he encouraged him to stand firm. "Take heed not to change thy mind on account of us." He was seventeen when his father was martyred, and he supported his mother and six younger brothers by teaching Greek literature. When the persecution broke out the catechetical school came to an end, but at the request of some who desired instruction he started it again, and was accepted by Bishop Demetrius as a catechist. Several of his pupils became martyrs, and Origen was noted for the fearlessness with which he visited them in prison, stood by them at their trial, and kissed them when led away to die, so that more than once he was nearly stoned by the mob.[1] His immunity from persecution may have been due to the fact that the law was apparently directed against converts to Christianity.

The number of his pupils became so great that he gave up his school of philosophy and devoted himself entirely to teaching the Faith. He lived a life of extreme asceticism, and sold his Greek books so as to secure for himself a trifling pension and be able to teach without a fee. He limited his sleep as well as his food, and always slept on the bare ground, wore no shoes, drank no wine, and ate only such food as was necessary to keep body and soul together. The fame of his asceticism seems to have attracted many, including "heretics and even philosophers of no mean account,"[2] who were prevailed upon to

[1] Eusebius, *H. E.* vi. 3.   [2] Ibid., 18.

adopt his doctrine. Many also imitated his way of life. His zeal led him into extremes in all he did, and his asceticism carried him to the length of self-mutilation, taking the words of Scripture, as Eusebius puts it, "in too literal and puerile a sense."[1] Demetrius, the bishop, was informed and bade him continue his work. His school became so popular that he was forced to enlist help, and employed Heraclas to instruct the beginners while he devoted himself to the more advanced pupils. At the same time he found it necessary to study Greek philosophy. As he himself put it : " When I had devoted myself wholly to the Word and my fame went abroad concerning my proficiency, as I was sometimes visited by heretics, sometimes by those who were conversant with the studies of the Greeks, especially those that were pursuing philosophy, I was resolved to examine both the opinions of the heretics and those works of the philosophers which pretend to speak of truth."[2]

Like Plotinus, he attended the lectures of Ammonius Saccas. Porphyry, the Neoplatonist philosopher, attended the same lectures, and gives the following account of Origen, "whom I happened to meet when I was very young, and who was very celebrated and is still celebrated by the writings which he has left. I mean Origen whose glory is very great with the teachers of those doctrines. For this man, having been a hearer of Ammonius, who had

[1] Eusebius, *H. E.* vi. 8.   [2] Ibid., 19.

The Catechetical School of Alexandria

made the greatest proficiency in philosophy among those of our day, as to knowledge derived great benefit from his master, but with regard to a correct purpose of life he pursued a course directly opposite. For Ammonius, a Christian, and brought up among Christians by his parents, when equipped with reason and knowledge changed his views and lived according to the laws. But Origen, a Greek, educated in Greek literature, fell away to this barbarian folly. To which he both consigned himself and his attainments in learning, living like a Christian contrary to the laws, but in regard to his opinions, both of things and the Deity, acting the Greek and intermingling Greek literature with these foreign fictions. For he was always in company with Plato, and had the works of Numenius and Cranius, of Apollophanes and Longinus, of Moderatus and Nicomachus, and others whose writings are valued, in his hands. He also read the works of Chaerenon the Stoic, and those of Cornutus. From them he derived the allegorical mode of interpretation, and applied it to the Jewish Scriptures."[1]

About A.D. 212 he visited Rome, "being desirous to see this very ancient Church." He was one of the earliest textual critics, and having learned Hebrew, searched for different versions in order to compare them with the Septuagint. He travelled widely, and his fame steadily increased.

He was sent for by the Governor of Arabia;

[1] Eusebius, *H. E.* vi. 19.

who wished to consult him about his soul. Later Mammaea, the mother of the future emperor, Alexander, was so impressed by his reputation that she summoned him to Antioch, and provided him with a military escort, "so desirous was she of conversing with him." The Emperor Philip corresponded with him. During the sack of Alexandria by the soldiers of Caracalla, Origen took refuge in Palestine, and was welcomed by the Bishops of Caesarea and Jerusalem, who invited him, though a layman, to address not only the catechumens, but the congregation in church. This was A.D. 215. Demetrius wrote to protest and recalled him to Alexandria.

Origen's first book—*De Principiis*, "On First Principles"—is the earliest attempt to form a synthetic Christian theology. The Apostles, he argues, had handed down certain facts and usages which are to be received, "leaving, however, the grounds of their statements to be examined into by those who should deserve the excellent gifts of the Spirit."[1] The Apostolic tradition contains the following points :—

There is one God Who created all things. Jesus Christ was born of a Virgin and the Holy Spirit, and was Incarnate although God; did truly die; and did truly rise from the dead; and was taken up into heaven. Thirdly, the Holy Spirit is associated in honour and dignity with the Father and the Son.

[1] *De Principiis*, Preface.

The soul has a life of its own and will be rewarded or punished. There will be a resurrection of the body. Every rational soul has free-will, and is opposed by evil spirits and assisted by angels.

The Scriptures are from the Spirit of God and have two meanings, the literal and the hidden, or spiritual.

Origen's business was to define, explain, co-ordinate, expand, and generally adapt to the needs of his contemporaries this Apostolic tradition. He was a daring thinker, and some of his speculations were eventually disallowed. But in this respect, as in so many others, he was a pioneer, and was sailing over seas as yet uncharted.

His literary output was prodigious. He is said to have produced six thousand works in all. He learnt Hebrew and wrote commentaries on the Scriptures. His great work was the *Hexapla* or sixfold Bible, which set out in parallel columns the Hebrew text in Hebrew, the Hebrew text in Greek characters, the Septuagint, and three other Greek texts. He was the pioneer of textual criticism as applied to the Bible, and took enormous pains to acquire texts and versions. " Those original works written in the Hebrew, and in the hands of the Jews, he procured as his own. He also investigated the editions of others who, besides the Seventy, had published translations of the Scriptures, and some different from the well-known translations of Aquila, Symmachus, and Theodotion, which he hunted up and traced to, I know not what, ancient lurking-places, where they had lain concealed from remote times, and brought them to the light. In which, when it was doubtful to him from what author they came, he only added the remark that he had found this translation at Nicopolis near Actium, but this other translation in such a place. "In the *Hexapla*, indeed, of the Psalms after those four noted editions, he adds not only a fifth, but a sixth and seventh translation, and in one it is remarked that it was discovered at Jericho in a tub in the time of Antoninus the son of Severus." [1]

His friend Ambrose, a man of wealth, provided him with seven amanuenses, who relieved one another, and seven copyists, besides girls who did other writing for him.

About A.D. 230 he was on a journey to Greece and went very much out of his way to visit his friends the Bishops of Jerusalem and Caesarea, who ordained him priest. It has not been suggested that the Ordination was arranged beforehand, but it can hardly have been otherwise. A serious-minded man like Origen would not be ordained casually, as an incident of a short visit. On his return to Alexandria he had to face a storm. Demetrius, according to Eusebius, was "overcome by human infirmity," or, in other words, became a prey to jealousy, and "wrote to traduce him to all the bishops of the Church, though he had nothing to

[1] Eusebius, *H. E.* vi. 16.

allege against him beyond the act done by him as a boy, nearly thirty years before."[1] It is not necessary, however, to impute jealousy. Rightly or wrongly Demetrius had acted on a deliberate and considered resolve in not ordaining Origen. If Origen desired Ordination, as presumably he did, his friends must have pressed it upon Demetrius. Whether Demetrius regarded the mutilation as a sufficient obstacle, which was quite a reasonable view to take, or whether he suspected his orthodoxy without feeling sure enough of his ground to challenge so redoubtable an opponent on that ground, or whether he had other reasons, good or bad, with which we are not acquainted, the decision must have been deliberate and maintained not without difficulty. Not unnaturally he was considerably provoked and summoned a Synod of Bishops and Presbyters, which condemned Origen to leave Alexandria. Demetrius then summoned a second Synod, by which Origen was excommunicated, a sentence which was enforced in Egypt and recognized in the West, but not in Palestine, Arabia, or Greece.

Origen retired to Caesarea, where he found shelter and protection. The school at Alexandria was taught first by Heraclas, and when Heraclas succeeded Demetrius as Bishop of Alexandria by Dionysius. It is significant that neither of them, though both were former pupils of Origen, and Heraclas had been his assistant,

[1] Eusebius, *H. E.* vi. 8.

when they in turn became Bishop of Alexandria did anything to bring him back.

The famous Alexandrian school was, however, in effect transferred to Caesarea, where many came, " not only of the residents, but also innumerable others from abroad, who left their country in order to attend his lectures." Thither came Gregory, afterwards called Thaumaturgus, and his brother Athenodorus. Firmilianus, Bishop of Caesarea in Cappadocia, summoned him "to benefit the churches" in his diocese. His own bishop, the Bishop of Jerusalem, we are told attended him like a pupil his master, and "allowed him to perform the duties of expounding the sacred Scriptures and other matters that pertain to the doctrines of the Church."

About A.D. 230 he wrote his work against Celsus.

In A.D. 250, during the Decian persecution, he was seized and put to the torture. " The nature and number of the bonds which he endured under an iron collar, and in the deepest recesses of the prison, where for many days he was extended and stretched to the distance of four holes on the rack, besides the threats of fire and other sufferings, he bore manfully."

He survived his tortures for two or three years, and died at Tyre, where for many centuries his tomb was the principal ornament of the cathedral of the Holy Sepulchre, and is still pointed out, though now only ruins remain.[1]

[1] C. Bigg, *Christian Platonists of Alexandria*.

He received no veneration after his death in spite of his stout confession and the austere asceticism of his whole life. In labours few scholars of any age have been more abundant. It may be that such labours did not make the popular appeal which was the necessary preliminary to the automatic canonization of those days, or that his unorthodoxy may have made more impression than appears, or his rash act may have been the bar, or there may have been something wanting in his character. But he remained uncanonized. He has never been reputed to be a saint.

Saint or not, he was one of the great men of his or indeed of any age, and a shining example to all students.

VIII

PAGAN ATTEMPTS AT RECON-
STRUCTION

FOR a long time the philosophers ignored Christianity, treating it as beneath contempt. When they did notice it, they named it as little as possible. Lucian, who was more a man of letters than a philosopher, scoffed at it in his *Death of Peregrinus*. But then he scoffed at all religions impartially.

Somewhere towards the end of the second century a Platonist called Celsus thought it worth while to write a book against the Christians, called *The True Word*. About the year A.D. 230, when Celsus "had long since departed," Origen wrote a reply, and the original attack survives only so far as it is quoted by Origen. The book is worthy of some examination, as it shows the objections to Christianity entertained by a pagan philosopher of that day, and gives some indication of the sort of reconstruction of the pagan religion which was to be attempted.

Celsus was well acquainted with the Scriptures of the Old Testament, with the Four Gospels, and with some of the Epistles of S. Paul. He probably knew the rest, though it did not answer

Pagan attempts at Reconstruction

his purpose to quote them. He fastens on the Incarnation and the Virgin Birth as the starting-point of Christianity, and further deals with the descent into hell, the Resurrection, the second coming to judge, as well as the creation—an interesting, because independent, witness to what were the salient features of Christian teaching in his day.

The Incarnation he thought preposterous. He scorns the thought that God should have come to earth at all. " God is good and beautiful and blessed.[1] . . . But if He come down among men He must undergo a change, from good to evil, from virtue to vice, from happiness to misery, and from best to worst. . . . God could not admit of such a change." " Why should He do it? Was it in order to learn what goes on among men?" That it should be to make men righteous he declares " a most shameless assertion." He sees no difference between men and animals. Bees and ants are not inferior to men.[2]

Jews and Christians are compared to a flight of bats, or to a swarm of ants issuing out of their nest, or to frogs holding council in a marsh, or to worms crawling together in a dung-hill and quarrelling with one another as to which of them were the greater sinners, and asserting that " God shows and announces to us all things beforehand ; and that, abandoning the whole world and the regions of heaven, He becomes a

Against Celsus, iv. 14.   [2] Ibid., 81.

citizen among us alone, and to us alone makes His intimations, and does not cease sending and inquiring in what way we may be associated with Him for ever." [1]

His account of the birth of Jesus is that He was "born in a certain Jewish village, of a poor woman of the country, who gained her living by spinning and who was turned out of doors by her husband, a carpenter by trade, because she was convicted of adultery; that, after being driven away by her husband and wandering about for a time, she disgracefully gave birth to Jesus, an illegitimate child, Who, having hired Himself out as a servant in Egypt on account of His poverty, and having then acquired some miraculous powers, returned to His own country and, by means of them, proclaimed Himself a god." [2] Celsus even went so far as to say that the father was a soldier called Panthera. On which story Origen makes the just comment that it at least admits that Jesus was not the son of Joseph and Mary.

The suffering, the lowly station, the affronts to which He submitted, culminating in the Cross, were inexplicable to Celsus, if Jesus were divine. He complains that Jesus received no assistance from His Father, and was unable to help Himself.[3] He considered that the rank of the Apostles was beneath divine dignity. "Jesus, having gathered round Him ten or eleven persons of notorious character, the very wickedest

[1] *Against Celsus*, iv. 23.   [2] Ibid., i. 28.   [3] Ibid., 54.

of tax-gatherers and sailors, fled, in company with them, from place to place, and obtained His living in a shameful and importunate manner."[1] He asks contemptuously: "Why did you not become a king instead of wandering about in so mean a condition, hiding yourself through fear, and leading a miserable life up and down?"[2]

He accuses Jesus, we do not know on what ground, of having attempted to hide after His condemnation, and "to escape in a most disgraceful manner"; and he goes on to assert that "a god could neither flee nor be led away prisoner; least of all could he be deserted and delivered up by them who had been his associates."[3] The betrayal was a very sore point. "No good general or leader was ever betrayed; nor even a wicked captain of robbers or commander of very wicked men, who was thought to be of any use to his associates."[4]

The descent into Hades and the Resurrection arouse his scorn and incredulity; but at the same time he called the Christians silly because they would not acknowledge that "a great multitude of Greeks and barbarians have frequently seen, and still see, no mere phantom, but Aesculapius himself, healing and doing good and foretelling the future."[5]

Christianity as *a way of life* he thought as bad as the Christian religion considered as a philo-

---
[1] *Against Celsus*, i. 62.   [2] Ibid., 61.
[3] Ibid., ii. 9.   [4] Ibid., 12.   [5] Ibid., iii. 24.

sophy. Not only the ignorant, but the sinful are welcomed. Others, when they invite to their mysteries, proclaim : " Every one who has clean hands and a pure tongue" approach. But the Christians say " Every one who is a sinner, who is devoid of understanding, who is a child, and to speak generally, whoever is unfortunate, him will the Kingdom of God receive. Do you not call him a sinner, then, who is unjust and a thief, a housebreaker, a prisoner, a committer of sacrilege, or a robber of the dead ? What others would a man invite if he were issuing a proclamation for an assembly of robbers ?" [1]

To which Origen rejoins that the Church invites the sick that they may be cured.

He complained that the Church made its appeal to the foolish and ignorant, in other words, to labouring folk, women, and children. In the market places they avoided philosophers, " but whenever they see young men or a mob of slaves or a gathering of unintelligent persons they thrust themselves in." [2] In private houses the manual workers became Christian, the fullers, the workers in wool and leather, and through them the leaven spreads. The children are told, according to Celsus, "to go with the women and their playfellows to the women's apartment or to the leather-shop or to the fuller's shop" to be taught.[3]

He accuses the Christians of repeating "Do not examine ; only believe," and "Your faith

[1] *Against Celsus*, iii. 59.   [2] Ibid., 52.   [3] Ibid., 53.

will save you," and that they also say "The wisdom of this life is bad, but foolishness is a good thing."[1] One can see how the words of S. Paul about the wisdom of this world to the Corinthians might be thus wrested by an adversary, and it is quite as likely that Celsus found the ground for this charge in the Epistle as in his actual experience.

He asserts that Christians "repel every wise man from the doctrine of their faith, and invite only the ignorant and vulgar"[2]; and that they lay down the following rules:—

"Let no one come to us who has been instructed or who is wise and prudent (for such qualifications are deemed evil by us); but if there be any ignorant or unintelligent or foolish or uninstructed persons let them come with confidence."[3]

Nevertheless, he has to admit that others besides the simple became followers of Christ, and that there were among them "persons of moderate intelligence and gentle disposition, and possessed of understanding and capable of comprehending allegories."[4]

He declares that their miracles are due to sorcery, magic, and demoniacal assistance.[5] He objects to the simplicity of the language of Scripture,[6] to the existence of heresies, to the doctrine of the resurrection of the body, and belief in prayer. "God is not to be reached

[1] *Against Celsus*, i. 9.   [2] Ibid., iii. 18.   [3] Ibid., 44.
[4] Ibid., i. 27.   [5] Ibid., 6.   [6] Ibid., vi. 2.

by word." But his principal charge against the followers of Christ, as against Christ Himself, is that of "lowness." They are an ignorant, credulous, low-born, and criminal rabble. He can hardly express the scorn he feels. Towards a constructive theory of life and religion Celsus does not give much help. He quotes Plato as saying, "It is a hard matter to find out the Maker and Father of the universe, and after having found Him it is impossible to make Him known to all."[1] Only the wise, in fact, says Celsus, are able to make out Him Who is the first, the unapproachable Being. And they endeavour to convey a notion of this Body by synthesis or by analysis or by analogy to those capable of understanding. But Christians, he thinks, would be incapable " being so completely wedded to the flesh as to be incapable of seeing aught but what is impure."[2]

It is right to serve demons and spirits because they belong to the Most High. It is right to sacrifice to them because " God is the God of all alike; He is good; He stands in need of nothing, and He is without jealousy. What, then, is there to hinder those who are most devoted to His service from taking part in public feasts?"[3] Moreover, these demons, " being set over the things of this world, we must give them thanks and first-fruits and prayers." The Supreme Being, it may be remembered, could not be reached by the word of prayer. If we fail to

[1] *Against Celsus*, vii. 42. [2] Ibid. [3] Ibid., i. 21.

do so they will be angry, and we shall suffer. " The satrap of a Persian or Roman monarch or ruler or general or governor, yea, even those who fill lower offices of trust and service in the State, would be able to do great injury to those who despised them ; and will the satraps and ministers of earth and air be insulted with impunity ? " [1]

He defends the worship offered by Egyptians to crocodiles and animals, on the ground that such acts of worship are really offered to eternal ideas, and not, as the multitude think, to ephemeral animals.

He believes in rewards and punishments after death though indignant with the Christian preaching of them. In one place he complains that God is made to come with fire like a torturer, and in another burns up the world like a cook. He held that God did not create the world nor the body of man, but only his soul. " God made nothing mortal, but immortal things alone; while mortal things are the work of others, and the soul is a work of God ; but the nature of the body is different, and there is no difference between the body of a man and that of a bat or a worm or a frog ; for the matter is the same and the corruptible part alike." [2]

The origin of evil was not difficult for the philosopher to fathom, but unnecessary for the multitude to know. They are to be told " that evils do not proceed from God, but cleave to

[1] *Against Celsus*, viii. 35.   [2] Ibid., iv. 55.

matter and have their abode among mortal things ; while the course of mortal things being the same from beginning to end, the same things must always agreeably to the appointed cycles recur in the past, present, and future." [1]

But Celsus, though he begins with abuse, ends with an appeal. He implores the Christians to rally to the support of the emperor, " to labour with him in the maintenance of justice, to fight with him," and " to take office in the government of the country." [2] How far Christians did their duty as citizens is discussed elsewhere. Here it will be enough to observe that Celsus admits the great influence of members of the Church, or appeals to them would not have been worth while.

But the work of Celsus is mainly destructive. His main purpose is to destroy and ridicule the Church, not to improve paganism. So far as that comes in at all it is incidental.

APOLLONIUS OF TYANA

Thoughtful pagans, whether religious-minded or not, saw the absurdity of the popular religion, of which Lucian made fun, and, like Celsus, the importance of religion as a prop of the Empire. Christianity was impossible, because it was exclusive ; but by the beginning of the third century it was becoming clear that persecution had failed, and that the Church must be met by

[1] *Against Celsus*, iv. 65. [2] Ibid., viii. 75.

Pagan attempts at Reconstruction

a reconstructed paganism. It must meet the demands of philosophy by postulating One Supreme Being, but at the same time be broad and comprehensive enough to include all deities or heroes popular with the multitude, of whatever kind, so that both popular feeling and philosophic honour could be satisfied. " There is no harm in kissing the hand to inferior deities."

An attempt was made at the suggestion of Julia Domna, the second wife of Severus and the mother of Caracalla, who left to her the direction of civil affairs while he occupied himself with the Army. She was the power behind the throne throughout his reign, and surrounded herself with a coterie of literary men and philosophers.

Severus married her because she had a royal nativity. Gibbon wrote of her : " Julia Domna (for that was her name) deserved all that the stars could promise her. She possessed, even in an advanced age, the attractions of beauty, and united to a lively imagination a firmness of mind and strength of judgement seldom bestowed on her sex. Her amiable qualities never made any deep impression on the dark and jealous temper of her husband ; but in her son's reign she administered the principal affairs of the Empire with a prudence that supported his authority and with a moderation that sometimes corrected his wild extravagances. Julia applied herself to letters and philosophy with some success and the most splendid reputation. She was the patroness

Y

of every art, and the friend of every man of genius. The grateful flattery of the learned has celebrated her virtues, but if we may credit the scandal of ancient histories, chastity was not the favourite virtue of the Empress Julia."[1]

Her religious sympathies were no doubt Oriental rather than Greek, and she seems to have wished to promote a grand amalgamation of all the religions of the Empire, a super-undenominationalism in fact. A visit of the Court to Tyana in the spring of A.D. 215 may have given her the idea of setting up Apollonius as a rival to Christ.[2] Among her circle of *littérateurs* was Philostratus, a young sophist, and he was given the commission; he wrote a book with the title *Philostratus on Apollonius of Tyana*. In it he tells us that one Damis, a disciple and companion of Apollonius, who had played Boswell to his Dr. Johnson, had left behind him memoirs, and "a person who was related to this Damis brought the originals of these memoirs, hitherto undiscovered, to the knowledge of the Empress Julia, and she laid on me the task of transcribing and editing these papers. It was her wish also that I should be responsible for the form of expression; for the Ninevite's language, though clear, was anything but a model of literary art."

Of the real Apollonius we know little. He

[1] *Decline and Fall*, v.
[2] *Philostratus in Honour of Apollonius of Tyana*, lxvii. See Translation and Introduction by Professor J. S. Phillimore.

Pagan attempts at Reconstruction 163

was born about the time that Christ died, and he died in the reign of Nerva. But he left no great name among his contemporaries and founded no school. Almost all we know of him we learn from Philostratus, and Philostratus' book is a romance written with a purpose. He seems to have travelled, and to have addressed the crowds at markets in Greek towns in Greece and Asia, to have had some claims to be considered a philosopher and a worker of miracles. Whether he was more a serious teacher or a charlatan and wonder-worker we cannot tell.

In reading the book in his praise it is best to take it as an attempt made A.D. 215 by a Greek philosopher to help on the great scheme favoured by the Court of promoting a general amalgamation of all religions and to point out the inferiority of the Founder of Christianity—the religion that obstinately refused to amalgamate—to Apollonius.

According to Philostratus, the birth of Apollonius was heralded by swans, and, though he would never acknowledge it, the countryside gave him Jupiter as a father. His parents were people of rank and fortune. He went to Tarsus to be educated and became learned in philosophy, and adopted the opinions of Pythagoras; he lived a life of asceticism, refusing to eat meat or wear any animal product, and going always barefoot. He used, according to Philostratus, to work miracles of healing at the temple of Aesculapius.

At the age of twenty-three his father died and

left him a fortune, of which he gave away half.
After that he kept the Pythagorean rule by
observing a five years' silence. The silence he
found inconvenient, but in spite of it was on one
occasion able to quell a tumult, save the governor
of a town from being burned alive, and compel a
number of food-hoarders to disgorge by waving
his hand and writing on his tablets.[1]

He afterwards set out on a journey to Babylon
and India, accompanied by the faithful Damis ;
he knew the languages of the countries to be
visited without having learnt them, and was also
able to converse with birds, as he told Damis,
though these useful accomplishments did not
make an interpreter unnecessary later on, nor are
his conversations with the birds on record. The
rest of the book is taken up mainly with his
travels, his miracles, and his discourses, principally his discourses. He discoursed without
pity, and improved every occasion. During a
prolonged stay in Babylon, on his way to the
Indians, he discoursed to the king at length
on religion and philosophy, and in addition gave
him advice on domestic and foreign policy,
which was gratefully received and acted upon
with docility. When the king was sick, he discoursed with so much eloquence on the nature of
the soul as to effect an immediate cure.

Unlike our Lord, he was not to be found
in the company of the outcast. At least this
prayer is put in his mouth : " O sun, grant

[1] *Philostratus on Apollonius,* I. xv.

me to know the virtuous only : as to the wicked, I wish neither to know them or to be known by them."

From Babylon he went to India and spent four months with the Indian sages. Here he seems to have found philosophers as loquacious as himself. They discussed their respective pre-incarnations, Apollonius describing an adventure with pirates when in a previous existence he was an Egyptian ship-master; they talked of creation, of pygmies who lived under the earth, of dragons, of griffons, winged animals as strong and large as lions, and of other things, and parted with expressions of mutual esteem. Afterwards he visited the principal towns of Asia Minor and Greece, dispensing advice to their inhabitants. At Ephesus he drove away a plague by persuading the inhabitants to stone an old beggar-man, who subsequently disappeared in the form of a hound. At Athens, to his credit, he rebuked the Athenians for their devotion to gladiatorial shows, and at Corinth he cast out a devil from one Menippus, an exorcism during which the demon implored not to be tormented, language which suggests familiarity with the Gospel of S. Luke.[1]

He found his way to Rome in the reign of Nero, and, meeting a bride being carried out to burial, raised her to life again. Towards the end of his life he was imprisoned by Domitian, and talked freely with his fellow prisoners. "As to

[1] viii. 28.

Apollonius," says Philostratus, " he never ceased giving advice."

Before his trial he dispatched the faithful Damis to wait for him at Puteoli. When summoned before the tribunal, which was presided over by Domitian and attended by all the great men of Rome, " he treated the emperor with a great degree of supercilious contempt." Not being allowed to make the speech he had written out for his defence, after a few words of advice to Domitian, he vanished from the court and appeared to his despairing companions at Puteoli.

For two years afterwards he discoursed triumphantly to admiring crowds in Greece and Asia Minor, and was able to announce at Ephesus the assassination of Domitian at the moment of its occurrence. Nerva invited him to come and teach him how to rule. He refused the request, but sent him a long letter by the hand of Damis, partly to get his disciple out of the way, as he knew that the hour of his own departure was at hand, and he wished to have no witnesses.

" Concerning the manner of his death, if he did die," says Philostratus, " various are the accounts." One says that he died at Ephesus, waited on by two handmaids ; another that he entered the Temple of Minerva at Lindus and then disappeared ; a third that he was last seen going into the temple of Dictymna in Crete, the gates of which were miraculously opened. " As soon as he entered them they shut of themselves, and the temple resounded with the singing of many virgins, the burden of whose song was 'Leave the earth, come to heaven—come—come,' which seemed as if they said 'Proceed from earth to heaven.'"

After his death he appeared to a young man who would not believe in the immortality of the soul, and was heard to declare for the last time " The soul is immortal. Immortality does not belong to you, but to Providence. After the dissolution of the body, the soul, like a mettlesome courser, when freed from all restraint, mingles in thin air, impatient of the servile state to which it was subject," with more to the same effect.

At some subsequent date he received divine honours. Caracalla built him a shrine, and Aurelian refrained from destroying Tyana through a vision of Apollonius, having recognized him by his likeness to the many statues he had seen in temples.

The points of likeness with Christ are so many that they must have been intentional. There is before the birth of Apollonius a kind of Annunciation, and miraculous singing attends the event. His parentage is left in doubt. He was believed, we are told by his biographer, to be the son of Jupiter, but he would not himself admit it. The vulgar might hold this opinion, but it need not be received by the philosopher. There are miracles suggestive of the Gospel miracles. There is a trial, foreknowledge of death, and at least one appearance after death.

The differences are fundamental. Philostratus and his friends found their stumbling-block in the lowliness of Jesus. He was not grand enough. His humble and mean birth, His lowly up-bringing, His unacquaintance with the systems of philosophy in vogue, the rusticity of the stage on which the scenes of His life were set, the falling away of His followers, the humiliation of His last days, and last and greatest, the crowning infamy of the Cross—all these things were offences and had to come out.

Apollonius worshipped the sun, and believed in one supreme being, who is to be worshipped above and through the lower gods, and himself needs neither sacrifice nor offering. This supreme being gives all but receives nothing. The inferior deities might be propitiated with sacrifices, though Apollonius himself would offer none. Unlike the God of the Jews and Christians, it cannot even be said of his supreme being " A broken and contrite heart thou wilt not despise."

" Indian theosophy, a natural science drawn chiefly from Stoic authorities, antiquarian ritualism in certain Greek cults, a great copiousness of moral sentiment, and certain asceticisms," are, according to Professor Phillimore, the main ingredients in his religion.

It may have had a success in Court and literary circles, but it is impossible to think that it ever had much effect of the sort intended. There was nothing to attract the great mass of suffering, striving, sin-laden men and women.

Neoplatonism

Thirty years after Philostratus began his work Plotinus, the founder of Neoplatonism, came to Rome and began to lecture. Plotinus was an Egyptian, who had studied at Alexandria and taught at Rome from A.D. 245 until his death in A.D. 270.

He would never tell the date or place of his birth, as he did not like to dwell on the details of that misfortune, " the descent of soul into body." We are told that he entered the University at Alexandria in order to study philosophy, and tried teacher after teacher, but left them all " with head hanging down." At last he attended a lecture by Ammonius Saccus, by trade originally a porter, by religion once a Christian, then a Platonist philosopher. When he heard him he exclaimed " This is the man I have been looking for," and for ten years he attended his lectures.

Unlike Celsus and Philostratus, who had other ends in view, Plotinus was disinterested. He sought the truth for its own sake, and not with the ulterior aim of injuring the Church or buttressing the Empire or making a literary reputation. He was concerned with philosophy rather than religion, but his teaching had the effect of showing how ancient beliefs might be reconciled with modern philosophy. He allowed the existence of subordinate deities — heaven and the heavenly bodies, nature, earth, and the demons. " All these in their degree are causes and desire worship. But the supreme cause, God, in the proper sense of the word, stands far above all these created deities, and embraces in itself a unity of Three Hypostases." The individual soul has to be purified by virtue and asceticism, and then through reason to attain communion with the nous or intelligence. Finally, through a kind of ecstasy the soul may attain communion with the One. Plotinus attained this four times in six years, Porphyry only once in his lifetime.

The teaching of Plotinus was difficult, and his moral standard high, and its influence must have been confined to a chosen few. He can hardly be said to have founded a religious system, much less a church. But some of his ideas have been fruitful. As his latest commentator has put it, the Church quietly carried off some of his honey into its own hive.[1] The theologians who had to formulate the doctrine of the Trinity seem to have been indebted to him; and the philosophical doctrine of matter underlying the theory of transubstantiation is his.

Porphyry, who was his disciple, and published his lectures, wrote a book against the Christians, which except for a few fragments has perished. It was the most formidable attack of that sort that the Church had to face. No less than four refutations were published, including one by Eusebius the historian, but none have survived.

After Plotinus, Neoplatonism became more

[1] W. R. Inge, *The Philosophy of Plotinus*, i. 67.

and more concerned with demonology and magic, and was therefore more popular, and its anti-Christian influence more seriously felt.

"Porphyry is the most devout believer in Hecate and her hell-dogs, in jinns, hobgoblins, spectres, amulets, spells, and can give the most philosophical reasons for the most ridiculous superstitions. Everything that the Christian alleged against Polytheism he admits in the coolest way. It was true that the Greek sacrificed to devils, not to God. It was true that the demons were corporeal, mortal, mostly maleficent. It was true that they were deceivers, and that philosophy was no safeguard. It was true that they demanded and received human sacrifices. He tells us that human blood was regularly poured on the altars in his time in Arcadia and at Carthage, and that even at Rome Jupiter Latiaris was annually sprinkled with the blood of a gladiator. What are we to say of this man who found the New Testament incredible and took the *Arabian Nights* for gospel?"[1]

Gibbon's description of the later Neoplatonists is not unfair. "They flattered themselves that they possessed the secret of disengaging the soul from its corporeal prison, claimed a familiar intercourse with demons and spirits, and by a singular revolution converted the study of philosophy into that of magic. The ancient sages had derided the popular superstition; after disguising its extravagance by the thin pretence of allegory,

[1] C. Bigg, *Neoplatonism*, p. 300.

the disciples of Plotinus and Porphyry became its most zealous defenders. As they agreed with the Christians in a few mysterious points of faith, they attacked the remainder of their philosophical system with all the fury of civil war." [1]

[1] *Decline and Fall*, xiii.

IX

RIVAL RELIGIONS

THE old religions of the Roman world, in spite of the reconstructions of the philosophers, were never any real menace to Christianity. They could destroy by instigating persecution, but they could not replace. One cannot imagine that the masses of mankind can conceivably have been attracted by the speculations of Plotinus, or even the romance of Apollonius. Very many people, perhaps the majority, were content with unreformed paganism, with local gods to protect the home, the camp, and the farm, without much inquiry into their morals or any searchings of heart as to polytheism. But these were people to whom religion was formal, a matter of custom and convention, which made no direct appeal to the heart or to the conscience. There were, however, many who did want something better and more satisfying. Man, who wants a real religion, wants an object of devotion; he wants to be able to give himself, and he demands a response. He gives himself, and he asks to receive. He is ready to die, but he desires to find life through death. With all the myriad

calls of the world sounding in his ears he
desires to find one voice that he must obey,
one leader he cannot choose but follow. At
the same time, in the troubles and pains and
perplexities of life, he looks for a Being to whom
he may go for comfort and sympathy and help.
In times of bereavement the help he feels the
need of most of all is some assurance of a life
beyond the grave. And often, though not
always, he needs deliverance from his sense of
guilt, the salvation offered to sinners by Christ.
In the face of such needs the third-century
philosopher was of as little use as was the nineteenth-century Rationalist a generation ago.

The three rival religions that seemed most
likely to satisfy those who really felt the need
of one in the second and third centuries were
Christianity, the worship of Isis, and Mithraism.

The Worship of Isis

Isis was an Egyptian goddess. Her husband,
the god Osiris, was killed by his brother Typhon.
Isis, brokenhearted, wandered over the marshes
of the Delta in her boat of papyrus and gathered
the fragments of his dead body. The son of
Osiris wanted to kill Typhon, but Isis cut his
bonds and let him go. Osiris then became Lord
of the Spirits of the Dead. Isis may be said
to have furnished the female element in the
object of worship. She was kind, gentle, full
of pity and sympathy. Like Jesus, and unlike

Mithra, she presented the idea of a suffering God, and this no doubt constituted a great part of her attraction. "She does not forget the sorrows which she endured, nor her painful wanderings, but ordains most holy rites in remembrance of her sufferings, for instruction in piety, for the comfort of men and women oppressed by similar misfortune."[1]

She had a regular priesthood, daily services, surpliced choirs, gorgeous ceremonial, and splendid rites; there were also religious orders. Apuleius, who was a convert, gives a description[2] of a procession in her honour. The occasion was a festival of the goddess. First came a body of masqueraders, dressed as soldiers, gladiators, magistrates, philosophers, and in other fancy costumes. There was an ape representing Ganymede, and a donkey with wings as Pegasus. "You would have enjoyed your laugh at both," said Apuleius. Then followed the procession proper. First came women gorgeously arrayed in white, some scattering flowers, others sprinkling the street with perfume. Then men and women carrying lamps and tapers. Musicians followed, with a choir of youths in snow-white garments. Then a body of the initiated, men and women clad in white, keeping up an incessant tinkling with their *sistra*, or rattles. The priests followed with the symbols of the goddess. There fol-

---
[1] Quoted by Bigg: *The Church's Task in the Roman Empire*, p. 45.
[2] *The Golden Ass*, Bk. xi.

lowed representations of the gods — including a cow borne erect on the shoulders of a man, an effigy of the divinity bearing no resemblance to bird or beast or man, and an urn with a live asp embracing its spout. After dedicating a ship the procession returned to the temple. One of the priests recited prayers and then dismissed the congregation, who departed after kissing the feet of a golden image of the goddess.

Apuleius also gives an account of his own initiation, which is too long to quote. He passed ten days in seclusion in the temple, eating no meat, in constant intercourse with the priests and attendance at the services. He had also to sell all he possessed to pay the fee. He had visions of the goddess, and the actual initiation was accompanied by a ceremonial bath and an ecstasy. "I approached the confines of death, and having trod on the threshold of Proserpine I returned therefrom, being borne through all the elements. At midnight I saw the sun shining with its brilliant light, and I approached the presence of the gods beneath and the gods above, and stood near and worshipped them."[1] The initiation was called a new birth. It was celebrated with a banquet, and afterwards he returned home.

Isis worship got a footing in Rome as early as the time of Sulla. The Emperor Tiberius pulled down her temple and crucified her priests. Juvenal complains of the attraction she had for

[1] *The Golden Ass*, Bk. xi.

the Roman ladies. Her cult spread fast, and traces of it have been found as far north as the Roman Wall in Britain. Its theology, like paganism, could be adapted to the philosopher or the peasant, but its attractiveness lay in its emotional appeal, which neither paganism nor Mithraism possessed, and which in Christianity was balanced and kept in check by the stern demand of moral renunciation. Perhaps Isis would have been a more serious rival to Christ if she had made more demands on her worshippers. It lacked the element of austerity found both in Mithraism and Christianity.

Mithraism

In the third century after Christ, from Commodus to Constantine, Mithraism was the most dangerous rival of Christianity, to which it had many striking resemblances. Like Christianity, it came from the East, and at about the same time. Plutarch tells us that the rites were first practised in Rome by men who had learnt them from Cilician pirates, captured by Pompey. But it was not until the end of the first century after Christ that it was fairly established in Rome.

Its appearance in the West was, in fact, contemporaneous with Christianity. It grew rapidly under the Flavians and the Antonines. Commodus, who was himself a devotee, gave it an enormous impetus, and by the end of the century it may have counted as many adherents as the Church. Both found their opportunity in the political unity, and the moral anarchy of the Empire. Both made their appeal to the world rather than to philosophers. They spread in different directions. Christianity tended to follow the trade routes, and was most strong along the coasts of the Mediterranean. Mithraism followed the camp, and was strongest in Italy and on the frontiers of the Rhine and the Danube. It was strong also in the valley of the Rhone. It seems to have made a special appeal to the Germanic races. Nowhere are its monuments more numerous than on the Rhine. They are nearly as thick in what is now Hungary, and next in order of frequency in Italy, and the most romanized of the provinces — the South of France and Dalmatia. Only one monument has been found in Greece, only four in Spain. In France they are almost confined to the valley of the Rhone. In Britain they have been found in the track of the legions.

Mithraism originated in Persia, and no doubt underwent many changes, but when it burgeoned in the West its theology seems to have been fairly established. There was One Supreme God, the first principle—unknown, unapproachable, called sometimes Aion or Saturn, generally represented in human form with a lion's head, his body entwined with a serpent. The first principle generated the earth and sky and ocean, which could easily be identified with Juno, Jupiter, and Neptune. These and their offspring inhabit heaven. A multitude of maleficent demons are however beneath the earth, whom it was necessary to appease. The active principles of nature, fire, water, light, were identified with gods, or were their manifestations. The sun was the object of special adoration as the giver of life, so were the moon and planets. But of all the heroes and objects of worship the most popular was Mithra.

Mithra was the god of light, and as such thought to dwell between heaven and earth, which gave rise to one of his titles, that of Mesites or Mediator. He is sometimes represented between two children, each carrying a torch, one uplifted, the other cast down. He was born of a rock, and shepherds hastened to adore him at his birth. He was born with the Phrygian Cap or Mithra, from which he took his name, and was armed with a dagger, and carried a flaming torch. His life began with a conflict with the sun, whom he overcame, and with whom he afterwards established an eternal league of friendship and mutual aid. His most striking adventure was his duel with the bull, the first living being created by Jupiter. The bull was feeding on a mountain alp; the hero seized him by the horns and bestrode him. Thrown by the violence of its plunges, he still held its horns. When the animal fell exhausted, he seized it by the hind legs and dragged it backwards into his cave, over many obstacles. This painful journey became an allegory of the pilgrimage of the human soul. The bull escaped and once more roamed the country. The sun sent a message by a raven to Mithra to slay the fugitive. Mithra, though much against his will, obeyed. He pursued the bull, came up with him and, seizing his nostrils with his hand, plunged his knife into his side.

Then ensued a prodigy. From the body of the dying bull grew the grass and healthful plants which cover the earth. From the spinal marrow wheat germinated, and the vine from its blood. From it also sprang all kinds of useful animals, and its soul, translated to celestial regions, became the special guard of soldiers. In this way the bull, by its death, became the source of life.

The first human pair now appeared on earth and were attacked by the powers of evil and protected by Mithra. Man survived drought, flood, and a devastating fire before he was left in comparative peace, and the temporal mission of Mithra was over. Then Mithra mounted to heaven in the chariot of the sun, but from the heavens continued to protect his faithful followers on earth. Mithra was therefore regarded as an emanation from God, who acted first as creator and then as protector of the world and mediator between its inhabitants and God. In this there are points of resemblance with the Logos.

The morals taught were lofty. A great point was made of sexual restraint, and absolute chastity was the ideal. Man was regarded as taking part in a struggle against evil. His good consisted in action. The ideal virtues were strength and courage rather than love and pity. The religion was hard. It was above all the religion of soldiers and extolled the military virtues.

Mithra is the sustainer of mortals in all difficulties and trials. He is the defender of truth and justice, the preserver of health, the antagonist of the powers of darkness. He is eternally young and vigorous, always vigilant, always victorious, giving victory to mortals alike over their enemies without and within. His followers believe in life after death, in a final judgement, in heaven and hell, and some kind of bodily resurrection. The secret of its attraction lay in its appeal to its votaries to take up arms against the forces of evil.

Mithraism had its liturgy and its offices, its sacred books and its sacraments. There were even degrees of initiation, the lowest that of the ravens, the highest the fathers, through which all the initiated passed on the way to attain perfect purity and wisdom. On ceremonial occasions the votaries wore vestments suitable to their degree. "Some flap their wings like birds, others roar like lions."[1] Only those who attained the fourth rank, that of lions, were actual partakers in the mysteries, which

[1] Cumont, *Textes et Mons. figurés rel. aux mystères de Mithra*, i, p. 314.

were presided over by the seventh order, that of fathers, who also admitted the novices.
There was a *pater patrum*, a kind of bishop.
All the initiated were brothers.
The ceremony of initiation to each order was known as a sacrament—*sacramentum*—because of the oath then taken. There were thus seven sacraments. Lustrations were a prominent feature of most of them.

There was also a solemn service in which consecrated bread and water, with wine added, were the principal features. The initiation to the order of soldiers including branding on the forehead with a hot iron, and had some resemblance to the anointing and the sign of the cross in Confirmation and Baptism. There was a regular order of priests and even orders of monks. The ceremonial baths, previous to initiation, were not parallel to Christian Baptism. They were for purification only. But the ceremony of the *taurobolium* had much more in common with the Christian sacrament. In it a bull, standing on a platform, had its throat cut, and the blood poured through the platform and bathed a mystic hidden in a ditch underneath, by which he was supposed to acquire a new birth.

They had temples and festivals, of which one, on December 25th, celebrated the birth of the sun, and another took place about the time of the Christian Easter.

The sense of brotherhood among the initiated was cultivated, and this, as among Christians, was no doubt a great attraction, especially with the poorer people, while the degrees of initiation were a constant interest and stimulus.

It had one fatal defect—it had no place for women.

From the succession of Commodus, for more than a century, Mithraism was actively patronized by the emperors. From the first years of the third century there was a priest of Mithraism in the palace. In A.D. 307 Diocletian, Licinius, and Galerius consecrated a temple to Mithra. This was due to the convenient support which it lent to the imperial theory of the divine nature of emperors. According to the Mithraic theory, the emperor was an emanation or effulgence of the sun, an incarnation in fact, selected by the gods independently of birth for that position, and therefore the emperor, *de facto*, could point to the fact as a proof of his divinity.

Mithraism had no quarrel with the religions it found in the Empire, or they with it. It was ready to find a place for their gods in its pantheon, and to modify its own dogma and ritual to suit local exigencies. But its essential features were unaltered. After all, no pagan would have objected to Christianity if room had been made for his deities alongside of Jesus Christ. It aspired to be universal, and would have established the universal domination of Mithra allied to the sun, but in the process would have assimilated local and national beliefs and deities.

The points of resemblance between Mithraism and Christianity are some of them real, others only superficial. The real resemblances are a common belief in a mediator, in a judgement, in a future life and the resurrection of the body ; also in the doctrine of brotherhood, and of the need of purity and renunciation in conquest of self. Mithraism had no redemption parallel to the Cross. The nearest approach was the slaughter of the bull by Mithra, a thing monstrous and repulsive. The resemblance in ritual, in festivals and sacraments, is only superficial, though the *taurobolium* claimed to have the effect of Baptism.

It is inconceivable that the Church should have borrowed from Mithra at that early date. Its horror of heathenism, its sense of separation and renunciation, was far too strong. But M. Cumont thinks that Mithraism may have borrowed the Adoration of the Shepherds, the Last Supper, and the Ascension from the Gospels. It certainly refrained from borrowing the Cross. Herein lay its weakness. It had little to win weak and suffering men and women. It preached a gospel to the strong, and had no invitation for the weary and heavy-laden.

X

THE PERSECUTIONS OF DECIUS AND VALERIAN

IN A.D. 248 Philip celebrated the thousandth anniversary of the foundation of Rome with immense pomp. The twenty years that followed were perhaps the most calamitous that the State had known. German armies crossed the Rhine and penetrated Spain. Hordes of Goths passed the Danube and invaded Illyria, while others sailed down the Euxine, plundered Trebizond, ravaged Pontus and Bithynia and even the cities of Greece, and Persian armies crossed the Euphrates. And as if these misfortunes were not enough, a pestilence of a most deadly kind ravaged the Empire from A.D. 250 to 265.

Philip fell in A.D. 249, and was succeeded by Decius, a Roman general of birth and merit. He seems to have desired to restore the virtues of the ancient State, and went so far as to revive the office of Censor in the person of Valerian. One of his domestic reforms took the form of a persecution of the Church on the grand scale. As a soldier and an upholder of the ancient ways, he objected, no doubt, to Christianity as a modern innovation, at deadly enmity with the gods that had made Rome great.

The exact wording of the edict is lost, but its meaning is plain. Its object was to produce apostates rather than martyrs. All men were to sacrifice to the gods and the genius of the emperor by a certain day. Bishops who refused were to be executed. Lesser persons to be imprisoned and tortured to make them recant, and to lose their property.[1]

Fabian, Bishop of Rome, was among the first victims, and on account of the persecution a successor could not be elected for a year. Alexander, Bishop of Jerusalem, died in prison, as did Babylas, Bishop of Antioch.

In Alexandria the persecution had preceded the edict by a year, a popular movement stirred up apparently by a local " prophet or poet." It consisted in outrages by the mob against the Christians, many of whom were killed, and a general plundering of their houses. " A certain prophet or poet, inauspicious to the city, whoever he was, excited the mass of the heathen against us, stirring them up to their native superstitions. . . . First seizing an aged man named Metra, they called on him to utter blasphemies, and, as he did not obey, beat his body with clubs and pricked his face and eyes; after which they led him away to the suburbs, where they stoned him. Next they led a woman named Quinta, who was a believer, to the temple of an idol, and attempted to force her to worship; but when she turned away in disgust they tied

[1] Cyprian, *On the Lapsed.*

The Persecutions of Decius and Valerian

her by the feet and dragged her by the hair through the whole city, over the rough stones of the paved streets. Then with one accord all rushed upon the houses of the faithful and despoiled and plundered them, setting apart the more valuable articles for themselves; but the commoner furniture they burnt in the streets, making the city look like one taken by the enemy."[1] When the edict arrived there were a large number of arrests and many recantations. "Some fled; others were taken, and of them some held out as far as the prison and bonds, and some after a few days' imprisonment abjured before they entered the tribunal. Some, after enduring the torture for a while, renounced their Lord. Others, however, firm and blessed pillars of the Lord, became admirable witnesses of His kingdom." A boy of fifteen named Dioscorus, stood firm against both torturer and argument and was released. But nearly all the accused, though kept in prison for some time and tortured to make them recant, were put to death in the end, many by fire. Women were especially prominent in this persecution, and many suffered. There were also soldier martyrs. Some who were present at the trial of a Christian encouraged him by gestures to stand firm when inclined to waver. They then gave themselves up and declared that they were Christians, and suffered in their turn.

Dionysius, Bishop of Alexandria, remained at

[1] Eusebius, *H. E.* vi. 41.

home awaiting arrest. The soldiers searched every possible hiding-place for four days, thinking it impossible that he should not have attempted to escape. At last they thought of going to his house, and found him there. He was seized and carried off. According to his own account, one of his friends, named Timothy, came to the house and found it empty. Then "a certain countryman met Timothy flying, and much disturbed, and asked the cause of his haste, and was told the reason. When the countryman heard it, he went his way, for he was going to a marriage festival, and when he arrived he told it to those who were present. These at once, with a single impulse, as if by agreement all arose, and came as quick as possible in a rush upon us, and as they rushed they raised a shout. The soldiers that guarded us immediately took to flight, and our rescuers came upon us lying upon the bare bedsteads. God knows I took them at first to be robbers come to plunder. Remaining, therefore, in my bed, only covered with a linen garment, the rest of my dress I offered them as it lay beside me. But they commanded me to rise and depart as quickly as possible. Then, understanding for what purpose they had come, I began to cry, beseeching and praying them to go away and to let us alone. But if they wished to do us any good to anticipate those who had led me away and to cut off my head. When I thus cried out, they tried to raise me by force, as my companions know; I cast myself back on the ground. But they seized me by the hands and feet and dragged me away, whilst Caius, Faustus, Peter, and Paul, who were witnesses of all this, followed behind. They, taking me up, bore me away from the town, and carried me off on an ass, bareback."[1] The chief interest of this incident is that it shows the tide had turned, and that Christians were no longer hated by their pagan neighbours, unless popular hatred had been stirred up, as in Alexandria itself.

In Carthage Cyprian was bishop. At the time of his conversion he had been the leader of the Carthaginian bar, renowned for his eloquence and success. He speaks of the liberal banquets and sumptuous feasts of his then life, of glittering in gold and purple, of being celebrated for his dress, and of delighting in the attendance of lictors and civic honours, and being accompanied by crowds of clients — all of which point to a considerable position.[2]

He was soon advanced to the rank of presbyter and in A.D. 248 became Bishop or Pope of Carthage. The Church had had peace for thirty-seven years since the death of Severus, February 4th, A.D. 211. Thirty-seven years seems a short time as we read of it, but it meant that no Christian under forty knew anything of persecution except by hearsay. They were unmolested; they knew their numbers were increasing. No doubt they looked on persecution as a thing of the past. The Church was therefore like the draw-net,

[1] Eusebius, *H. E.* vi. 40.   [2] *To Donatus.*

full of all sorts of fishes, bad as well as good, much as it is to-day. Many, no doubt, were faithful. Many more only needed the trumpet call of persecution to rouse them from slumber. But many others were leading careless and worldly lives. Cyprian, writing after the event it is true, paints a somewhat black picture of the pre-persecution Church.

Among other things he complained that bishops had so far forgotten their sacred calling as to become agents in secular business, to desert their people, and wander over foreign countries on commercial quests, and had even lent money on usury.[1]

The Decian Edict of persecution required that every one should give evidence of not being a Christian by a certain day. Something like a panic seized the Church. Large numbers, without waiting for the persecution to begin, hastened to sacrifice. " They, indeed, did not wait to be apprehended ere they ascended, or to be interrogated ere they denied. Many were conquered before the battle, prostrated before the attack. Nor did they permit it to be said of them that they seemed to sacrifice to idols unwillingly. " They ran to the market-place of their own accord ; they willingly hastened to death, as if they had long wished for it, as if they would embrace an opportunity they had fervently desired." The officials could not keep pace with the crowd of would-

[1] *To Donatus*, vi.

be sacrificers. "How many were put off by the magistrates at that time, when evening was coming on, how many asked that their destruction might not be delayed." [1]

Others only broke down after enduring many tortures, who might plead as Cyprian suggests: "The scourges were lacerating my already worn-out body, the clubs bruised me, the rack strained me, the claw dug into me, the fire roasted me, my flesh deserted me in the struggle, the weakness of my bodily frame gave way in the struggle—not my mind, but my body, yielded in the suffering."

In some cases heads of households obtained a certificate as having sacrificed and so secured immunity, not only for themselves, but for their families and dependants, and were even able to receive fugitive Christians into their houses, thus "offering to the Lord many souls living, and safe to entreat for a single wounded one." Others received certificates without actually sacrificing. Either in person or by deputy they appeared before the magistrate, stated that they were Christians and were not allowed to sacrifice, but were willing to pay for a certificate, which seems to have been granted.

Cyprian himself withdrew from the storm. As there is no reason to question his readiness to face death, or to suppose that he was unwilling to become a martyr, his moral courage in withdrawing is remarkable. Its

[1] *To Donatus*, viii.

expediency was undoubted. Decius had struck principally at the bishops, and it was playing into his hands for bishops to let themselves be killed too easily. Moreover, the flock needed a shepherd; never had the need of rule been greater. Besides, his presence in Carthage would have still further excited the already frenzied mob. The Roman presbyters, when Bishop Fabian had been martyred, wrote a letter of pained sympathy and good advice to the Carthaginian clergy on Cyprian's withdrawal. They were to be good shepherds and not hirelings, in the absence of their bishop. The advice was unnecessary as Cyprian was discharging his functions of government and oversight with diligence. He exhorted the presbyters and deacons "to discharge your own office and mine that there be nothing wanting to discipline or diligence." They were also to see that nothing in the way of money was to be lacking to those in prison, or to the poor, and he himself had provided money for the purpose. They were to be careful not to be provocative and were to see that the brethren did not visit the confessors in crowds, and that only one presbyter and one deacon at a time should celebrate the Eucharist in the prisons, and that they should take turns "because by thus changing the persons and varying the people suspicion is diminished."[1]

The systematic and thorough nature of the persecution is shown by some certificates of

[1] *Ep.* 5.

heathenism recently discovered near Alexandria. These state that "the bearers have always sacrificed to the gods, and have now done so in the presence of certain commissioners, whose signatures are appended."[1]

Decius was slain in battle with the Goths in the Dobrudja, A.D. 251. Gallus succeeded, and though the persecution ceased for the moment, it was renewed in the following year as a result of a pestilence which, beginning in Egypt, spread over the Roman world, for which the Christians were blamed.

Meantime a serious difficulty was brewing in the Carthage Churches. The martyrs and confessors were recognized as the saviours of the Church. The brethren visited them in crowds, and Cyprian addressed them in terms of lyrical enthusiasm. Every death is to be communicated to him that he might commemorate them in the Eucharist and place their names in the calendar for future observance. He recognizes that the martyrs have a certain privilege (*prerogativa*) with God. It is not surprising that some of them had their heads turned. Indeed, Cyprian had already written to this effect that they were to be exhorted to be humble and modest and peaceable.

The trouble arose over the lapsed, many of whom wished to come back to Communion. It had been the custom for martyrs to intercede with bishops for the restoration of sinners. Ter-

[1] Gwatkin, *Early Ch. Hist.*, ii. 256.

tullian protested against the custom—"No sooner has any one put on the bonds than adulterers beset him, fornicators gain access to him ; prayers echo round him ; pools of tears from the eyes of the polluted surround him. . . . Let it suffice the martyr to have purged his own sins, it is the part of ingratitude or pride to lavish upon others what one has obtained at so high a price. Who has redeemed another's death by his own but the Son of God alone ? "[1]

Now aided and abetted by four disaffected presbyters who saw their opportunity of creating a formidable faction the practice threatened to grow beyond all bounds. Cyprian laid down that those who had received a letter from a martyr, and were in danger of death, after confession and the imposition of hands in token of forgiveness, might receive Communion. All others must wait until after the restoration of peace, when the bishops, with the clergy in the presence of the faithful laity (the plebs who stand fast) would order all things after consultation.

This did not go nearly far enough for the friends of the lapsed. Great pressure was evidently brought to bear on the bishops, and the bishops remaining firm, recourse was had to the confessors. One Lucian, while in prison, was asked by Celerinus that he or one of his fellow martyrs, " whichever is first crowned, should remit this great sin to our sisters Numerica

[1] *Apology* xxii.

The Persecutions of Decius and Valerian

and Candida." Lucian replied that "while the blessed martyr Paulus was alive he called him and said 'Lucian, in the presence of Christ I say to you, if any one after my summons shall ask for peace from you, grant it in my name.'" Accordingly Lucian went on to grant peace to the two women, with the proviso "the case being set forth before the bishop and confession being made."[1]

But that was not the worst. The confessors appear to have felt that their letters were receiving inadequate attention from the bishops. At any rate, they met and sent Cyprian a joint letter, written by Lucian: "Know that to all concerning whose conduct since the commission of their sin, has been in your estimation satisfactory, we have granted peace. We wish you to inform the other bishops."[2]

Here we see an advance. It is not the bishop who grants peace on the intercession of the martyr, but the confessors who grant peace if the subsequent behaviour of the lapsed has been satisfactory to the bishop. Such a grant of absolutions *en bloc* would have reduced the matter to an absurdity. Cyprian stood firm and refused to be carried away. His reply was to repudiate absolutely the absolution *en bloc*. Each case must be considered on its merits. Peace might be given to those who, after having sacrificed, were tried a second time and stood firm. Others must wait until all the bishops could be gathered

[1] Cyprian, *Ep.* 22.   [2] Ibid., 23.

together, and each case could be considered on its merits.

A schism was begun by the friends of the laxity, headed by a presbyter called Novatus and a deacon Felicissimus.

When at length the Council of Bishops met, it decided that those who had actually sacrificed could only be restored at the hour of death. Others might be restored after a process varying in length according to the circumstances. Those who would not undergo their penance were not to be restored even in the hour of death.

In Rome Novatian headed a rigorist schism, and got himself elected antipope in opposition to the Bishop Cornelius.

When a fresh persecution seemed to threaten, the African bishops met May, A.D. 252, and wrote by Cyprian to inform Cornelius of their decisions. " We have decided," he wrote, " that peace is to be given to those who have undergone penance, that they may be armed and equipped for the battle which is at hand. That we may not leave those whom we stir up and exhort to the battle unarmed and naked, but may fortify them with the protection of Christ's Body and Blood ; and as the Eucharist is appointed for this very purpose, that it may be a safeguard to the receivers, that we may arm them whom we wish to be safe against the adversary. For how do we teach or provoke them to shed their blood in confession of His Name if we deny to them the Blood of Christ ? Or how do we make them fit for the cup of martyrdom if we do not first admit them to drink in the Church the cup of the Lord by the right of Communion?"[1]

Valerian became emperor A.D. 253, and began by favouring the Christians. "Never was there any emperor before him so favourably and benevolently disposed towards them. Not even those who were openly said to be Christians so plainly received them with such civility and friendship in the beginning of his reign. All his house was filled with Christians, and was indeed a congregation (*ecclesia*) of the Lord."[2] The change is attributed by Dionysius, Bishop of Alexandria, to Macrianus, his prime minister, and chief of the Egyptian magi, whom he accuses of having instigated his master to practise magical rites, "to sacrifice children and search the bowels of newborn babes and to mutilate and dismember the creatures of God."[3] We may take it that Macrianus was an enemy of the Church, and found his opportunity in the military disasters that befell the Empire on every frontier to suggest that the Christians were to blame.

The persecution began A.D. 257. Valerian's first edict was directed mainly against bishops and priests, and forbade assemblies for worship and the entrance of Christians into their cemeteries, still used apparently as places for worship by Christians.

[1] Cyprian, *Ep*. 57.   [2] Eusebius, *H. E.* vii. 10.
[3] Ibid.

Cyprian was banished to Curubis, and Dionysius to Cephro, a village in the desert.
Dionysius gives some particulars of the persecution in letters quoted by Eusebius. "We did not keep aloof from assemblies, but I gathered together all the more diligently those left in the city, as though I were present." At Cephro " at first we were persecuted and stoned ; at last not a few of the heathen abandoned their idols and turned to God." Again, " It is superfluous to recount our brethren by name, as they are numerous and unknown to you. They are men and women, young and old, young virgins and aged matrons, soldiers and private men, every class and every age, some that obtained the victory under stripes and in the flames, some by the edge of the sword. . . . In the city Maximus, Demetrius, and Lucius, presbyters, concealed themselves, and Dioscurus secretly visited the brethren. It was Eusebius, a deacon, whom God strengthened from the first and prepared to minister strenuously to the confessors in prison and to bury the bodies of the blessed martyrs made perfect at the risk of his own life. For up to the present time the governor does not cease killing in a most cruel manner, torturing, scourging, wasting with imprisonment and bonds, and commanding that no one shall go near them, and looking to see if any one should do so. Yet God, by the alacrity and kindness of the brethren, has afforded some relief to the afflicted." [1]

[1] Eusebius, *H. E.* vii. 11.

Carthage had escaped more lightly. But in August, A.D. 258, Cyprian wrote that Valerian had sent a new rescript to the senator, ordering that bishops, presbyters, and deacons be summarily put to death; that senators, men of rank, and Roman knights be deprived of both their rank and their property, and, if afterwards they persisted in being Christians, be executed; that matrons lose their property and be banished; that all imperial officials who have either confessed before or confess now have their property confiscated, be reduced to slavery, and sent to work on the imperial estates.

It is worthy of note that Cyprian's anxiety was now no longer lest Christians should fail to confess, but only that they should keep the peace, and that none should voluntarily give themselves up.

He returned to Carthage to await arrest, and was ordered to confine himself to his country house near by, as Galerius the governor was detained at Utica. He refused all solicitations to seek safety in flight, but disappeared when he heard that he was to be tried at Utica. He did this because he wished to die in Carthage, because "the city in which he presides over the Church of the Lord is the place where a bishop ought to confess his Lord and to glorify his whole people by the confession of their prelate in their presence." Some years before he had written to Lucius that "the victim which has to set before the brotherhood the pattern of manliness and of faith ought to be offered up in the presence of the brethren."

When Galerius came to Carthage, Cyprian came out of hiding and returned to his villa. On September 13th two officers drove up in a chariot and carried him off to Carthage. Round the house where he spent the night a vast crowd assembled, pagan as well as Christian, to do him honour.

The next day he was brought before Galerius, the proconsul, who began :—

"You are Thascius Cyprianus."

Cyprian. " I am."

Galerius. " You have given yourself to be a bishop to people of sacrilegious views."

Cyprian. " I have."

Galerius. " Consider."

Cyprian. " Do what you are ordered to do. In such a simple matter there is nothing to consider."

Galerius then passed sentence : " Your life has long been one of sacrilege ; you have been associated yourself with a great number of persons in a criminal conspiracy. You have constituted yourself an antagonist to the gods of Rome, and to their sacred observances. As you have been detected as the instigator and standard-bearer in heinous offences, you shall be in your own person a lesson to those who have been associated with you. Our pleasure is that Thascius Cyprianus be executed with the sword."

This sentence Cyprian acknowledged by saying

"Thanks be to God." The crowd, all greatly moved, shouted "Let us also die with him."

Accompanied by an immense crowd he was taken to the place of execution. Arrived at the spot he took off his woollen cape and knelt down and prayed. Then he rose, removed his dalmatic, and in his white linen alb prepared for death. He placed the bandage over his eyes, and his deacon fastened it. The executioner trembled so that he could not perform his task. But the centurion took the sword and severed his neck at one stroke.

In Rome the Pope Sixtus was found teaching in the Catacombs, and there executed with six of his seven deacons. Four days later S. Laurence, with others, met their death. S. Laurence was Archdeacon of Rome. The story is that when he saw Sixtus being led to execution he exclaimed "Why do you leave me, holy father? Should the priest go to the sacrifice without his attendant deacon?" Laurence, as keeper of the treasures of the Church, was ordered by the authorities to produce them. He asked for a day in which to collect them, and spent the time in visiting the poorest quarters of the city. The next day he appeared at the tribunal, attended by a crowd of beggars and cripples. "These," he explained, "are the treasures of the Church!" He was ordered to be burnt on a gridiron.

The persecution came to an end with the capture of Valerian by the Persians under Sapor. Gallienus, who succeeded, issued an edict of toleration, A.D. 260. The edict is lost, but it allowed the clergy to perform their accustomed ministrations unmolested, and granted permission to the bishops to recover the cemeteries. It was addressed to them, and therefore recognized the Church as a corporation. This edict remained in force until the last and greatest persecution under Diocletian, A.D. 303.

For forty-three years the Church had peace.

XI

THE ROMAN CHURCH

HOW Christianity was first introduced into Rome we do not know. But we know that on the day of Pentecost among those addressed by S. Peter there were "the sojourning Romans, Jews as well as proselytes," that is, a body of Jews from Rome resident for the time at Jerusalem. These Jews may probably be identified with the Synagogue of the Libertines, or Roman freedmen, to whom, in the first place, S. Stephen addressed his preaching. There can be no reasonable doubt that Christianity found its way to Rome within a year or two at most. But we do not know who first organized the Church there, or who laid its foundations. We know that S. Paul had left it alone "because he would not build on another man's foundation," and that when he wrote, A.D. 57–58, it was a large and flourishing community. Who was "the other man"? The universal tradition of the Christian Church answers S. Peter, and there is no sufficient reason for rejecting this testimony. It has also of late years received the support of archaeological investigation.

Mr. Edmundson[1] suggests that when S. Peter vanishes from S. Luke's history in the Acts, after his escape from prison in the spring of A.D. 44, he went to Rome. If so, the suggestion may have come from Cornelius, who belonged to the *Cohors Italica*. There is a strong tradition that S. Peter spent some years there, though, if so, his residence would hardly have been continuous. On the authority of Justin Eusebius tells us[2] that he followed on the heels of Simon Magus, who had preceded him there and was regarded as a god. Hippolytus tells us that S. Peter successfully opposed Simon Magus in Rome, as he had previously in Samaria.[3]

In A.D. 51 or 52 Claudius expelled the Jews from Rome, and the Acts tell us that S. Paul found Aquila and his wife Priscilla in Corinth, who had come there in consequence of the edict, being at the time already Christians. Suetonius gives the further information that the Jews were expelled on account of their continual tumults, *impulsore Chresto*, Chrestus being the instigator. So it is not unreasonable to assume that the disturbances arose through the introduction of Christianity.

S. Paul spent two years (A.D. 61–63) as a prisoner at Rome, and S. Peter probably wrote there his First Epistle, which ends with a greeting

[1] Edmundson, *The Church in Rome in the First Century*.
[2] *H. E.* ii. 13, 14.
[3] For the whole subject of S. Peter's connection with Rome, see *The Church in Rome in the First Century*, Lecture ii.

from "Babylon"; and Babylon is almost certainly a synonym for Rome. It is reasonably certain that both Apostles were martyred there, probably between A.D. 64 and 67. It was therefore fitted by its Apostolic connections, as by its central position and the associations and glory of its name, to become the centre of Christendom when Jerusalem was destroyed. Rome was not only the capital of the world : it was the only Apostolic see in the West.

A great source of influence may be traced to its hospitality. One of the most elementary charitable duties of the Christian, as we have seen, was hospitality. The world flocked to Rome as the English-speaking world flocks to London to-day, and the Roman Church became by its position the hostess of visiting Christians from all over the Empire and beyond.

Owing, perhaps, to their exceptional opportunities of knowing the needs of other Churches, Roman Christians seem to have been distinguished for their generosity. Dionysius, who was Bishop of Corinth, writing "to the Romans," addressing his letter to Soter, the bishop of that city, is quoted by Eusebius as saying :—

"For this practice has prevailed with you from the beginning, to do good to all the brethren in every way and to send contributions to many churches in every city, thus refreshing the needy in their want and furnishing necessaries to the brethren condemned to the mines ; you preserve by these contributions the practices of your ancestors the Romans. Which was not only observed by your Bishop Soter but also increased, as he not only furnished great supplies to the saints, but also encouraged the brethren that came from abroad with words of consolation as a loving father his children." [1]

It is noteworthy that at first it is the Church rather than the Bishop of Rome which is prominent. Clement wrote a letter to the Corinthians on certain disorders in their Church, with which the Roman Church was closely connected, as Ignatius wrote to Churches in Asia Minor, and Dionysius of Corinth wrote to remonstrate with the Church at Athens. It was a part of the general sense of brotherhood. If your neighbour was in difficulties or sin you had to try to help. What was true of the individual was equally true of the Church. It was the most natural thing in the world that Clement should write to the Corinthian Church. What does seem strange is that Clement writes, not in his own name as bishop, but in the name of "the Church of God which sojourns in Rome." Again, Ignatius, the last man to slight the office of a bishop, writing about twenty years later, addressed his letter to the Church and not to the bishop. Dionysius, of Corinth also, in acknowledging the generosity of the Roman Church, wrote "to the Romans" instead of to Soter their bishop.[2] Ignatius describes the Roman Church as "having the presidency in the country of the land of the Romans," and as

[1] Eusebius, *H. E.* iv. 23.   [2] Ibid.

being famous for good works. There is no word of the bishop, and no hint of more than a presidency of honour among the local Churches.

Among the famous Christians who visited Rome was Polycarp, who came in the time of Anicetus, and disputed with the followers of Valentinus and Marcion, and brought many of them to the Faith. He and Anicetus had many arguments about the proper date of Easter, but neither could persuade the other. However, they agreed to differ amicably, and Anicetus allowed Polycarp to celebrate in his place.

Soter, who succeeded Anicetus, wrote the letter to the Corinthians which has already been mentioned.

We get the first clear picture of the Roman Church as a natural guide and arbiter from Irenaeus, though he too speaks of the Church and not the bishop. It would be, he says, too tedious to refute the Gnostics by reckoning up the successions of all the Churches, so it will be enough to show the Apostolic tradition "of the very great, the very ancient, and universally known Church founded and organized at Rome by the two most glorious Apostles, Peter and Paul. . . . For to this Church every Church—that is, the faithful everywhere—must needs resort on account of its greater pre-eminence, since the Apostolic tradition has always been preserved therein by the faithful, who resort to it from everywhere." [1]

The words are obscure and the translation diffi-

[1] *Against Heresies*, III. 3.

cult, but the meaning apparently is that Christians looked on the Church of Rome as an arbiter on disputed points of faith, because from her position she was in touch with the faithful everywhere, and in a position to know the truth generally professed.

In A.D. 177 Irenaeus was sent with a letter from Lyons to bring intelligence of the martyrdoms in Gaul to Eleutherus, who was the Bishop of Rome, and also to protest against the errors of the Montanists. Eleutherus seems to have condemned the Montanists. At least Tertullian claims that a subsequent Bishop of Rome "acknowledged the claims of Montanus, Prisca, and Maximilla, and bestowed his peace on the Churches of Asia and Phrygia," but afterwards withdrew his approval at the instigation of Praxeas, who "insisted on the authority of the bishop's predecessors in the see."[1]

Victor, bishop A.D. 189–199, took a much stronger line than any of his predecessors. There had long been a controversy as to the correct day for keeping Easter. The Churches in Asia were quartodecimans; that is, they ended their fast before Easter on the fourteenth day of the Jewish month Nizam, so as to coincide with the conclusion of the Jewish Passover. Elsewhere Easter was always observed on a Sunday. Anicetus and Polycarp had had, as we have seen, a friendly difference on the subject, but the feeling of the Church was consolidating against the quartodecimans everywhere except in Asia. The

[1] *To Prax.* i.

question was specially felt at Rome, because of the number of strangers who kept Easter there, and Victor seems to have made up his mind to procure uniformity. Councils were held in Gaul, in Pontus, in Palestine, and in Asia. Everywhere except in Asia the quartodecimans were condemned. Polycrates, Bishop of Ephesus, and the Bishops of Asia were alone recalcitrant. Polycrates quoted the examples of the "great lights in Asia," whom they followed—of Philip the Apostle and his virgin daughters, of John who rested in the bosom of our Lord, and of other great men. Moreover, seven of his own relatives had been bishops, and they "always observed the day when the Jews threw away the leaven." Nothing, therefore, would induce him to give way. Victor, who seems to have been the chief mover in promoting these gatherings, "forthwith endeavoured to cut off the Churches of all Asia, together with the neighbouring Churches, as heterodox, from the common unity. And he published abroad by letters that all the brethren there are wholly excommunicated."[1] But this, continues Eusebius, was not the opinion of all the bishops. On the contrary, they exhorted Victor with much severity to promote peace and unity. Irenaeus in particular wrote in the name of the Churches in Gaul, "admonishing Victor not to cut off whole Churches of God, who observed the tradition of an ancient custom." He urged the example of Victor's

[1] *H. E.* v. 24.

predecessors in allowing the difference, notably the instance of Anicetus and Polycarp. "With all these maintained peace, and we have maintained peace with one another; and the very difference in our fasting establishes the unanimity in our faith."

It is probable that Victor afterwards withdrew from an untenable position.

Hippolytus, who died A.D. 235 or 236, is the outstanding figure in the Roman Church during the first quarter of the third century. He was a disciple of Irenaeus, and a man of immense learning. Under Victor he seems to have been in favour, but in the time of Zephyrinus, A.D. 199–217, he lost influence. Zephyrinus was succeeded by Callistus, who had once been a slave. Hippolytus had been on bad terms with Callistus, and was infuriated by the appointment of his enemy. The subsequent history is obscure, but Hippolytus went into schism, and is possibly the first anti-pope. At least, he never speaks of Callistus as bishop, but as having set up a "school," and made himself the head of it. In the following entry in the Liberian Catalogue he is referred to as a presbyter, not as a bishop. "At that time the Bishop Pontianus and the Presbyter Hippolytus were deported to Sardinia, a pestilential island, in the consulship of Severus and Quintianus, A.D. 235."[1] His death probably

[1] Liberian Catalogue. For the view that Hippolytus was Bishop of Portus see Lightfoot, *Apostolic Fathers*, I, vol. ii. 427–36.

occurred in this year or the next. He is not, however, reckoned among the anti-popes, and he is counted among the martyrs, so it may be that he was reconciled with his rival Pontianus in the marshes of Sardinia, and his schism forgotten. He was laid to rest in the time of Fabian by the Via Tiburtina, where a statue was found in 1551, perfect except for the head. He is seated in a chair on which are inscribed his tables for finding Easter. As this cycle went wrong from A.D. 237 the statue cannot have been put up later. There is also a catalogue of his writings. Among them are a large number of exegetical works and the *Philosophumena*, a voluminous book against heretics. He also wrote a book of *Chronicles*, and is probably the author of the so-called *Egyptian Church Order*.[1]

Hippolytus is the Roman Tertullian at a distance. He had immense learning, and was deficient in charity; but is far below Tertullian as a writer of vivid and nervous prose. He attacked Callistus in the most savage manner for past scandals in his private life, the truth of which we have no means of judging, but they bear marks of gross exaggeration. He also attacked his policy, principally in respect of his leniency to sinners. Hippolytus, like Tertullian, was a rigorist, and would allow no absolution for grave sins. Callistus had issued

[1] See article in *Texts and Studies*, viii. 4, by Dom R. H. Conolly.

an edict allowing repentance to those guilty of adultery, which called forth one of Tertullian's characteristic protests. "You introduce," he writes, addressing the pope, "into the Church in order to melt the brotherhood by his prayers the penitent adulterer. You lead him into the midst and prostrate him, all in haircloth and ashes, a compound of disgrace and horror, before the widows, before the children, suing for the tears of all, kissing their footprints, clasping their knees. Meantime you harangue the people and excite their pity for the sad fate of this suppliant. O good shepherd, O blessed pope, you relate the Parable of the Lost Sheep in order that this goat may be returned to you." [1]

Callistus decreed that if a woman of high birth married a slave the marriage should be recognized by the Church. The State did not recognize the marriage of a slave at all.

Hippolytus accused him of allowing men who had been twice or thrice married to continue in holy orders, and of allowing those already ordained to marry. He also says that during his pontificate a second baptism was attempted. This must mean a re-baptism of heretics, but if so the attempt was not successful, as not long after Stephen stated that re-baptism had never been allowed by his predecessors.

After the death of Hippolytus his mantle fell on Novatian. Like Hippolytus, he was a man of real learning, and, like him, was contentious

[1] *On Chastity* xiii.

The Roman Church 213

and unruly. According to Cornelius, he had been baptized on his sick-bed, and had never been confirmed; and for this reason objection was made to his ordination as presbyter.[1] He produced a learned work on the Trinity, and—again according to Cornelius—expected to be made pope. But, being disappointed, he persuaded three obscure Italian bishops to consecrate him, and headed a second rigorist schism during the troubles that followed the Decian persecution. He made common cause with Novatus, of Carthage, so we have the surprising result that Novatian, at the head of a rigorist schism in Rome, was allied with Novatus at the head of a laxity schism in Carthage. It gave rise to a good deal of correspondence between Cyprian and the Roman Bishop Cornelius, which has been preserved.

Cyprian wrote to give an account of his own troubles with schismatic presbyters, and sympathized with Cornelius in his difficulties, even going so far as to write a letter to the confessors at Rome who were causing them. In reply Cornelius wrote to tell him of the submission of some of the rebellious presbyters, in order, he explains, that he may give thanks.

When expecting a second outbreak of persecution, Cyprian and the assembled African bishops decided to admit the penitent lapsed to Communion "that they might be armed for the fray." This decision was communicated to

[1] Eusebius, *H. E.* vi. 43.

Cornelius, partly for his information and partly, apparently, for his example.

Fortunatus and Felicissimus, two of the African insubordinate presbyters, went to complain at Rome. Cyprian then wrote to urge Cornelius, whom he evidently thinks wanting in firmness, to have nothing to do with them. It had evidently not entered his head that they had a right to appeal to Rome. They had wandered about making trouble all over the province of Africa, and, being now too well known there, had gone to try their fortunes at Rome.

Later, when Stephen was pope, Marcian, Bishop of Arles, announced that he adhered to Novatian, and separated himself from the rest of the bishops. Whereupon Cyprian advised Stephen, now pope, to write to "our fellow bishops in Gaul not to suffer any longer that Marcian . . . should insult our assembly because he does not yet seem to be excommunicated by us." In other words, Stephen was to write to the bishops of the province and to the people at Arles that Marcian might be excommunicated and a successor appointed. Cyprian urges Stephen to act instead of acting himself, presumably because Rome was much nearer than Carthage to Arles and its communications with the province much closer.

His letter went on to descant on the duties of bishops, and gave Stephen some excellent advice. Among other things he wrote : " Although we are many bishops we feed one flock, and ought to collect and cherish all the flock which Christ by His Blood and Passion sought for; nor ought we to suffer our suppliant and mourning brethren to be despised"—words which show plainly enough that any idea of papal jurisdiction, of the one bishop over all, was not in his mind.

In another case of discipline Stephen was in conflict with Cyprian. Basilides and Martial, two Spanish bishops, had given way in the persecution and were expelled by their flock, who elected Sabinus and Felix in their place. Their deposers wrote to Cyprian, informing him of what had happened, and to be relieved "by the comfort or by the help of our judgement." Cyprian and his fellow bishops warmly approved their conduct. Basilides had aggravated his offence by appealing to Stephen, who, "placed at a distance and ignorant of what had been done and of the truth," had been induced to canvass that he might be replaced unjustly in the episcopate from which he had been righteously deposed.[1]

On the question of the re-baptism of heretics there was an acute difference. In the second century such baptisms had been administered by Gnostic sects, which were definitely outside the Church, and the refusal to recognize them was almost a matter of course. Later, after the rise of the Montanists and the Novatianists, who were schismatics, the question came up for decision. Novatian himself had begun by re-baptizing his

[1] Cyprian, *Ep.* 67.

disciples. Cyprian, adopting the traditional view, refused to recognize any baptism given outside the Church. He was followed by most of the African bishops. Stephen, Bishop of Rome, was as emphatic on the other side. Cyprian's position was logical and clear.[1] Those outside the Church are dead. No one can be made alive by that which is dead. Therefore no baptism outside the Church can be baptism at all. How can dead waters give life?

The controversy was acute, and lasted for some time. The Eastern Church seems to have been in favour of re-baptism, though Dionysius of Alexandria was firm on the other side. Firmilian, Bishop of Caesarea, wrote: "All powers and grace are established in the Church when the elders preside, who possess the power both of baptizing and of imposition of hands and of ordaining. For as a heretic may not lawfully ordain or lay on hands, so neither may he baptize."[2] From which we see incidentally that no one maintained the validity of confirmation or ordination if administered by heretics.

Stephen, Bishop of Rome, strongly opposed Cyprian and those who thought with him, and went so far as to excommunicate them. Firmilian was much shocked by this breach of charity, and pointed out that previously there had been differences with the Church of Rome in respect of the date of Easter and other matters without producing any breach of "the peace and unity of

Cyprian, *Ep.* 71, 1.   [2] Ibid., 75, 7.

the Catholic Church, such as Stephen has now dared to make."¹ The controversy was for the moment ended by the death of Stephen and the martyrdom of Cyprian ; but the Eastern Church was slow to give in, though the Roman view prevailed in the end.

It is worthy of note that the Church in Rome was at first a Greek and not a Latin Church. Clement wrote in Greek, and down to Hippolytus all who wrote at Rome wrote in Greek. Hippolytus was the last great writer of the Roman Church who wrote in Greek.²

¹ Cyprian, *Ep.* 75, 6.
² NOTE.—No attempt has been made to deal with the theory of Papal Supremacy, though certain facts that bear on it have been given. To go into the question at any length would be beyond the scope of this work. For this reason the passages in Cyprian's Treatise *On the Unity of the Catholic Church*, have not been discussed. For its discussion, see Benson's *Cyprian*, 180 sqq.

XII

LIFE IN THE CHURCH

THE ante-Nicene fathers tell us little of the Church life of their day; of its internal organization, its officers and their duties, the ministry of its women, the ordering of its services, its social life, its charities, and its discipline, though we are able to glean some valuable and interesting information. But scholars in recent years have added considerably to our knowledge of these things by bringing into the light what are known as the Church Orders. These are Manuals of Church Order and Discipline for the use and instruction of local bishops. The earliest is probably the *Didaché*, on which was afterwards based the seventh book of the *Apostolic Constitutions*. Next came a manual commonly known as the *Egyptian Church Order*.[1] Its original seems to have been written in Greek by Hippolytus, and was called the *Apostolic Tradition*, somewhere during the first quarter of the third century. The Greek original is lost, but we have some fragments of a Latin version, published by E. Hauler and commonly called the Verona fragment, and four

[1] See *Texts and Studies*, viii. 4, by Dom R. H. Conolly.

Oriental versions [1] translated from the Latin, two of them Coptic, one Arabian, and one Ethiopian. Fourth or fifth-century adaptations of these are found in the so-called *Canons of Hippolytus*, Book viii of the *Apostolical Constitutions*, and the *Testament of the Lord*. Later still came the *Epitome* and the *Constitutiones per Hippolytum* derived from Book viii of the *Apostolic Constitutions*. We have also a third-century manual in Syriac, though this is not to affirm that Syriac was the original language in which it was written, called the *Didascalia Apostolorum*, which reappears later, brought up to date and revised, in the first six books of the *Apostolic Constitutions*, written towards the end of the fourth century.

So far as our period is concerned, we have to rely on the *Didaché*, the *Egyptian Church Order*, and the *Didascalia*. Between them we learn a good deal of the inner Church life of the third-century Christian.

Baptism

Admission into the Church was by Baptism. About that there is no doubt. We have no very early description of the service. Justin Martyr gives some account in his *First Apology*,[2] but does not enter into details.

---

[1] See *The Statutes of the Apostles*, by Rev. G. Horner; H. Tattam, *Apostolical Constitutions*; also Funk's *Didascalia et Constitutiones Apostolorum*.

[2] lxi.

"As many as are persuaded and believe that what we teach is true, and undertake to live accordingly, are instructed to pray and entreat God, with fasting, for the remission of their past sins, we praying and fasting with them. Then they are brought by us where there is water, and are regenerated in the same manner in which we were ourselves regenerated. For in the Name of God, the Father and Lord of the universe, and of our Saviour Jesus Christ, and of the Holy Spirit they then receive the washing with water. For Christ also said 'Except ye be born again ye shall not enter into the kingdom of heaven.'"

In the *Didaché* there was a direction to baptize in running water in the Name of the Father and of the Son and of the Holy Spirit : "If thou hast not running water, baptize in some other water ; and if thou canst not baptize in cold then in warm water ; but if thou hast neither" (that is neither a stream of running water or a pool of standing water), "pour water three times on the head."[1]

By the middle of the third century the preparation for Baptism and its ritual had developed considerably. The candidates, or catechumens, had to serve a long and arduous apprenticeship. First of all, they "were brought to the teachers before the people came in ; and they shall ask them for what reason they sought the Faith."[2]

[1] *Didaché*, vii.
[2] Horner, *Statutes of the Apostles*, p. 148.

They were also examined as to their trades and way of life. A slave might not be admitted unless he could bring a good character from his master. Four classes of people are to change their way of life or to be rejected:—

1. Those leading immoral lives or living on the immorality of others.

2. Those having to do with heathen worship, " whether a priest, or a maker of idols, or a painter or gilder of them."

3. Those who have any connection with the Shows or Games of the circus. "A man or a woman who is concerned in a theatre, or a charioteer, or an Olympic contender, or a chorus flute-player, or a harp-player, or a piper, or a dancer, or one who goes to the games or who is a gladiator or teaches gladiators to fight."[1]

4. Sorcerers and soothsayers of all kinds—star-gazers, diviners, serpent-charmers, " one who augurs by the birds of heaven."

If the catechumens answered the questions satisfactorily they were admitted by the imposition of hands. They were then placed under instruction, and allowed to attend the first part of the Eucharist—called later the Mass of the Catechumens. They stood at the back of the church and heard the readings of the Scripture and the sermon, but were dismissed before the celebration of the Mysteries.

The teaching was moral and doctrinal. The moral teaching seems to have been mainly on the

[1] Horner, *Statutes of the Apostles*, p. 312.

lines of "The Two Ways," which are given in the *Didaché*, as the groundwork of a catechetical instruction. The teacher might be a layman, and was appointed for the purpose. He was called the Doctor. After each instruction they prayed by themselves, the women separately from the men ; the instructor then laid his hands on them and dismissed them with a prayer.

The preparation lasted normally for three years, but it varied with the individual candidate. " Yet if he were a good scholar and one who knows good conduct no length of time need be required of him, but the conduct alone shall decide for him." [1]

Candidates imprisoned for their religion before the end of their catechumenate were not to be apprehensive at the prospect of dying unbaptized, as martyrdom was considered to have the effect of baptism. " If a catechumen is arrested for his religion he is not to fear, because if put to death he is baptized in his own blood." [2]

On the fortieth day before the Easter on which they were to be baptized, their lives were examined, " if they lived in the fear of God, if they honoured the widow, or visited the sick, or if they did all good, and if there is witness in their favour from those who bring them," [3] and if the result was satisfactory, the Gospel was read

[1] Horner, *Statutes of the Apostles,* p. 150.
[2] Ibid., p. 151.
[3] Ibid., p. 152.

over them, and they were admitted to a more intensive preparation.

They were now daily instructed and exorcized with the imposition of hands. Some day shortly before Easter they underwent an examination at the hands of the bishop. " And if one is found who is not pure they shall put him aside by himself; for he has not hearkened to the voice of instruction with faith." [1]

Those who are accepted are directed to bathe on the Thursday, and to begin their fast on the next day. On the Saturday they were once more brought to the bishop, and knelt before him. " And when he has laid his hand upon them, let him exorcize all alien spirits to flee away from them and not to return to them henceforward. And when he has done exorcizing, let him breathe in their face." [2] At nightfall they assembled with the faithful for the devotions of the Paschal vigil, a prolonged service of lessons, hymns, and a sermon. It included the first part of the Eucharist, and lasted until dawn. They then went to the baptistery. The baptism began with the blessing of the water. " At the hour when the cock will crow let them first pray over the water. Let the water be flowing along into the tank or descending upon it. . . . But if there be a scarcity then use the water which ye shall find." [3]

At the same time the oil has to be blessed, and

[1] Horner, *Statutes of the Apostles*, p. 152.
[2] Ibid., p. 316. [3] Ibid.

the candidates undress. " Let the bishop give thanks over the oil and put it into a vessel and call it the oil of thanksgiving ; and take also other oil and exorcize it and call it the oil of exorcism. . . . And a deacon shall carry the oil of exorcism, and stand on the left hand of the presbyter. And another deacon shall take the oil of thanksgiving and stand on the right hand of the presbyter." [1]

The children are to be baptized first. "And ye shall first baptize the children. All who can speak for themselves, let them speak. But for them who cannot speak, let their parents speak for them, or any other belonging to their family." [2]

Then followed the renunciation. " And when the presbyter has taken hold of each one who will be baptized, let him command him to renounce, saying, 'I renounce thee, Satanas, and all thy service and all thy works.'" In the *Canons of Hippolytus*, a later work, the catechumen turns to the west and says, "I renounce thee, Satan, and all thy works." [3]

The candidate is then exorcized. "And when he has renounced all these, let him anoint him with the oil of exorcism, saying, 'Let every foul spirit remove far from thee.'" The anointing presbyter then hands him over, naked, to the presbyter or bishop, who is to baptize. " Like-

[1] Horner, *Statutes of the Apostles*, p. 317.
[2] Ibid., p. 316.
[3] Cabrol and Leclercq, *Monumenta Ecclesiae Liturgica*, p. 267.

wise also let the deacon go with him into the water, and let him say to him, helping him to say it, 'I believe in the only true God, the Father, the Almighty, and His only Son Jesus Christ, our Lord and Saviour, and His Holy Spirit.'"

Then the act of baptism takes place. "And he who gives the baptism shall put his hand on the head of him who receives, and dip him three times; and he who is baptized shall make declaration every single time that he is dipped."

Afterwards apparently he repeats his profession of faith. He is asked: "Dost thou believe in the Name of our Lord Jesus Christ, the only Son of God the Father, that He became man in an incomprehensible miracle by the Holy Spirit and by our Lady Mary the Virgin without seed of man, and that He was crucified in the time of Pilate the Pontian, and He died; and He died by His own will to save us, and He rose from the dead on the third day, and released the captives, and ascended into the heavens and sat down on the right hand of the Father, and He shall come to judge the living and the dead at His appearing and His kingdom?"

"Dost thou believe in the Spirit, the holy, the good, the sanctified in the holy Church, and dost thou believe in the resurrection of the body which shall happen to every man, and the kingdom of the heavens, and eternal judgement?"

And he shall answer for all these things, saying "Verily I believe in this."[1]

After the act of baptism and the profession of faith the candidate is anointed with the oil of thanksgiving.

Confirmation

They then dry themselves and put on their clothes, and go into the church and are immediately confirmed.

"Let the bishop lay his hand upon them with great desire, saying 'Lord God, according as Thou hast made these worthy of receiving the forgiveness of their sins unto the future life, make them worthy of being filled with Thy Holy Spirit, and send down upon them Thy grace that they may serve Thee according to Thy will, because Thine is the glory, Father, Son, and Holy Spirit, in the holy Church now and always and for ever and ever.'"

He then anoints the candidate.

"And he shall pour some oil of the thanksgiving upon his hand, and lay his hand upon his head, saying 'I anoint thee with an unction in holy oil by God the Father Almighty, and Jesus Christ and the Holy Spirit.' And he shall seal him upon his forehead, kissing him, and shall say 'The Lord be with thee.' And he who has been sealed shall answer 'And with thy spirit.'"[2]

[1] Horner, *Statutes of the Apostles*, p. 254.
[2] Ibid., pp. 318–19.

The whole congregation then pray silently, and give one another the kiss of peace.

It should be noticed that the outward sign of Confirmation consists of unction, imposition of hands, and signing. Dr. Brightman says that the unction in the West was probably peculiar to Rome, and was not found in Africa, the imposition of hands being the essential part of the rite. In the East the unction was the central act. Origen does not mention the laying on of hands.[1]

The Eucharist was now continued, and the baptized received their first Communion.

THE EUCHARIST

When the newly-baptized received their first Communion a cup containing water and another containing honey and milk were consecrated at the same time as the wine. The water was to symbolize the washing of the inner man, and the honey and milk the Promised Land into which they were now entering. They received first the Bread with some such words [2] as " This is the Body of Christ." The communicant saying *Amen*. Then the cups containing water and milk and honey. Then the Wine.[3] " He

---

[1] *Early History of the Church and Ministry*, pp. 349–50.

[2] In the Ethiopic version, Horner, *Statutes of the Apostles*, p. 178.

[3] This is the order in the Verona fragment. Later, by the time of the so-called *Canons of Hippolytus*, the cups of water, etc., were given *after* the chalice.

who administers the cup shall say 'This is the Blood of Christ,'" the communicant again saying *Amen.*

It was the great privilege of the baptized to be present at the Eucharist Sunday by Sunday. Justin Martyr records that "on the day called Sunday, all who live in cities or in the country gather together into one place." In later times some Christians required urging. The writer of the *Didascalia* urges the faithful to be regular in their attendance, to see that no one diminishes the Church by not assembling, or makes smaller by a member the Body of Christ.[1] They are "to leave everything on the Lord's Day, and run eagerly towards your church, for this is your glory. If not, what excuse will you have before God for those who have not assembled on the Lord's Day to hear the Word of Life and to be nourished with the divine Food which endureth for ever?"

It was the custom for all who were present to receive, unless undergoing penance, and in some parts of the Church those who wished could carry away with them some portion of the consecrated Bread, and possibly of the consecrated Wine, with which they might communicate themselves during the week. The *Egyptian Church Order* gives directions as to its safe custody when in the house: "Every one shall be most careful not to let any but the faithful receive of the

[1] *Didascalia Apostolorum*, translated from the Syriac by M. D. Gibson, xiii.

Mysteries, nor a mouse nor any other creature, and not to let any be spilt and lost, since it is the Body of Christ and His Blood, and all the faithful shall eat of it—it is not proper to neglect it." [1]

It is to this custom that Tertullian alludes when he warns his wife in speaking of the inconveniences of marriage with a heathen that he will want to know "what it is which you secretly taste before taking any food." Daily Communion was thus made possible, and was no doubt the practice of many. We do not hear much of the daily celebration, though Cyprian alludes to it as being apparently his custom.

At first the Eucharist succeeded the agape. But by Tertullian's time it seems always to have been received fasting. The Church Order lays down that "All believers shall accept the admonition that they should receive of the Mystery before that they taste anything." [2] In the *Canons of Hippolytus* the faithful are to fast before Communion, "especially on the days of the sacred fast." [3]

The seating of the congregation was ordered with due care. In the east of the building the seats of the presbyters were to be placed, and the bishop's throne in the middle. The deacons, when not engaged in guarding the doors or seating the congregation or keeping watch over the

---
[1] Horner, *Statutes of the Apostles*, p. 261.
[2] Ibid., p. 180.
[3] R. H. Conolly, *Texts and Studies*, viii. 4, p. 68.

offerings, stood close at hand.[1] The writer of the *Apostolical Constitutions* says they must wear tightly-girt garments, like the mariners of a ship, to which he compares the Church. But this was later. West of the clergy sat the laymen, and behind the laymen the women, who were arranged in classes. The old women and widows sat by themselves, and virgins and deaconesses no doubt had their special places not long afterwards. Tertullian complains bitterly that a virgin was seated among the widows, which shows that there were not then special places for them, but that such places were felt to be required.

Children are to sit with their parents, or in a place by themselves. Girls are to sit apart by themselves, or if there is not room stand behind the women.

A deacon is to stand at the entries for men, and later on a deaconess at those for women. "Every one has his own place, and if any one sits out of it he must be admonished by the deacon and put in his proper place."[2] The deacon has to see that they go to their places and do not sit at the entrance. He has also to keep an eye on their behaviour "lest any one whisper or sleep or laugh or make signs. For a church is not a place of confabulation, but of reverent prayer."[3]

Careful arrangements are made for the reception of visitors. "If there come a person from

[1] *Didasc.* xii. [2] Ibid. [3] Ibid.

another assembly, a brother or a sister, let the deacon ask and learn if she be a wife or a believing widow, if she be a daughter of the Church, or if it be one of the heresies, and then let him conduct her to the place that befits her."

A presbyter is to be received by presbyters, and seated among them; a deacon is to sit with the deacons. If a bishop comes he is to sit with the bishop, and is to be asked to preach, "for the admonition of strangers is very acceptable, and no prophet is acceptable in his own country."[1] He is to be asked to offer the Eucharist. If he be wise and gives honour to the local bishop by refusing to officiate, yet "over the cup let him speak."[2] Later he is to give the blessing.

"If, after the congregation is set down, any person arrives who has honour in the world, either man or woman, whether he be a stranger or one of your own country, neither do thou, O bishop, if thou art speaking the Word of God or hearing him that sings or reads, accept persons so far as to leave the ministry of the Word, that thou mayst appoint a place for him; but continue quiet and let the brethren receive him. Let one of the brethren who is full of love and loves his brethren and would do honour rise and give his place."[3] But if no one rises, then, "O deacon, look thou at those who are sitting for him who is younger than his comrades or her who is younger; make them rise and seat him who rose

[1] *Didasc.* xii.   [2] Ibid.   [3] Ibid.

and gave up his place. Lead him whom thou hast made to rise and put him behind his comrades, that others also may be educated and learn to give place to those who are more honourable than they."[1] If a poor man or poor woman of a mean family come, especially one of advanced years, a place must be found. In the *Didascalia* the bishop must find a place even if he himself has to sit on the floor; but later this is left to the deacon in the case of a man, while the deaconess has to do it for a woman.

Good behaviour in church could apparently no more be taken for granted then than it can now. The *Didascalia* speaks of those who "not even in the communion of the assembly on Sunday, when they come, are attentive; the women and the men, they either sleep soundly or talk about something else."

The Agape

The agape was originally a solemn meal which immediately preceded or followed the Eucharist. During the second century the agape was separated from the Eucharist and became a social meal; one might almost call it a sanctified parish tea. It took place in the evening, and was partly religious and partly social. Tertullian has given a vivid account of it in his *Apology*. After speaking of the lavish feasting associated with heathen worship, he goes on: " Yet about the

[1] *Didasc.* xii.

modest supper-room of the Christians alone a great to-do is made. Our feast explains itself by its name. The Greeks call it love. Whatever it costs, our outlay in the name of piety is gain, since with the good things of the feast we benefit the needy; not as with you do parasites aspire to the glory of satisfying their licentious propensities—but, as it is with God Himself, a peculiar respect is shown to the lowly. As it is an act of religious service, it permits no vileness or immodesty. The participants before reclining first pray to God. As much is eaten as satisfies the cravings of hunger; as much is drunk as befits the chaste. They eat as remembering that during the night they have to worship God; they talk as knowing that the Lord is one of their auditors. After the washing of hands and bringing in of lights each one is asked to stand forth and sing, as he can, a hymn to God, either one from the holy Scriptures or one of his own composing—a test of the measure of our drinking. The feast is closed, as it began, with prayer." [1]

The agape seems to have begun with a prayer of thanksgiving and an address by the bishop, if present. In his absence a presbyter or, in default of either, a deacon would preside, and say the prayers and distribute the *Eulogia*, the *pain bénit*, or blest bread, sometimes called the bread of exorcism. Catechumens were not allowed to sit down at the feast, but were

[1] *Apol.* 39.

given a share of the *Eulogia*. In the absence of any of the clergy a layman might preside, but in that case there was no distribution of *Eulogia*.

In the Ethiopian Church there seems to have been a rule of silence, the object for which was that those present might ask the bishop questions. " Those who are invited shall eat without conversing, but when the bishop allows they shall speak and ask what is suitable."

The bringing in of lights at the agape was the signal for the Psalms and hymns which closed the feast, and was at one time attended with some ceremony. The Ethiopic version of the Church Order has some interesting directions " concerning the bringing in of lamps at the supper of the congregation."

" When the evening has come, the bishop being there, the deacons shall bring in a lamp, and the bishop, being about to give thanks, standing in the midst of the faithful, shall first give us the salutation, thus saying, ' The Lord be with you all.' And the people also shall say ' With His Spirit.' And the bishop shall say ' Let us give thanks to the Lord ' ; and the people shall say ' Right and just, both greatness and exaltation with glory are due to Him ' ; and they shall not say ' Lift up your hearts,' because that shall be said at the time of the oblation. And he prays thus, saying,

" ' We give Thee thanks, God, through Thy Son Jesus Christ our Lord, because Thou hast enlightened us by revealing the incorruptible Light. We having therefore finished the length of a day, and having come to the beginning of the night, and having been satiated with the light of the day which Thou hast created for our satisfaction, and now since we have not been deficient of the light of the evening, by Thy grace we sanctify Thee and we glorify Thee through Thine only Son our Lord Jesus Christ.'[1] And they shall all say Amen."

The feast then ends with the recitation of Psalms and the solemn offering and sharing of a cup.

The prayer given in the *Apostolical Constitutions* to be used at the lighting of the lamps in church after the dismissal of the catechumens or penitents is evidently taken from the one used here. " Thou Who has brought us through the length of the day and has brought us to the beginning of the night, afford us a peaceable evening and a night free from sin ; preserve us by Thy Christ, through Whom glory, honour, and worship be to Thee in the Holy Spirit for ever." With this may be compared the evening hymn alluded to by S. Basil as being in his time already ancient : "Hail, gladdening Light of the pure glory of the Father, Who is immortal, holy, heavenly, Jesus Christ the blessed ; now, having come to the setting of the sun, beholding the light of evening we hymn the Father, Son, and Holy Spirit of God. Worthy art Thou at all times

[1] Horner, *Statutes of the Apostles*, p. 160.

to be hymned with holy voices, Son of God, Giver of Life, therefore the world shall own Thy glory."[1]

But already the agape was beginning to degenerate from the parish tea in which all meet on the basis of brotherhood into the parish treat organized on a basis of charity. It had become a private affair. The partakers are there by invitation of a well-to-do member of the congregation. The feasters must eat and drink with decency and not with inebriety, that "*he who invited you* may not be distressed." The fragments of the feast are to go to the poor, and the feasters are urged to moderation in their repast that the fragments may be abundant. "Eat with moderation and drink with moderation, that there may be some left; and that that which is left from you may be sent by him who invited you to whom he will: and he shall say that this meat is the leavings of the holy ones."[2]

---

[1] With this may be compared the metrical translation by Mr. Keble—

Hail, gladdening Light, of His pure glory poured
  Who is the Immortal Father, Heavenly, Blest,
Holiest of Holies, Jesus Christ, our Lord.
  Now we are come to the sun's hour of rest,
    The lights of evening round us shine,
We hymn the Father, Son, and Holy Spirit Divine.

  Worthiest art Thou at all times to be sung
    With undefiled tongue,
  Son of our God, Giver of life, Alone!
Therefore in all the world Thy glories, Lord, they own.

[2] *Didasc.* ix.

The *Canons of Hippolytus* speak of *agapai* prepared for the poor, as well as those given to widows. Those who entertained widows had to send them away before dark. If this could not be done the food and wine was distributed to them and eaten at home. " If this is not possible because of the clergy who have been invited, he shall give to them food and wine, and having given them send them away immediately."

The cessation of persecution killed the agape. When churches could be built and used it was no longer necessary to conduct worship secretly in private houses. Before, it had been safer to meet for a meal and take advantage of the meeting for common prayer and praise. But when churches were there and could be used, it was equally natural to use the church for prayer and the house for food, and to separate the two. We see by the Church Orders that the sparing use of food and drink was not easily obtained. Already in the fourth century we find the beautiful ceremony and prayers at the lighting-up of the lamps transferred to church. No doubt there were other reasons. The unfortunate taint of pauperism was on it. The gospel of brotherly love and charity can demoralize giver and recipient alike. The Christians of the first days were as fully awake to these dangers as were the founders of the Charity Organization Society, who have added little to the warnings against the abuse of charity contained in the New Testament and the Church Orders. The love-feasts afforded an irresistible temptation to the spirit of patronage on the part of the giver, and to greed and deceit on the part of the receiver. They were doomed.

There also seems to have been a distinct agape with a close connection with the memorial of the departed. " Now when you are invited to their memorials do you feast with good order and the fear of God, as disposed to intercede for those who are departed." [1] Presumably it took the same form as the other, except that their devotions were explicitly for the soul of the departed. In this case the memorial began with a Eucharist and was followed by the memorial agape.

FASTING

From the beginning it is probable that fasting formed part of the discipline and devotional life of the Church.

Irenaeus, writing to Victor, Bishop of Rome, with reference to the date of Easter, alludes to the difference, not only as to the day, but also as to the fast preceding it. " Some think they ought to fast one day, some two, some more days; some compute their day as consisting of forty hours day and night; and this diversity is not a matter that has just sprung up in our time, but long ago among those before us." [2] As

[1] *Apos. Con.* viii. 44.   [2] Eusebius, *H. E.* v. 24

Irenaeus had been a disciple of Polycarp, who was the disciple of S. John, his statement points to the extreme antiquity of the practice. It was connected with the Death and Passion of Christ. "When the Bridegroom shall be taken away, then shall ye fast."

Tertullian seems to assume that until the rise of Montanism only the days immediately before Easter were fasting days of obligation. "They think that those days were definitely appointed for fasts in which the Bridegroom was taken away." Other fasts were to be "of choice, not of command." However, there had sprung up the custom of fasting on Wednesdays and Fridays up to 3 p.m., the hour of our Lord's death on the Cross, the days being chosen as those of His Betrayal and Crucifixion. They were called station days, and those who observed the fast on them were said to keep a station. The name seems to have been a military term, and is thus explained by Ambrose: "Our fasts are our encampments (*stationes*) which protect us from the devil's attack; they are called 'stations' because, standing in them, we repel our foes."

In the earliest Church Orders, we find directions to fast on the Friday and Saturday before Easter. No other fasts are mentioned, except for those preparing for Baptism. The fast is an absolute fast. No food at all is to be taken from Thursday night until after the Easter Communion. Sick persons need only fast on one day, and on that day were allowed bread and water. Travellers who omitted to fast before Easter had to make up for it by fasting after Pentecost.[1]

In the *Didascalia* Christians are directed to fast from Monday in Holy Week until Easter. " From the tenth day, which is Monday, during the days of the Passover, ye shall fast, and be nourished by bread and salt and water at the ninth hour (3 p.m.), until Thursday. But on Friday and Saturday ye shall fast completely and eat nothing ; but assemble yourselves and wake and pray the whole of the night with prayers and supplications, and with the reading of the prophets, with the Gospel and the Psalms, with reverence and fear and intercession until the third hour of the night after the Sabbath, and then ye shall leave your fast," presumably after the Easter Eucharist.

The extension of the Holy Week fast so as to become the Lent fast of forty days was a later development, probably arising out of the custom of catechumens beginning their strict preparation forty days before Easter.

One of the Montanist innovations was the introduction of novel fasting days. They introduced two weeks of abstinence from all except dry food, extended the station from three until six p.m., and make their observance compulsory, instead of leaving it a matter of free choice for the individual.

[1] Horner, *Statutes of the Apostles*, p. 260.

The Sick

Care was taken that the sick should be visited. They were anointed with oil which had been blessed by the bishop, but might be administered by any person, clerical or lay;[1] in the *Egyptian Church Order*, by the deacon. A prayer is given for the blessing of the oil by the bishop, in which he prays "that for those who shall be anointed therewith it may be for healing and safety and benefit in all diseases and sicknesses and for extermination of the Satanic adversary."

Women who were sick were in some places visited by a widow or deaconess. In the *Didascalia* we find rebukes addressed to the widows who neglect this duty. "Thou seest the widows, thy companions, and thy brethren in sicknesses, and thou carest not to fast and pray for thy members, to put to thy hand, and to visit them."[2]

Some Christians were looked on as possessing the gift of healing, though we do not hear very much about it, and it does not seem to have filled a very large place in the popular mind. There seems to have been an order of healers, into which new members were admitted only after giving proof of their powers. "As for the grace of healing, if some one says 'I have acquired the grace of healing and prophecy,' they shall not lay hand on him until his deed make evident that he is trustworthy."[3]

---

[1] Horner, *Statutes of the Apostles*, p. 159.
[2] xv.   [3] Horner, *Statutes of the Apostles*, p. 147.

The healer was soon merged in the exorcist. When dead the Christian could be buried in a Christian cemetery which was maintained by the bishop out of the offerings of the faithful for the benefit of the poor members of the community. Those who could afford it were expected to pay the wages of the gravedigger.

Marriage

Marriage remained throughout this period the business of the State. Its legality depended on civil and not religious sanction. But pagan rites and religious ceremonies accompanied it among the heathen, so at an early stage Christians substituted for such ceremonies those of the Church. At marriage Christians received the blessing of the Church on their union. The Church seems to have in some formal way approved the marriage through the presence of its representative at the betrothal, the legal contract, and by a subsequent blessing in the Church. " Whence are we to find words enough fully to tell the happiness of that marriage which the Church brings about and the oblation confirms and the benediction signs and seals—which the Father holds for ratified. For even on earth children do not rightly and lawfully wed without their father's consent."[1]

Ignatius had already written eighty years before that " men and women who marry ought to be

[1] Tertullian, *To his Wife*, ii. 8.

united with the consent of the bishop, that the marriage be according to the Lord, and not according to lust."[1]

Not that the marriage would not have been valid without, for the contracting parties then, as now, were held to be the ministers of the Sacrament of Marriage, but the Church gave its approval and afterwards its blessing in the communion of the newly married.

Organization of Charity

Christ had told His disciples they were to love one another, and their neighbour as themselves, and had insisted on the necessity of giving. Brotherly love was not so much an emotion as practical assistance given to those who were in need. It was feeling realized in action. The kindness shown by Christians to one another excited the attention and aroused the exasperation and envy of pagans. The heathen Caecilius, in his dialogue with Octavius, is made to assert: "They know one another by secret marks and signs, and they love one another almost before they are acquainted." To which Octavius retorted: "We do not distinguish our people by some small bodily mark, as you suppose, but easily enough by the sign of innocency and modesty. We love one another, to your regret, because we do not know how to hate. We call one another brethren, to your envy, as being

[1] Ignatius, *To Polycarp*, v.

born of one God and Father, and companions in faith and fellow heirs in hope. You, however, do not recognize one another, and are cruel in your mutual hatreds ; nor do you acknowledge one another as brethren, unless for the purpose of parricide."

So Tertullian. "'See,' they say, 'how they love one another,' for they themselves are animated by mutual hatred. 'How they are ready to die for one another,' for they themselves will sooner put to death. And they are angry with us because we call each other brethren." [1]

The giving of alms was a feature of the Eucharist on the first day of the week. "They who are well to do and willing give what each thinks fit ; and what is collected is deposited with the president, who succours the orphans and the widows, and those who through sickness or any other cause are in want, and those who are in bonds, and the strangers sojourning among us, and in a word takes care of all who are in need." [2]

Such passages might be multiplied. Tertullian apparently knew of a monthly not a weekly collection.

Even if there is a Church fund it is not made up of fees as though of a religion which has its price. "On the monthly collection day each, if he likes, puts in a small donation ; but only if willing and able. These gifts are piety's deposit fund. For they are not taken

[1] *Apol.* 39.   [2] Justin Martyr, *Apol.*, 67.

out to be spent on feasts and drinking bouts and eating houses, but to support and help poor people, to supply the wants of boys and girls destitute of means and of parents, and of old persons confined to the house; such as have been shipwrecked or are in the mines, or banished to the islands or shut up in the prisons for their fidelity to the cause of God, become the nurselings of their confession."[1]

We see from this and similar passages that the Church took care that none of its sick or indigent or unfortunate members should suffer want. The regular Church fund seems to have been administered by the bishop, assisted by the deacons. Hence the importance attached by S. Paul to the presbyter-bishops not being "lovers of money."

"When I was in prison ye visited Me," was a text taken to heart and acted upon with zeal. The pagan Lucian scoffs at Christians for visiting Peregrinus in prison and supplying him with meals. Tertullian begins his exhortation *To the Martyrs* with the words: "Blessed martyrs designate.. Along with provision that our Lady Mother, the Church, makes from her own breasts, and each brother out of his private means, for your bodily wants in prison, accept also from me some provision for your spiritual sustenance."

Instances occur again and again in the acts of the martyrs. The gaoler of Perpetua and her companions allowed them to receive visitors, who

[1] Tert., *Apol.* 39.

ministered to their needs. Eusebius[1] records that Licinius, when he became a persecutor, devised illegal laws, by which prisoners were forbidden to receive visitors or food in prison, and those who transgressed the edict were to receive the same punishment as the prisoners they visited.

The care of the Church for its needy members was liable to abuse, a fact which did not escape Lucian. But the Church was fully awake to the danger. "If a man receive being in need, he shall be free from guilt; but he who receiveth when not in need shall pay a penalty as to why he has received and for what purpose; and when he is in tribulation he shall be examined as to what he has done, and shall not depart till he has paid the uttermost farthing. For of a truth it has been said on these matters 'Let thy alms-giving abide in thy hands until thou knowest unto whom thou art giving.'"[2]

The prophet who remains as a guest for three days and takes money as well as food for his journey is a false prophet. "Whosoever shall say in the spirit, 'Give me money or things of that kind,' listen not to him."[3]

Further, it was laid down that the Church must provide work rather than alms for the able-bodied. "For those able to work provide work, and to those incapable of work be charitable."[4]

"Let every one that cometh in the Name of the Lord be received. . . . If he be a wayfarer

[1] H. E. v. 8.   [2] Didaché, i.   [3] Ibid., xi.   [4] Clem., Hom. viii.

assist him so far as ye are able, but he will not remain more than two or three days unless there be a necessity. But if he wish to settle with you, being a craftsman, let him work and so eat; but if he know not any craft provide ye according to your own discretion that a Christian may not live idle among you. But if he is not willing to do so he is a trafficker in Christ. From such keep aloof." [1]

Cyprian also assumes that any one who has been living by an art forbidden by the Church must be provided with work, or if unable to work outside his profession with the necessaries of life.

There are directions in the Church Orders for the care of orphans and children. In the *Didascalia* the bishop is to persuade the rich and childless members of his flock to adopt orphans. " If one of the children of the Christians be an orphan, either a boy or a girl, it is well that, if there be any of the brethren who hath no children, he take the boy in place of children." [2]

If they are not willing to do this, the bishop is to see to it himself. " Ye therefore, O bishops, take up the burden of them that they may be brought up so that nothing be wanting to them, and when it is the time for the maiden give her in marriage to one of the brethren. And let the boy when he is grown up learn a handicraft, and when he is a man let him take the wage that is meet for his craft, and acquire the necessary tools that he may no longer be a burden on the charity

Didaché, xii.   [2] Ibid., xvii.

of the brethren. Truly, blessed is he who is able to help himself, and does not straiten the place of the widows and orphans and the poor." [1]

Three instances, at least, are on record of ministrations by the Church on the grand scale in time of plague.

In A.D. 259 there was plague in Alexandria, of which Bishop Dionysius wrote: "Most of our brethren by their exceeding great love and brotherly affection, not sparing themselves, were constantly superintending the sick, ministering to their wants without fear and without cessation.... Among the heathen it was the reverse. They both repelled those who began to be sick and avoided their dearest friends. They would cast them out into the roads half dead, and throw out their bodies without burial." [2]

During the plague in Carthage we are told by Cyprian's biographer that when "all were shuddering, fleeing, shunning the contagion, and bodies lay about the whole city," Cyprian summoned the Christians and exhorted them to minister to the heathen sick as well as to the brethren. As a result, "good was done to all men, not only to such as are of the household of faith." [3]

The third instance is recorded by Eusebius [4] as having occurred in the government of Maximin Daza, after his defeat by the Armenians, though he does not specify the exact place:

[1] *Didaché*, xvii.   [2] Eusebius, *H. E.* vii. 22.
[3] *Cypr. Life*, x.   [4] *H. E.* ix. 8.

"Then also the evidences of the zeal and piety of the Christians became manifest to all, for they alone showed sympathy and humanity amid so much distress. They continued all day; some in the care and burial of the dead, for numberless were they for whom there was none to care; others collected the multitude of those wasting by famine, and distributed bread among them all, so that the fact was cried abroad, and men glorified the God of the Christians."

Discipline

No question caused the Church of the third century more trouble than that of discipline. Strict probation and a stern renunciation were required of the catechumen before he could be admitted by baptism. It followed that if he relapsed into immoral ways or pagan practices he must be disowned and separated from the communion of the faithful.

We find the principle enunciated by Christ in the gospel. "If he neglect to hear the Church, let him be unto thee as a heathen man and a publican."[1] The commission given by our Lord to bind and loose had a recognized meaning to frequenters of the synagogue. It had a definite reference to exclusion from the privileges of religious membership and admission to them.

S. Paul bids the Corinthians "not to keep company, if any man that is called a brother be

[1] S. Matt. xviii. 17.

a fornicator, or covetous, or an idolater, or a railer, or a drunkard, or an extortioner ; with such an one no not to eat."[1] They are to put away from themselves that wicked person. He commands the Thessalonians in the Name of Christ " that ye withdraw yourselves from every brother that walketh disorderly, and not after the tradition which he received from us."[2] " If any man obey not our word by this epistle, note that man, and have no company with him, that he may be ashamed."[3]

It was acted on from the beginning by the Church, and is thus explained by Origen to Celsus :—

" And this is their method of procedure both with those who are sinners and those who lead dissolute lives, whom they exclude from their community. . . . The venerable school of Pythagoreans used to erect a cenotaph to those who had apostatized from their system of philosophy, treating them as dead ; but the Christians lament as dead those who have been vanquished by licentiousness or any other sin because they are lost and dead to God, and if they change, they receive them afterwards as risen from the dead, though after a greater interval than was the case of those admitted at first, but not placing in any office or post of rank in the Church of God those who after professing the Gospel lapsed and fell."[4]

[1] 1 Cor. v. 11.   [2] 2 Thess. iii. 6.
[3] Ibid., 14.   [4] *Against Celsus,* iii. 51.

The sins which incurred the penalty of exclusion were of the sort that the candidate for baptism had to renounce, such as idolatry, magic, serious offences against the law of purity, fraud, violence, and false witness; also heresy and schism.

In many cases the sinner would excommunicate himself; either because his sin was self-evident or because his own sense of shame would not allow him to face the congregation. "If he who sinneth see that the bishop and deacons are free from accusation, and all the flock are pure, he will not dare to go up to the congregation because he is reproved by his own mind." [1] If he does venture to appear, the bishop is to reprove him before the whole congregation; "he will blush therefore, and with much shame he will go out quickly weeping and be in penitence of soul."

When a definite accusation was made and guilt was denied, something like a judicial prosecution took place with the bishop as judge, the presbyters and deacons as assessors, and the congregation as jury. If guilty the accused was excommunicated. [2]

The object of excommunication was to preserve the Church from impurity and to afford an example to the faithful. "They also who see them and hear that they have gone out like publicans may fear and take heed to themselves

[1] *Didasc.* v.
[2] Ibid., xi. F. E. Brightman, *Early History of the Church and Ministry*, p. 365.

that they sin not, lest it happen thus to them also, and they go out of the Church being reproved for sin and for falsehood."[1]

It had for its third object the restoration of the sinner. The bishop is constantly exhorted to keep this end in view. The sinner is compared to a man who has fallen in the river, and the bishop is to stretch out his hand so as to pull him out. Prayers are to be offered in church for the sinner, and the bishop is to try to move him to repentance. " Him that is abandoned in sins or excommunicated as for reproof leave not without, but teach and admonish and convert and receive him into thy flock . . . do not allow him to perish utterly. But do thou visit him, admonish and teach and convert him, command him and encourage him to awaken ; tell him that there is hope."[2]

Sinners who repented were admitted to penance, the severity and duration of the penance varying according to the Church and the nature of the sin. The object of the penance was that the penitent sinner might bring forth fruits of repentance ; in other words, give an earnest of the sincerity of his penitence. " By penitence amends are made ; of penitence repentance is born ; by penance God is appeased."[3] Miriam is quoted as an example of penance. " If her father had but spit in her face would she not have been ashamed and separated for seven days without the camp, and then she would have come in ?"

[1] *Didasc.* x.   [2] Ibid., vii.   [3] Tert., *On Penance*, ix.

The procedure seems to have been that the sinner, when willing to submit to penance, first applied privately to the bishop, and then sent emissaries to the bishop and assembled congregation formally asking for their prayers. The bishop then commanded him to come in, and asked if he repented; if so he admitted him to penance. "If he be worthy to be received into the Church, appoint him days of fasting according to his fault."[1] As a penitent he stood once more in definite relationship to the Church. He was, in fact, in the position of a catechumen. He had a special place assigned to him at the back of the church, and was not allowed to communicate. "Thus also we do not communicate with these until they show the fruits of repentance; for they can certainly come in, if they wish to hear the Word, that they may not perish utterly, but in prayer they take no part, but go outside."[2] They are not to be "utterly prevented from hearing the discourse of the bishop"; but were sent out before the Eucharistic prayers. This was in Syria.

In Africa the place of the penitents was outside the church, in the porch or vestibule. "Before her doors it stands,"[3] says Tertullian of penitence. But they do not seem to have been dismissed at any period of the service.

In Asia Minor there were three or four grades or stages of penitence. The lowest was that of the "Hearers"; these were admitted to the

[1] *Didasc.* vi. [2] *Ibid.*, x. [3] *On Modesty* iii.

Mass of the Catechumens and dismissed after the sermon. Then came the "Kneelers," who were also dismissed before the Eucharistic prayers, but only after the faithful had prayed over them as they lay prostrate on the ground. The final stage was that of the "Consistents," who stood with the faithful throughout the service, but did not communicate. But Dr. Brightman thinks that this system did not extend beyond Asia Minor.

The course of penance, or exomologesis, as it was called, is described in lively terms by Tertullian. "This exomologesis is a discipline for man's prosecution and humiliation, enjoining a demeanour calculated to move mercy. With regard to the very dress and food it commands the penitent to lie in sackcloth and ashes, to cover his body in mourning, to lay his spirit low in sorrows, to exchange for severe treatment the sins which he has committed; to know no food and drink but such as is plain—not for the stomach's sake but for the soul's; for the most part, however, to feed prayers with fastings, to groan, to weep, and roar unto the Lord your God; to roll before the feet of the presbyters and kneel to God's dear ones; to enjoin on all the brethren to be ambassadors to bear his supplication to God."[1] "What if," he continues, "besides the humiliation which they make the most account of, they dread the bodily inconveniences; in that unwashen, sordidly attired,

[1] Tert., *On Penitence*, ix.

estranged from gladness, they must spend their time in the roughness of sackcloth and the horridness of ashes and the sunkenness of face caused by fasting ? "

But, after all, the austerities of the penitent are no worse than the annoyances sustained by seekers of office. " Why, they who go about canvassing for civil office feel it neither degrading nor irksome to struggle for the attainment of their desires with annoyance to soul and body and contumelies of all kinds. . . . Do we hesitate when eternity is at stake to endure what the competitor for consulship or praetorship puts up with ? Shall we be tardy in offering to the offended Lord a self-chastisement in food and raiment which Gentiles lay upon themselves when they have offended no one at all ? "[1]

So perhaps penance was not so severe as it sounds.

The length of penance varied from a few weeks to a lifetime, the penitent in that case being given communion only when at the point of death. In Syria apparently the longest term was seven weeks.[2]

At the end of the appointed time the penitent had to appear in the church and make his exomologesis or confession, when he appeared before the clergy and congregation, confessed his sins, and implored forgiveness. The congregation then implored the bishop to pronounce absolution, which was done. It seems that the bishop

[1] Tert., *On Penitence*, xi.   [2] *Didasc.* vi.

had previously satisfied himself of the penitent's earnestness.

This confession probably took place in the Eucharist after the dismissal of the catechumens, so that the penitent could communicate during the service. This restoration was never granted more than once. Tertullian calls penance and baptism the two planks of salvation. Neither could be repeated.

Discipline as practised in the Church not unnaturally gave rise to difficulties. The system was severe and it was public, and, especially during the persecutions, produced hard cases.

The first controversy was over the question whether the Church had any right to grant absolution for certain grave sins. *The Shepherd* of Hermas was written to plead for forgiveness for all sins. The question whether certain sins could be forgiven was much debated. Some of the African bishops, we learn from Cyprian, had decided that "peace was not to be granted to adulterers, and wholly closed the gate of repentance against adultery."[1]

About A.D. 220 the pope, Callistus, apparently included among absolvable sins adultery and fornication. "I absolve such as have discharged the requirements of penitence from the sins of adultery and fornication."[2] This drew furious protests from Tertullian, now a Montanist, and from Hippolytus. Tertullian in his tract *On*

[1] Cyprian, *Ep.* lv. 21.
[2] *On Penitence*, i ; *Refutation of all Heresies*, ix. 7.

Penitence maintained that all deadly sins were non-absolvable. That is, while counselling life-long penance to the guilty, he declared that the Church had no power to restore them to communion, but they must be left to the mercy of God.

By a strange perversity the Church has often been accused of "shutting the gates of mercy on mankind" by denying the possibility of forgiveness to those who were not admitted to penance. The Church did nothing of the kind. Even the rigorist Tertullian is far from doing that. His point is not that such sins as adultery are unforgivable, but that their forgiveness belongs to God alone and is beyond the scope of the judgement of the Church. The penance of such sinners, he declares, "believes not that man's peace is adequate to its guilt," and, as far as regards the Church, "it prefers the blush of shame to the privilege of communion. For before her doors it stands, and by the example of its own stigma admonishes all others and calls to its aid the brethren's tears and returns with their compassion—merchandise even richer than their communion. And if it reaps not the harvest of peace here, yet it sows the seed of it with the Lord : nor does it lose but prepares its fruit." [1]

Origen seems to have held the same view as to the non-absolvability of certain deadly sins. It was based on 1 S. John v. 16 : "There is a sin unto death ; for that I do not say that he shall pray."

[1] *On Modesty*, iii.

Tertullian lays down that there are two classes of sins—those absolvable by the Church and those non-absolvable. By the middle of the third century, in Africa at least, the rigorist view had been given up. At least we find Cyprian, in a letter [1] about Novatian, assuming that even to adulterers " repentance is granted and the hope of lamenting and atoning is left." The persecutions under Decius and Valerian gave rise to bitter controversies on this vexed question, of which some account has already been given. They were revived again after the Diocletian persecution. But the inevitable tendency was in the direction of lessened severity and even of laxity.

[1] *Ep.* iv. 26.

XIII

THE OFFICERS OF THE CHURCH AND THEIR DUTIES

IT is clear that from the very earliest times the Church had its regular officials, its Apostles, presbyters, and bishops, its deacons and widows, not to mention evangelists, prophets, and teachers, whose status and duties are more disputable.

The Church Orders give some interesting information about their admission to office, and their duties when admitted, during the third century, by which time some changes in the procedure had taken place.

The Bishop

The bishop, of course, comes first. He is the source of authority in each diocese. He is the high priest, the *sacerdos*, who is the customary celebrant at the Eucharist; he holds the purse and dispenses the offerings of the faithful; he is the teacher of his flock and also holds the keys, in other words administers discipline.

His duties are set down in the Ordination Prayer,[1] to be said at his consecration by the

---

[1] Horner, *Statutes of the Apostles*, p. 139. Compare the Verona Fragment. Funk, *Didascalia et Constitutiones Apostolorum*.

bishops present, when they pray that " he may feed Thy flock, and minister as priest to Thee without blame . . . that he may offer Thine Oblation in Thy holy Church, in the Holy Spirit of the priesthood, having authority to forgive sin according to Thy commandment, and to give ordination according to Thy command, and loose all bonds of iniquity according to the authority which Thou gavest to Thine Apostles."

The bishop was considered to be chosen by the Holy Spirit. This choice might be immediate, as when the lot fell on Matthias, or the prophecies [1] were made over Timothy, or the dove alighted on the shoulder of Fabian. It was generally indicated by the personal worthiness of the chosen candidate, confirmed and ratified by popular assent. Therefore stress was laid on his election. His character also is to be carefully examined. If there was no one in the diocese competent to examine the proposed bishop help must be got from outside. " If it is a place with few people in it of the faithful, and the assembly not large enough to elect a bishop, being not more than twelve men, then let them write to the Churches of the neighbourhood to bring three of the faithful, trustworthy men, and they shall test carefully as to which is worthy of the work. If he has a life of good repute among the peoples, and without sin or anger, a lover of the poor and kind, not a drunkard or adulterer, not a railer or hypo-

[1] 1 Tim. i. 18.

The Officers of the Church and their Duties 261

crite.[1] He shall have a share of all sound doctrine and be able to expound the Scriptures; and if he should be one who cannot expound the Scriptures, he should be humble and abound in love to all men, that the bishop may be condemned in nothing whatever, nor let him be reproved in anything." He need not be unmarried, but "it is good that he be without wife, though if he have married one before he is ordained bishop, he shall live with her."[2] He would have a principal part in disposing of the alms of the faithful, therefore he must not be "a lover of the greater share for himself." From the above quotations we see incidentally that the numbers in the diocese might be tiny and the bishop almost illiterate.

The election was not carried out in the exact modern way. It was rather an acclaim or an assent of the faithful to the person put before them by their leaders and the neighbouring bishops. It was effective as is shown by an instance given by Dr. Frere.[3] At Cirta, A.D. 305, Silvanus, who had surrendered books in the persecution, was proposed, and the people shouted, *Alius fiat*—"Let another be appointed," and they had their way.

Cyprian[4] says that in order to preserve the divine and Apostolic tradition at ordinations, all

---

[1] Horner, *Statutes of the Apostles*, p. 239.
[2] Ibid., p. 133.
[3] *Early History of the Church and Ministry*, p. 300.
[4] *Ep.* 67, 5.

the nearest bishops in the same province are to assemble, and the new bishop is to be chosen in the presence of the people because they are fully acquainted with the life and character of all who are present. It is, in fact, a power of veto, rather than election. The choice was probably made beforehand by the presbyters and deacons, or the influential lay people, and later on in times subsequent to the period under review, by the king or some great civil authority, as is the case to-day. But the veto was a real thing. It has survived in the *Siquis* for priests and deacons and the citation to objectors which is part of the confirmation ceremony for bishops.

The presence of the neighbouring bishops was a guarantee to the rest of the Church that the ordination was valid, and a witness to the new bishop and his flock of their participation in the unity of the Catholic Church.

We have also an account of the Ordination Service.[1] " The bishop shall be ordained as we have already spoken ; one who has been chosen by all the people together, with the presbyters and deacons on the Lord's day. And all the bishops shall go with mutual consent and lay their hands upon him ; and the presbyters, standing by, keep quiet, and all of them together in silence and praying in their hearts that the Holy Spirit may help them and descend upon him. And every one of the bishops shall pray, and all of them severally, standing up, shall

[1] Horner, *Statutes of the Apostles*, pp. 138-39.

lay their hands upon him who is ordained bishop, and they shall pray over him thus." Then follows the consecration prayer, which, after the exhortation, goes on to pray: "And now pour out from Thee the might of the Holy Spirit, which Thou gavest to Thy beloved Son Jesus Christ, which Thou grantest to us the holy Apostles, Thy helpers in Thy Church, working with the plough of the Cross and in the place of Thy holiness. . . ." Then follows the prayer for the graces required for the special duties of the episcopate, which has been given already.

After the consecration prayer came the kiss of peace. "Every one of them shall salute him with the mouth, kissing him who has become a bishop." A deacon then brought him the oblations, upon which the other bishops and the presbyters laid their hands, and he then began the Communion Service with the *Sursum Corda*.

The consecration prayer which followed immediately contains, in the Ethiopic version, one beautiful phrase which is worth recording. "Spreading out His hands for suffering that He might release the sufferers who trust on Thee."[1]

The Presbyters

The presbyters were, in the second and third centuries, very much overshadowed by the bishop and the deacons. It is not until, in the fourth

[1] Horner, *Statutes of the Apostles*, p. 140.

and fifth centuries, when the organization of the Church made it necessary for them to have independent cures, that they begin to assert themselves. We find Jerome, for instance, asking what a bishop can do that a presbyter does not do except ordain. In the third century they are still comparatively submerged.

There is one interesting bit of evidence in the Church Orders illustrating the rise of the presbyterate between the beginning of the third and the end of the fourth centuries.

In the *Egyptian Church Order* there is a direction that the bishop's prayer should be used over the presbyter. "In the form which we said before he shall pray," and then follows the same *exordium* as that in the bishop's prayer; but the prayer itself is different and appropriate to the presbyter. Mr. C. H. Turner suggests that the direction only means that the same *exordium* should be used.[1]

However that may be, the *Canons of Hippolytus*,[2] a fourth or fifth century adaptation of the *Egyptian Church Order*, directs that the same prayer should be used for the presbyter as for the bishop, with the exception of the name, and adds the significant explanation: "The bishop is equal in all things to the presbyter, except for the throne and ordination. For the power of ordaining is not given to the presbyter." There is also the preliminary direction that " All things

[1] *Early History of the Church and Ministry*, p. 284.
[2] Cabrol et Leclercq, *Reliquiae Liturgicae Vetustissimae*, p. 264.

are to be done with the presbyter as in the ordination of a bishop, except that he is not enthroned." This plainly implies an advance in the position of the presbyter.

It is also laid down in the *Canons of Hippolytus* that the deacon is to minister to the bishop and to the presbyters. But in the *Egyptian Church Order* there is nothing said about their ministering to presbyters. They are the servants of the bishop alone. These changes are all for the greater glory of the presbyter, and—given the earlier date of the *Egyptian Church Order*, which may be considered to be established by the researches of Dom Conolly—show his rise in position and prestige between A.D. 225 and 375 approximately.

The Church in towns was organized on the plan of a cathedral, and not of a modern diocese. Instead of a large number of small and more or less independent parishes there was the one Church presided over by the bishop, assisted by presbyters and deacons. The presbyters were in some respects like the canons of a modern cathedral, where the bishop is also dean. They were generally elderly, always in residence, always present at the services, but neither celebrated or preached in the presence of the bishop. And the bishop nearly always was present. As to absolution, it seems unlikely that they were ever authorized to give it so early as this. They were the bishop's advisers and assessors, his Chapter in fact, and no doubt if men of ability found enough to do. But we hear little of them, and it is likely that they were generally ordained when elderly [1] from among the more devout and religious deacons, minor officials, or laymen, and quite possibly, on the analogy of widows, some were ordained, if of unblemished character, that they might receive an honourable and suitable provision in their old age.

The Church Order says that a bishop is to have three always with him. It also says that the proper number of presbyters in a church is twenty-four. "And it is proper for the presbyters that they should be like old men . . . and they shall partake of the Mystery with the bishops, and help with him in everything whatsoever, and gather round him with love of their shepherd. And the presbyters who are on the right shall be careful to give assistance at the altar. . . . And the presbyters who are on the left shall attend to all the people, that they may be quiet and not in commotion." [2]

At his ordination the bishop "shall lay his hand upon his head; and all the presbyters shall touch him and pray over him."

At one time the custom prevailed of allowing confession involving torture to take the place of ordination, just as martyrdom was allowed to count as baptism. The Ethiopian text of the Church Order [3] lays down that "if the confessor has been in the place of punishment, in chains,

---

[1] Horner, *Statutes of the Apostles*, p. 134.
[2] Ibid., p. 142.   [3] Ibid., p. 146.

for the Name of Christ, they shall not lay hand on him for a ministering, for that is the honour of a deacon; but as for the honour of the presbyterate, though he hath the honour of the presbyterate by that which he hath confessed, yet the bishop shall ordain him, having laid his hand upon him." In the Arabic [1] and Saidic [2] versions the confessor may be advanced to the presbyterate without laying on of hands, but "if he is appointed bishop the hand shall be laid on him." It is not clear how far this rule was carried out in practice. We know that Cyprian only made the confessor Celerinus a reader, though he was given "the honour" and allowances of a presbyter.

THE DEACON

The deacon was a most important person, and, unlike the presbyter, whose principal qualification was age, or at least the chastity and sobriety that age should bring, a long list of more positive qualities is required of him. "They shall be tried concerning all the service, having the testimony of all the people, that they live with one wife, and have reared their children in purity, and such as are merciful and humble, and such as are not murmurers, and such as are not doubletongued nor wrathful, because wrath depraves a wise man. And they shall not respect the person

[1] Horner, *Statutes of the Apostles*, p. 246.
[2] Ibid., p. 308.

of the rich, nor act unjustly to the poor ; nor drink much wine ; and they shall work hard for the Mysteries, the hidden, the beautiful, the cheering. And they shall honour all with all honour and modesty and fear, and they shall keep themselves in all purity. And some of them they shall teach, and some of them they shall question, and some of them they shall reprove, and some they shall console. As for the rejected, they shall also expel them at once, and they shall know that those who oppose, the revilers, the rejected, are your adversaries." [1]

He was, in fact, the bishop's chaplain, secretary, man of business, and almoner ; and as all the offerings of the Church came under the control of the bishop, the deacon had enough to do. He had both to make inquiries and distribute the alms. He was also responsible for most of the duties in church, which now would be divided between the sacristan, the verger—the doorkeeper and acolyte came later—and the old-fashioned parish clerk. He bid the prayers. For instance we read : " The deacon shall say ' Pray ye for those who gave their names.' " In fact he seems to have combined all these ecclesiastical functions with those of an agent of the Charity Organization Society.

In the deacon's ordination prayer the bishop prays that "he may obtain the exalted priesthood " ; so it is not unreasonable to assume that when too old to carry on the work of deacons

[1] Horner, *Statutes of the Apostles*, p. 135.

efficiently they were raised to the priesthood if their lives were satisfactory, just as a parish priest to-day, when getting too old for the work of a big parish, is sometimes made the canon of a cathedral.

At his ordination the bishop alone is to lay his hand on his head. "And why do we say that the bishop alone is he who lays his hand upon him? For a sign it is of this thing that he was not ordained for priesthood, but only for the service of the bishop. And he was not ordained to be a teacher of those who are in Orders, but to be one who will think of what is proper, and to inform the bishop. And he was not ordained to acquire the Great Spirit of which the presbyters partake, but to occupy himself with that which is proper, that the bishop may trust him, and that he may acquaint the bishop with that which is fitting for him to know." [1]

The archdeacon later on was called the *oculus episcopi*. We see the beginning of it here. The modern archdeacon, stript of the accidental and extraneous functions which sometimes devolve on him as a canon or parish priest, is the descendant of the ancient deacon.

The Minor Officials

Outside the Orders of Bishop, Priest, and Deacon the first official to appear is the reader. His duties, except so far as they are indicated

[1] Horner, *Statutes of the Apostles*, p. 144.

by his name, are obscure, and he soon lost his importance. We read in the Church Order [1] that "a reader shall be ordained after he has been first tried. He shall not be of many words, or a drunkard or a scoffer. And he shall be of good character, and a lover of the good; one who is quick to go every day to the church, who remembers the judgement; and he shall be obedient and one who reads well, and who knows the duty of him who reads, that he should do according to what he reads; and one who fills the ear of others with his word, ought he not to do it himself?"

At this time, at any rate, he was appointed rather than ordained. "To the reader who is ordained the bishop shall deliver the Scripture, and shall not lay hand upon him." [2]

The Subdeacon

The subdeacon at this period came after the reader, and apparently after the widow and the virgin. His duties were to assist the deacons. "He shall not lay hand upon a subdeacon, but he shall make mention over them of the Name, that they may minister to the deacons." The fourth and fifth century witnessed a great expansion of the duties of the deacons, and the importance of the subdeacon grew accordingly. The reader and subdeacon were paid and may have

[1] Horner, *Statutes of the Apostles*, p. 155.
[2] Ibid., p. 174.

ranked as clergy, but Cyprian says they were *clero proximi*—next to the clergy.

Acolytes

We hear little of acolytes. They are not mentioned in the first Church Order, but we learn that in Rome in the third century there were seven deacons, one for each ecclesiastical district, and under each deacon one subdeacon and six acolytes.[1]

The Widow

"It is not permitted to a woman to speak in the church; or to teach, or to baptize, or to offer, or to claim to herself a lot in any manly function, nor to say in any sacerdotal office."[2] This probably represents not untruly the negative attitude of the Church as a whole. Nevertheless, there had been from the beginning a ministry of women.

From very early days there was an order of widows. "Let not a widow be enrolled under three score years of age, having been the wife of one man, well reported of for good works; if she have brought up children, if she have lodged strangers, if she have washed the saints' feet, if she have relieved the afflicted, if she have diligently followed every good work. But the younger widows refuse."[3] They are to continue

---
[1] *Early History of the Church and Ministry*, p. 302.
[2] Tert., *On the Veiling of Virgins*, ix.   [3] 1 Tim. v. 9–11.

in prayer night and day. They were not, however, to teach apparently or to usurp authority over the men.

The widow was enrolled partly as an act of charity. For if she has nephews or children, they are to support her. She is not to be a burden on the Church. Only if she is desolate and without means of support, in addition to more spiritual qualifications, can she be enrolled. Later on the qualification of destitution seems to have tended to oust the other.

The agape seems to have survived latest as a treat for widows. The most afflicted are to be invited oftenest.[1]

One of the reasons for not appointing young widows is that by reason of indigence they might marry again.[2] In the first Church Order there are directions for the ordination of widows. Only those whose husbands have been dead a long time are to be ordained. They are to be ordained by word only. " They shall not lay hand upon her, because she does not offer the sacrifice, nor has she a (sacred) ministry. For the sealing is for the priests because of their ministry, but the duty of widows is about prayer."[3] A later edition adds that a widow must remain a long time, keeping apart with good works, with fasting and prayer, before she is admitted into the order.

In the *Didascalia* they are not to be less than

[1] *Didasc.* ix. [2] Ibid., xiv.
[3] Horner, *Statutes of the Apostles*, p. 147.

fifty. Tertullian gives sixty as the age limit. Those who contribute to their support are not to give to the widows with their own hands, but are to contribute through the bishop, who knows the circumstances of each; and when they receive the gift they are to be told the name of the giver.

"Take care of them therefore, O bishop, and remember also the poor. . . . Therefore those who bring gifts are not to give to widows with their own hands, but are to offer to thee on their behalf. . . . And when thou distributest tell them the name of the giver, that they may pray for him by his name." [1]

She is to be humble, peaceful, and quiet. She is not to be a great talker, or lift up her voice when she speaks, or to have a long tongue or love quarrels. She is to care for nothing else but to pray for her benefactors and the whole Church.

She is not to teach, because if "it is declared to them (heathen under instruction) by a woman about how our Lord became incarnate and about the Passion of the Christ they will mock and joke. . . . Therefore it is not necessary or right that women should be teachers, especially about the Name of the Lord and about salvation by His Passion, for women were not appointed to teach, especially not a widow; but that they should make prayer and supplication to the Lord God." [2]

[1] *Didasc.* xiv. [2] Ibid., xv.

As a class they do not seem to have been satisfactory, which is not altogether ׳ surprising. There are bitter complaints of widows who gad about and are grumblers, quarrelsome, and have no shame, "for not even in an assembly on Sunday are they attentive ; . . . they either sleep soundly or talk about something else."[1] By them their order is considered a merchandize, and they care only for money. "She who is assiduous to gad about cannot please God." "When she stands up to pray she recollects where she should go to receive something, or that she has forgotten to say some word to her friends."

But "the widow who wishes to please God sits within her house and meditates in the Lord night and day without ceasing, at all times offering prayer and supplication. She does not gad about, her prayer is not impeded, and her peacefulness, quietness, and purity are accepted of God."[2]

This system of providing for widows not unnaturally fomented jealousy. "The wise widow, when some old widow, thy companion, has received a garment or a gift, thou, O widow, oughtest to say 'Blessed be God Who comforteth the old woman my comrade.'" The woman who received the gift will like.a wise woman conceal the name of the donor. But if the recipient is without sense she will reveal the giver's name, and if she to whom it is

[1] *Didasc.* xv.   [2] Ibid.

revealed is one of those who only care to beg or gad about, "she grumbles and blames the bishop who made the provision, or the elder or him who gave the gift, and says 'Dost thou not know that I am nearer to thee, and I am much more destitute than she?'" Some disappointed widows seem to have so far forgotten themselves as to curse the bishop who was responsible.

The widows were, in fact, an order of destitute persons with a claim on the charity of the faithful, which they were expected to requite with prayers.

The Deaconess

The deaconess seems to have been evolved from the widow. We come across the phrase "widows who are deaconesses." In some cases, at any rate, they anoint the bodies of women in baptism, and take communion to sick women, visit women in houses when men would not be admitted, put women in their places in church, and have generally a recognized ministry to women. "A woman is required for the service of women; for there are houses where thou canst not send a deacon on account of the heathen. Send a deaconess for many things."[1] She was also to visit the sick and anoint those who were healed from sicknesses. The *Didascalia* says they are to be appointed. The compiler of the *Apos-*

[1] *Didasc.* xv.

tolic Constitutions, Books i–vi, who produced a revised and amplified edition of the *Didascalia*, says they are to be ordained. The same editor lays down that widows are to be subject to deaconesses. By the fourth century there are directions for the bishop to ordain her by laying on of hands, and a special prayer is provided. Her ordination follows that of deacons, and comes before those of subdeacons and readers. In the *Testament of our Lord* there are directions for the appointment of widows and also of presbyteresses or widows "who sit in front," who are presumably much the same as deaconesses, and have been evolved in the same way.

The deaconess does not appear until towards the latter half of the third century, and not often then. The Church Order (in a later edition) speaks of subdeaconesses and women readers, but gives no particulars.[1]

Virgins

The virgin is the woman who voluntarily undertakes to lead a celibate life for the sake of greater devotion to our Lord.

The idea is not exclusively Christian. Consecrated virgins, of whom the Vestal Virgins of Rome are the best-known example, are found in heathen religions.

In the Church there are three ideas underlying the life. There is first that, which is prominent

[1] Horner, *Statutes of the Apostles*, p. 201.

in S. Paul's mind, of serving the Lord without distraction; in his case emphasized by his expectation of the Second Coming as being imminent. Then there is the idea of a mystical union with Christ, Who is the bridegroom, and the virgin may take no other; an idea which has been prominent in ascetic literature and lives for centuries. We find it in Tertullian, in his treatise *de Virginibus Velandis*. "You do not belie yourself in appearing as a bride, for wedded you are to Christ: to Him you have surrendered your flesh; to Him you have espoused your maturity." Cyprian has the same idea. The third development later than our period is the idea of leading this life in common with others who are in the same condition—in other words, of leading the community life.

We find them mentioned as an order in the first Church Order, when we read that "he shall not lay hand on a virgin [in ordination], but it is with her heart alone that she became a virgin."[1] In the next century we read: "A virgin is not ordained, for we have no such command from the Lord; for this is a state of voluntary trial, not for the reproach of marriage, but on account of leisure for piety." Later, "They are to communicate after the deaconesses and before the widows."

In the fourth century the Empress Helena found a company of holy virgins or Church virgins at Jerusalem, and waited on them at supper.

[1] Horner, *Statutes of the Apostles*, p. 147.

But women had much earlier consecrated themselves to Christ with a vow or at least a resolution of continence. Tertullian wrote to urge them to wear veils both in church and in the streets. He seems to urge the veil on all women, married and unmarried, those looking to marriage, and those regarding themselves as espoused to Christ; but he plainly regards the last as a special class. He also mentions that he knew a virgin of twenty placed in the order of widows, which he not unnaturally considered an unsuitable arrangement. It seems to point to the fact that women who were under a pledge of chastity were regarded as a class apart, and worthy of special honour, and further that in his time in Africa there was as yet no regular order for them to enter.

XIV

MINISTERIAL AUTHORITY AND ITS TRANSMISSION

SOME attempts must be made to answer the much vexed question of the source from which the ministers of the Church derived their authority. There are three theories. The first, that it came from above, that is from the Apostles, who were themselves sent from Christ, and they in their turn commissioned others, like Timothy and Titus, who were given authority to hand on the power of ordaining to their successors. The second, that authority came from below, that the Church, or at least the ministry, elected to vacant offices, and that election, followed by the laying on of hands, was all that was necessary. The third theory is that no external authority was required; that each ministered as moved by the Spirit, and their fruits, as seen in their prophesying or teaching or healing, were their only and sufficient credentials?

All that will be attempted will be to summarize the facts, and give such explanations as seem to be necessary.

The last theory may be dealt with first. It

was evolved by Professor Harnack from the *Didaché* and is sometimes called the charismatic theory of the ministry, derived from charisma, a Greek word translated *grace-gift* by the Dean of Wells.

In the *Didaché* [1] the local churches are ordered to elect bishops and deacons, bishop being apparently used in its New Testament sense as a synonym for presbyter; but the prominent ministers are the Apostles, prophets, and teachers —Apostles and prophets may refer to the same order, as seems to be implied in this passage, "Let the Apostle take nothing but bread; if he ask for money he is a false prophet." [2] This, however, is not the usual view. These officials take precedence of the bishop or presbyter. They are to celebrate the Eucharist "so far as they are willing to do so." [3] The local churches are warned not to despise the bishops and deacons, "for they also render to you the ministry of the prophets and teachers." It has therefore been suggested that these itinerant Apostles, prophets and teachers were the original type of minister who were replaced later on by the local ministry of presbyter-bishop and deacon which was just coming into prominence. The chief passage in the New Testament that can be urged in its support of this theory is 1 Corinthians xii. 28 ff :—

"And some God hath set in the church, first Apostles, secondarily prophets, thirdly teachers,

[1] xv.   [2] Ibid., xi.   [3] Ibid., x.

after that miracles, then gifts of healings, helps, governments, diversities of tongues. Are all Apostles? are all prophets? are all teachers? are all workers of miracles? Have all the gifts of healing? do all speak with tongues? do all interpret? But covet earnestly the best gifts."

Here it is said we have first of all the three orders of Apostles, prophets, and teachers, and then S. Paul diverges to impersonal gifts. But S. Paul has been speaking of the spiritual gifts of the Spirit in the Church, and has been exalting edifying gifts such as prophecy at the expense of speaking with tongues. It is much more natural to take Apostles, prophets, teachers, as denoting qualification or function rather than office. God hath sent Apostles with the Apostolic qualifications of being witnesses of the Resurrection; others—they may be presbyters, deacons, or laymen—with the gift of prophesying, yet others who have the gift of teaching, others again with the gift of healing, others who can work miracles, and so on. To-day a bishop, writing a letter in his Diocesan Magazine, might say: " God has given us in this diocese men of learning, missioners, diligent parish priests, others who have the gift of conducting retreats, others who are skilled in hearing confessions, some even who devote themselves to spiritual healing. Therefore we have every right to be encouraged." He would hardly say: " We have a bishop, priests, and deacons, so take courage and go forward."

Another passage of S. Paul is also quoted in favour of this charismatic theory. " And he gave some, Apostles; and some, prophets; and some, evangelists; and some, pastors and teachers. . . ." [1]

Here we note first of all that the list has developed. Evangelists and pastors have been added. But if it is really a list of office-bearers, it is difficult to account for the fact that later on still, in the *Didaché*, they have again shrunk to two or three at the most—Apostles, prophets, and teachers. Secondly, it must be repeated that an Apostle was probably a prophet, certainly an evangelist and teacher, and that a presbyter was probably both pastor and teacher. In the Pastoral Epistles the presbyter who teaches is to be doubly honoured.

This charismatic theory has little support from the New Testament, and none from any other Christian literature except the *Didaché*. The *Didaché* appears to belong to some obscure Palestinian group of Christians, and may easily have been isolated and peculiar. Nor is there anything in its pages to show that these itinerant Apostle-prophets or Apostles and prophets were not ordained and given authority to ordain others in their turn. Whatever their position was, it seems to have been very exceptional and irregular.

There were not two forms of ministry—the ministry of gifts and the ministry of office—but

[1] Eph. iv. 11.

one form, including Apostles, bishops, or presbyters, and deacons, any member of which might be endowed with one or more of the many gifts of the Spirit, prophesy, miracles, teaching, tongues, or any other.[1] The source of authority was not then within each minister. Was it from above or below?

Now, when Church history opens with the first chapter of the Acts, all ministerial authority is centred in the Apostles. They are the undisputed rulers of the Church, and all authority to minister in the congregation, except as regards certain endowments such as speaking with tongues, seems to come from them. There may be exceptions, but we do not hear of them. When in the first days the Eucharist was celebrated κατ' οἶκον, that is in private houses, it is difficult to believe that the celebrant was not either an Apostle or some one authorized by an Apostle. Though they are never mentioned there must have been many among the seventy mentioned by S. Luke as being appointed by Christ,[2] who would seem to have been ready to hand for the purpose.

There is no hint that the Apostles looked forward to a distant future and provided a scheme of government and a regular ministry to meet its needs. They lived and acted as though the Second Coming was imminent and no long

[1] See J. A. Robinson. Essay ii, *The Early History of the Church and Ministry.*
[2] S. Luke x. 1.

views were required. Whatever offices were established we should expect to find provided to meet the needs of the moment as they arose. Their conviction of the nearness of the end made their Church policy of necessity opportunist and " hand-to-mouth." This view is borne out by the appointment of the Seven, whether we are to take the traditional view that the Seven were the first deacons, or to hold that they were exceptional officials created to meet a need that did not recur. The Apostles found that the work of superintending the distribution of alms interfered with their more spiritual functions, so the Church was told to choose seven men, and authority was given them by the Apostles through the imposition of hands.

With the dispersion that followed the death of Stephen the situation was altered. The disciples were scattered abroad, and wherever they went they preached the Word. We know there were bodies of Christians in Samaria and at Antioch ; we do not know whether any official ministers were appointed to superintend these scattered congregations and to preside over their Eucharists.

We first hear of a body of Church officials called *presbyters* or *elders* at Jerusalem, when the brethren at Antioch determined to send relief to the Mother Church, " sending it to the presbyters by the hands of Barnabas and Paul."[1] Again, when the dispute arose at Antioch, the brethren appointed Paul and Barnabas and

[1] Acts xi. 30.

other delegates to go to Jerusalem "unto the Apostles and presbyters." The deputation was received "of the Church and the Apostles and presbyters," and later on we read that "the Apostles and presbyters were gathered together to consider of this matter." Paul and Barnabas on their missionary journey appointed presbyters in every city. The title was probably adopted from the synagogue, as every Jewish synagogue was presided over by a council of elders. It no more implied age than the Roman title "senator" or our "alderman."

Later on we come across *episcopi* or bishops. The word is Greek, and is found both in the Septuagint and in classical Greek. Bishop Lightfoot gives "inspector" as the nearest English equivalent. Though a different view has been held, there seems no sufficient reason to doubt that in the New Testament the terms presbyter and *episcopus* or bishop are identical.

By the death of S. Paul the presbyter or *episcopus*, with deacons, may be considered to be everywhere established as the local church officials. The letter to the Philippians is addressed to the Church in Philippi "with bishops and deacons." S. Peter exhorted "the elders who are among you"[1] to feed the flock of God. In 1 Timothy iii S. Paul gives directions for the appointment of bishops and deacons. In his letter to Titus he tells him to appoint elders in every city. We are not told explicitly as to

[1] 1 S. Pet. v. 1.

their appointment or their duties. But there can be no reasonable doubt that they were appointed by Apostles or Apostolic delegates. It is unlikely that so important a class would have been formed without Apostolic appointment, and in the Acts and the Pastoral Epistles we find that such is the case.

As to their duties we are told little, and it is easy to see that their most obvious and pressing duties are the least likely to be mentioned. S. Luke in the Acts does not expatiate on things that were familiar and a matter of course to his readers. The Holy Communion is only mentioned incidentally; so is Baptism. The appointment of the Seven is mentioned at some length. It represented a new departure. The appointment of presbyters followed so closely upon Jewish usage that their existence was assumed and their duties were known to all.

The writers of the Reformation period in England frequently use the phrase "preaching ministers," or mention that a particular priest was a preacher. No one mentions that they were celebrants. No one writing to-day would mention either. It is taken for granted. So with New Testament writers.

S. Paul tells Timothy that elders "who rule well be counted worthy of double honour, especially those who labour in the Word and in teaching."[2] So it is plain that some do not teach.

[1] 1 Tim. v. 17, R.V.

The candidate for episcopal office must rule his own house well; if not, how will he care for the Church of God? They were to be no lovers of money, so probably they were in charge of the treasury of the Church. They were to be lovers of hospitality, and were no doubt the representatives of the congregation whom visiting brethren would naturally seek out first of all.

But there can be little doubt that their principal duty was to preside over the Eucharist. This no doubt accounts for their early appearance at Jerusalem, where the number of Christians was large from the beginning, and for their appointment by Paul and Barnabas in each infant Church.

The question to be solved is "How, then, were the Apostles replaced, either as rulers or as transmitters of authority?" What were the stages to be traversed before the monarchical and local bishop took the place of the equally monarchical but itinerant Apostle? Was it a descent by a regular act of devoluted authority? Or was it an ascent? Did the bishops or elders, compelled by the needs of the time, choose one of their own number, and, under God, themselves invest him with the necessary power, or is the power transmitted and devolved from above?

In the Pastoral Epistles we find Timothy and Titus acting as temporary bishops in Ephesus and Crete respectively. The appointment is temporary; they are rather episcopal delegates than bishops, but their position and duties are those of a bishop.[1] Their work is to rule and to ordain. Moreover, S. Timothy is reminded to "stir up the gift of God" which is in him "by the putting on of my hands." It is true that he is also warned not to neglect the gift given him "by prophecy with the laying on of the hands of the presbytery," which might appear to favour a presbyteral ordination if we did not know that from the earliest times of which we have any record it was the custom for the presbyters to be associated with the bishop in the laying on of hands.

The evidence afforded by the sub-apostolic Church is scanty, but the first epistle of Clement seems to bear out the theory of transmission from the Apostles. The author of this epistle, addressing the Church of God at Corinth in the name of the Church of God "which sojourns at Rome," wrote in order to put an end to strife which had arisen in consequence of the extrusion of certain presbyters at Corinth by a faction in that Church. The pertinent passages are as follows :—

"Christ therefore was sent forth by God, the Apostles by Christ. . . .

"And thus, preaching through countries and cities, they appointed the first-fruits of their labours, having first proved them by the Spirit, to be bishops and deacons of those who should afterwards believe.[2] Our Apostles also knew through our Lord Jesus Christ that there would

[1] 1 Tim. iv. 14.   [2] i. 42.

be strife for the office of the episcopate. For this cause therefore, inasmuch as they had obtained a perfect foreknowledge of this, they appointed those ministers already mentioned, and afterwards gave instructions that when these should fall asleep other approved men should succeed them in their ministry. We are of opinion, therefore, that those appointed by them, or afterwards by other eminent men with the consent of the whole Church, and who have blamelessly served the flock of Christ cannot be justly dismissed from the ministry. For our sin will not be small if we eject from the episcopate those who have blamelessly and holily fulfilled its duties. Blessed are those presbyters who, having finished their course before now, have obtained a fruitful and perfect departure."[1]

It is plain that *presbyter* and *bishop* are still synonymous terms. Also that stress is laid on their appointment originally by Apostles. The controverted point turns on the alternative method of appointment — "or afterwards by other eminent [approved] men." The Apostles, we are given to understand, made arrangements for the future provision of clergy. When the present clergy should die others should succeed. Those then appointed, either by Apostles or other approved men, must not be extruded. Taken by itself, the "other approved men" might be prophets, and not "ordered" ministers at all. But, read with the context, it can hardly

[1] *First Epistle of Clement*, i. 44.

be so. His argument is that God has fixed all things belonging to His worship. Christ is from God, the Apostles are from Christ, the presbyters are from the Apostles. Therefore their ejection is a sin. If the "approved men" do not derive their authority from the Apostles, like Timothy and Titus, the argument falls to the ground. Clement was, after all, appealing to facts perfectly well known, and if the "other approved men" were of Apostolic descent it would be unnecessary to use some such clumsy periphrasis as "men authorized by Apostles to ordain," which would have been the alternative.

The *Didaché* has one reference to the subject. "Appoint for yourselves bishops and deacons." The Greek word means properly to elect by a show of hands, but it is used of the appointment and ordination of elders by S. Paul and S. Barnabas. So that the writer of the *Didaché* may well be speaking of the election of fit persons to serve as bishops and deacons, leaving their formal ordination on one side.

S. Ignatius is silent on the subject of Apostolic appointment, but his complete silence, if it proved anything, would prove that Apostolic appointment was unknown to him, which is absurd. He probably took it for granted. Nor did he need it for the purpose of his argument. The bishop is like God, the presbyters like the Apostles at the Last Supper. It would have been an anti-climax to have gone on to ascribe the authority of either to Apostolic descent. It is quite possible that Ignatius and others accepted the fact without attaching any particular importance to it. But his silence certainly does not show that he was ignorant of the fact. Moreover, he implies the theory of the transmission of authority in the following passage :—

"Let that be held a valid Eucharist which is under the bishop or one to whom he shall have entrusted it."

It is noteworthy that there is no mention of a *bishop*—in the later sense—either at Rome or Corinth, by Ignatius or Clement. The evidence of the papal lists, which Bishop Lightfoot has marshalled with such skill, is fairly conclusive proof that there was a Bishop of Rome, though Ignatius, writing twenty years later, seems to ignore his existence. The case of Corinth is more doubtful. It may be that the Church was ruled by presbyter-bishops, some at least with the power of ordination, or there may be some other explanation which has not yet come to light. There is the same ambiguity in the case of the Philippian Church, as Polycarp, writing to that Church about the year A.D. 150, makes no mention of a bishop.

With these exceptions, episcopacy, as we understand it, with the possible exception of Alexandria, seems to have been the rule in every Church from the beginning. At least we have no evidence of any other form of government.

In Jerusalem we find James, the Lord's

brother, established as ruler of the Church; and Hegesippus records that he was succeeded by Symeon. Eusebius further gives a list of thirteen bishops who succeeded.[1] The Syrian Antioch had Evodius as its first bishop, after the Apostle S. Peter, and he was succeeded by Ignatius. In proconsular Asia Clement of Alexandria distinctly states that S. John went about from city to city " in some places to establish bishops, in others to consolidate whole Churches, in others to appoint to the clerical office some one of those who had been signified by the Spirit." Polycarp was said by his pupil Irenaeus to have been "established as bishop by the Apostles in Asia in the Church at Smyrna."[2]

By the third quarter of the century the Church had to face a new development of the Gnostic heresy. The Marcionites made out that theirs was the true Apostolic doctrine and the Catholic version the false. The peril was great, and the Church met it by affirming the Apostolic character of its Creed, its Scriptures, and its ministry. For the first time the word succession (*diadoche*) is used.

Hegesippus of Palestine, writing about A.D. 175, after travelling through Greece on his way to Rome, states that he " conversed with most of the bishops when he travelled to Rome, and that he received the same doctrine from all."[3] Then " in every succession and in every city the preaching of the law and the prophets is faithfully

[1] *H. E.* iv. 5.   [2] Ibid., iv. 14.   [3] Ibid., 22.

followed," and when he came to Rome he began to make out a succession (*diadoche*) up to Anicetus. *Diadoche* is plainly a technical term used to describe the succession of the bishops, and though he does not say succession from the Apostles it is plainly implied.

Irenaeus was born in Asia Minor A.D. 125 to 130, and was a pupil of Polycarp, Bishop of Smyrna. He was in Rome when Polycarp was martyred, A.D. 155–156, and afterwards went to Gaul. As bishop he had to contend with Gnostics, and found that they claimed to teach an esoteric doctrine handed down secretly from the Apostles, and that the Creed of the Church was only a debased and vulgarized version of the true teaching. In his great work commonly known as *Against Heresies* he appealed to the successions of bishops from the Apostles as a proof that the Church taught the Apostolic doctrine, and that the Gnostic had no case when he appealed to an alleged secret Apostolic tradition as over-riding the Scriptures. "It is within the competence of all, therefore, in every Church, who may wish to see the truth, to contemplate clearly the tradition of the Apostles manifested throughout the whole world; and we are in a position to reckon up those who were instituted bishops in Churches by the Apostles and the successions of these men to our own times. . . ."[1] Since, however, "it would be very tedious to reckon up the successions of all the Churches,"

[1] Irenaeus, *Against Heresies*, iii. 1–4.

he contents himself "by indicating that tradition derived from the Apostles of the very great, the very ancient, and universally known Church founded and organized at Rome by the two most glorious Apostles, Peter and Paul, as also the faith preached to men, which comes down to our time by means of the successions of the bishops. . . . The blessed Apostles, then, having founded and built up the Church, committed into the hands of Linus the office of the episcopate. Of this Linus Paul makes mention in his Epistle to Timothy. To him succeeded Anencletus, and after him, in the third place from the Apostles, Clement was allotted the bishopric. This man, as he had seen the blessed Apostles, and had been conversant with them, might be said to have the preaching of the Apostles still echoing in his ears. . . . "To this Clement succeeded Evarestus. Alexander followed Evarestus; then sixth from the Apostles Sixtus was appointed; after, Telesphorus who was gloriously martyred; then Hyginus; after him Pius; then after him Anicetus. Soter having succeeded Anicetus, Elentherus does now in the twelfth place from the Apostles hold the inheritance of the episcopate. In this order, and by this succession, the ecclesiastical tradition of the Apostles and the preaching of the truth have come down to us."

Later on, dealing with the marks of the true presbyter, he says, "Wherefore it is incumbent to obey the presbyters who are in the Church—

Ministerial Authority and its Transmission 295

those who, as I have shown, possess the succession from the Apostles."[1]

Tertullian, the great African, wrote to the same effect :—

"Let the heretics display the origins of their churches ; let them unroll the lists of their bishops in unbroken succession from the beginning, showing that their first bishop was created and preceded by one of the Apostles or of the Apostolic men who continued with the Apostles."[2]

Hippolytus was the first to write of the bishops in general as being successors of the Apostles. Hitherto the particular bishop had been spoken of as the successor of the Apostle who founded his particular see.

Cyprian was Bishop of Carthage A.D. 148–158. His language on the authority of bishops resembles that of Ignatius. He is accused of using sacerdotal language ; but he is not more sacerdotal than Tertullian. To Cyprian the bishop is the *sacerdos*, the clergy are the senators, the laity the plebs. He is as clear as previous writers on the subject of the succession. Writing to Pupianus, who had accused him of unworthy conduct, he says, " You constitute yourself a judge of God and of Christ, who says to the Apostles, and therefore to all prelates who succeed to the Apostles by appointment in their room, He that heareth you, heareth Me."[3]

---
[1] Irenaeus, *Against Heresies*, iv. 26.
[2] *Objection against Heretics*, 21.   [3] *Ep.* 68.

As against this body of testimony there is only the case of Alexandria, where, according to Jerome, from Mark the Evangelist down to the times of the bishops Heraclas, A.D. 233–247, and Dionysius, 247–265, "the presbyters always nominated as bishop one chosen out of their own body, and placed in a higher grade ; just as if an army were to appoint a general, or deacons were to choose from their own body one whom they knew to be diligent, and call him archdeacon." This, however, is not to say that the presbyters were not endowed with the episcopal authority to ordain. Further, Bishop Lightfoot quotes Hilary to the effect that " In Egypt the presbyters seal (i.e. ordain or consecrate) if the bishop be not present." But seal undoubtedly means confirm not ordain, and in the East to this day the presbyters confirm though using oil previously blessed by the bishop.

Bishop Gore also quotes [1] Severus, an intruded Bishop of Antioch, who was expelled about A.D. 518, and settled at Alexandria, as saying that the Bishop of Alexandria had in old times been appointed by presbyters. But he thinks that Jerome and Severus and those, who in modern times have adopted their view, have been led astray by a blunder, for which some Arian heretics were responsible. These heretics visited the Abbot Poemen, and disparaged the Archbishop of Alexandria by saying that he had been ordained by presbyters. The archbishop in

[1] *The Church and the Ministry*, p. 122.

question, however, was Athanasius, of whose consecration by bishops we have satisfactory evidence. It is quite possible that Jerome and Severus were led astray by this story. At any rate Origen, who had every reason to disparage the position of the Bishop of Alexandria, appears to know nothing of this presbyteral succession, and in the first Church Order, which goes back to the early part of the third century, and survives in two Coptic versions, it is very clearly laid down that the bishop is to be elected by the people, but consecrated by one of the bishops present. Later on this rule is altered, and three bishops are required for a consecration.

So far as the principle of *succession* is concerned it does not matter whether Jerome was right or not. It would only mean that the presbyters of Alexandria were all bishops with the right to ordain, but elected one of their number to exercise the main functions of the episcopate.

There is one other fact of history that tells against Bishop Lightfoot's theory that the bishop rose out of the body of presbyter-bishops by ascent, and received his authority from them instead of from an Apostle or bishop, and that is the comparative insignificance of the presbyters in early days. Nowhere are the presbyters at all prominent. In the Church Order, about A.D. 225, they are plainly almost honorary officials in comparison with the bishop and the deacons, as we have seen in the last chapter. It is unlikely that if the presbyters were the real Church-rulers early in the second century they should have been so completely suppressed within a hundred years, and that the fourth and fifth centuries should have witnessed their slow and gradual rise into power.

To sum up, the position seems to be that, by the middle of the second century, episcopacy as we understand it, that is one bishop over each diocese with authority to rule and ordain, was everywhere established with the possible exception of Alexandria. That it had been established in Apostolic times, at least in Antioch, in Jerusalem, in Asia, and in Rome. It is possible, though unlikely, that in Corinth, Philippi, and possibly one or two other Greek cities with democratic prejudices, the Church was ruled by presbyter-bishops, of whom some at least had power to ordain. It is not improbable that between the time that the Apostles died and the time that the bishops were everywhere localized there were itinerant officials with powers of supervision and ordination like those conferred on Timothy and Titus, called variously Apostles, prophets, evangelists. But the evidence shows pretty clearly that the authority to minister was given by the Apostles to a class, by whatever name called, afterwards known as bishops, who were themselves the only authorized transmitters thereof.

CHAPTER XV

THE TRUCE, A.D. 260–303

FROM the capture of Valerian by Sapor, A.D. 260, down to the issue of his first edict of persecution by Diocletian in February, A.D. 303, the Church enjoyed a period of peace, comparative which was undoubtedly a time of very considerable growth. The Gospel reached new countries and was listened to by many in provinces, where it had long been preached, with an attention never shown before. Decius and Valerian had tried a fall with the Church and had been worsted. Persecution may very well have seemed a thing of the past.

The history of the Church during this period is somewhat obscure, but some names stand out. Of these the most notable are Dionysius of Alexandria; Paul of Samosata, the heretic; Manes, the founder of Manicheeism; Gregory, the Wonder-worker, and Gregory the Illuminator, though the last is a very shadowy figure.

DIONYSIUS OF ALEXANDRIA

Dionysius we have already met as the Bishop of Alexandria during the Decian and Valerian persecutions. He was a pupil of Origen, and, like his master, of an inquiring mind. "I perused," he wrote, "the works and traditions of the heretics, defiling my mind for a little with their execrable sentiments. . . . When a certain brother of the presbyters attempted to dissuade me, saying my mind would be corrupted, in which, as I thought, he spake the truth, I was confirmed in my original purpose by a vision from heaven, when a voice came to me and commanded me in words as follows : 'Read all that thou takest in hand, for thou are qualified to correct and prove all, and this very thing has been the cause of thy faith in Christ from the beginning.' I received the vision as consistent with the Apostolic declaration which says to the more competent 'Be ye skilful money-changers.'"[1]

He was ordained presbyter, and succeeded Heraclas as head of the Catechetical School, A.D. 232, where he remained until he became bishop, A.D. 247.

Unlike most of the Eastern bishops, he allowed heretical baptism, but he opposed Stephen when that prelate proceeded to excommunicate those who, like Cyprian, took the opposite view.

He also had his troubles concerning the treatment of the lapsed, and adopted much the same measures as Cyprian and Cornelius. In a letter to Fabius, Bishop of Antioch, who was inclined to join the rigorist party of Novatian, he gave some account of his methods which is worth

[1] Eusebius, *H. E.* vii. 7.

repeating. "There was a certain Serapion, an aged believer, who had passed his long life irreproachably, but as he had sacrificed during the persecution, though he frequently begged [to be admitted to penance], no one would listen to him. He was taken sick, and continued three days in succession speechless and senseless. On the fourth day he recovered a little, and called his grandson. 'I beseech you hasten and get me absolution. Call one of the presbyters.' The boy ran to the presbyter. But it was night, and the presbyter was sick. I had already given an order that those at the point of death, if they desired it, and especially if they had asked for it before, should receive absolution, that they might depart from life in comfortable hope. I therefore gave the boy a small portion of the Eucharist, telling him to dip it in water and to drop it into the mouth of the old man. The boy returned with the morsel. Serapion said at once 'Thou hast come, my son, but the presbyter could not come. Do what you are told quickly and let me go.' The boy moistened it and dropped it into the old man's mouth. And he, having swallowed a little, immediately expired."[1]

Though peace was restored to the Church with the accession of Gallienus in A.D. 260, there was little enough of it in Alexandria. There was first of all civil war, so that Dionysius says he could not pass from one side of the city to the other. This was succeeded by pestilence and famine.

[1] Eusebius, *H. E.* vi. 44.

He has left a vivid account of the noble conduct of the Christians during the plague, which is given elsewhere.

He was a wise and loving ruler, full of the spirit of reasonableness and conciliation. We get a vivid picture of him in this character in his treatment of Nepos, an Egyptian bishop who had promulgated certain chiliastic heresies. These views had attained considerable vogue in the neighbourhood of Arsinoe. "So, when I was at Arsinoe, where, as you know, this doctrine was afloat, so that schisms and apostasies of whole Churches followed, I called the presbyters and teachers of the brethren in the villages and exhorted them to examine the doctrine publickly. When they had produced this book of Nepos as a kind of armour and impregnable fortress, I sat with them for three days from morning till evening attempting to refute what it contained."

At length his moderation and reasonableness carried the day.

He rejoiced "at the moderation and conciliatory spirit" displayed by all. It is doubtful, however, if these qualities would have been so prominent if the matter had been handled by a Tertullian, or even a Stephen.

He was also, which is more surprising, an acute critic of the New Testament, a higher critic before his time. The fragment of his criticism that has survived concerns the Apocalypse. He tells us that some had set aside the book altogether, and attributed it to Cerinthus. Dionysius would not reject it, but thought it should be understood symbolically and felt that he did not himself possess the key to the symbolism. " For though I do not understand, yet I suspect that some deeper sense is enveloped in the words ; . . . but, allowing more to faith, I have regarded them as too lofty to be comprehended by me, and those things which I do not understand I do not reject, but I wonder the more that I cannot understand."

He was of opinion that the author was John, but not the John who wrote the Epistle and Gospel ; he gives his reasons, all of them sound, though not necessarily conclusive. He ends his argument by saying " The attentive reader will find the expressions, the *life*, the *light*, frequently occurring in both ; in both he will find the expressions *fleeing from darkness*, *the truth*, *grace*, *joy*, *the flesh and blood of the Lord*, *the judgement*. . . . And throughout it will be obvious that there is one complexion and character in the Gospel and Epistle. Very different and remote from all this is the Apocalypse."

He remarks that John was a common name and that many assumed the name out of devotion to the Apostle, and that there were two monuments in Ephesus, each bearing the name of John.

He died A.D. 265.[1]

[1] Eusebius, *H. E.* vii. 25.

Paul of Samosata

Paul had succeeded Demetrius as Bishop of Antioch about A.D. 260. He seems to have been of obscure birth but considerable talents, and was not only bishop but a financial official (*procurator decenarius*) with a large salary. His conduct gave offence and caused scandal. He was accused of having amassed immense wealth by bribes and extortion, of being full of pride and ostentation, " wishing rather to be called a magistrate than a bishop, strutting through the forum and reading letters and repeating them as he walked in public, escorted by multitudes. In church he prepared himself a throne and struck his thigh and stamped on the floor with his feet and reproved and insulted those who would not clap or applaud."

He was said to have stopped the hymns that were sung in honour of Jesus Christ as recent compositions, and prepared a choir of women to sing hymns in his own honour at Easter. His conduct in another respect gave rise to scandal, as two beautiful women accompanied him wherever he went. By bribes and threats he had every one in his power. Besides all this, he was accused of the heresy of Artemas.[1] It is not quite clear what Paul's heresy was, but it had to do with the divinity of Christ. " He entertained low and degrading notions of Christ, and taught that He was in nature a common man."[2]

[1] Eusebius, *H.E.* vii. 30.   [2] Ibid., 27.

In A.D. 265 a council was summoned to deal with him. It was attended by Firmilian of Caesarea in Cappadocia, Gregory Thaumaturgus from Pontus, Hymenaeus, Bishop of Jerusalem, and many others. Dionysius was summoned, but could not come on account of age and infirmity. The council seems to have concerned itself with his doctrinal rather than his moral irregularities. Possibly, as is often the case to-day, witnesses are shy, and moral charges very difficult of proof. The doctrinal charges were not much easier to substantiate. Paul was acute and subtle, and many questions about the person and nature of Christ were not yet defined. At first he could not be pinned down to any definitely heretical statement. More than one council was held, but at last, in the reign of Aurelian, the bishops took with them a presbyter named Malchion, who had been at the head of the Sophist Greek School at Athens. It was a case of setting a sophist to catch a sophist. " This man, indeed, was the only one who, after opening a discussion with him—which was taken down by several reporters—was able to ferret out his cunning and deceitful sentiments."

Accordingly the council proceeded to depose and excommunicate Paul, and appointed another bishop in his place, by name Domnus. This was A.D. 267 or 268. Paul, however, refused to submit; he was supported by Zenobia, and remained in possession of the church and the temporalities of the see.

Zenobia, the celebrated queen of Palmyra and

the East, was a remarkable woman. With her husband Odenathus, she had driven back the victorious Persians, and Odenathus was accepted as a colleague by Gallienus. After the death of Odenathus in A.D. 267, Zenobia ruled alone, and throwing off her allegiance to Rome, defeated the Roman general who came against her. But in A.D. 272 the Emperor Aurelian defeated her armies, shut her up in Palmyra, and took her prisoner. One of the by-products of his victory was that the Church appealed to him to recover the ecclesiastical buildings of Antioch from Paul. Aurelian decided that the bishop who was in communion with the Bishops of Rome and Italy was the rightful possessor of the church, which was accordingly handed over to Domnus. This is the first instance of an appeal being made to the secular arm. It is a shock to find it made to a heathen emperor, at a time when Christianity was rather connived at than permitted. But as long as the Church holds property it cannot entirely escape State control, and in the course of exercising that control the State will sometimes be forced to define the faith or lay down terms of communion. If in any given case the price is too high the Church must forgo its claim to the property in dispute.

Gregory Thaumaturgus

The episcopate of Theodorus or Gregory, afterwards named Thaumaturgus, or the Worker of

Wonders, throws some light on the work of a missionary bishop in a remote and uncivilized region. Gregory was born A.D. 210, and while still quite young spent five years with his brother Athenodorus as the pupil of Origen at Caesarea, of which he has left an interesting account. His biographer and relative, Gregory of Nyssa, writing about a hundred years afterwards, asserts that he spent some time studying in Alexandria; but he may have studied there while under Origen's direction.

Somewhere about A.D. 240 Gregory returned to Neocaesarea, in the east of Pontus, his native city, and became, as Eusebius tells us, one of the most famous bishops of his age. Unfortunately the biography of Gregory of Nyssa belongs to the order of ecclesiastical romances, and is almost confined to tales of the marvellous. But enough may be gleaned to give some valuable and interesting information.

Before he would consent to be ordained he desired time for meditation, during which he is said to have had a vision, in which S. John was told by "the Mother of our Lord" to declare to him the mystery of the Faith. This declaration became the foundation of his preaching, and his biographer tells us that those who wish to be reassured may refer to the original, written down and preserved "in the writing of that blessed hand," in the actual church at Neocaesarea in which he preached. The creed alluded to in this story may have been Gregory's, but the story of how it came to his knowledge almost certainly belongs to a later date. For one thing, far too authoritative a position is given to Mary.

Of his administration of his see we know little, but can infer a good deal. He seems to have swept in the heathen *en masse*. We are told that shortly before his death, A.D. 270, there were only seventeen heathen left, whereas he only found seventeen Christians when he came. The country round Neocaesarea was certainly very heathen when he arrived there. "The city and country alike were full of idols and temples; the whole nation was devoted to heathenism and given over to an insane worship which stained their altars with impurities and abominations."

His biographer attributes his success to his miracles. One may be permitted, perhaps, to attribute his miracles in a great measure to his success. Like Aidan, he is credited with the gift of second sight. At the beginning of his ministry there was a great heathen festival at Neocaesarea; the theatre was crammed, and fresh crowds came flocking in from the country, all praying with one accord, "Zeus, make room for us." When Gregory heard this reiterated prayer he exclaimed "You shall have more room than you pray for or have ever known." Almost immediately the plague broke out with devastating results. It may have been already on some of the spectators, and if so the infection would have been spread by the crowd. In any case Gregory's reputation seems to have been made, and conversions began.

On a later occasion, during the Decian persecution, he foresaw the torture and death of a martyr, and told his deacon, who would not believe until he had gone to the spot and verified the account.

Among his other wonders he is said to have dried up a lake which was a matter of contention between two brothers, diverted the course of the Lycus, which had overrun and devastated fertile and inhabited country, exercised supernatural powers over demons, moved a rock without touching it, and worked many miracles of healing. Some of the wonders appear far less incredible now than they did twenty years ago, for modern science has been busy investigating admitted facts, such as cures by faith or suggestion, which appear to transcend the hitherto known course of nature.

The more impossible wonders seem rather to show that Gregory was a man of vivid personality who had an enormous influence over ignorant people. If he gained a great reputation as an arbitrator it is easy to understand that stories were told of his signal success in one case—when a lake was in dispute—and the stories grew until he was credited with drying up the lake. He might even have threatened that God would dry it up. The story of the diversion of the course of the Lycus reminds one of Wilfrid, who when Bishop of the South Saxons saved the inhabitants from starving in time of drought by teaching them to fish. Gregory had studied mathematics, and conceivably the diversion was a feat of engineering, miraculous enough to the primitive sufferers from the devastated regions.

One class of miracles which impressed his biographer with his powers, and would have impressed most people until lately with the extreme gullibility of his biographer, is that in which his powers as an exorcist were displayed. To take an instance. He was on one occasion driven by the weather to spend a night in a heathen temple. By his prayers the demons were exorcised, so that when the heathen priests arrived in the morning their customary incantations were ineffective until Gregory, in answer to their remonstrances, gave them a parchment with the words on it, "Gregory to Satan—enter." This would, one imagines, be regarded to-day by a large number of people as a commonplace manifestation of spiritualism. Gregory was hostile, and in his presence there could be no manifestations.

Gregory of Nyssa gives a picture of his work which has the air of truth. Whenever he arrived at a place and only a few heard his discourse over-night, by dawn the next morning a large crowd would have collected. The next morning again there would be outside his doors "a crowd of men with their wives and children, with old people and those who suffered from demons or ailments of the body. And according to the need of each, discriminating by the power of the Spirit, he preached, argued, admonished, taught, or healed. He used to attract masses to his preaching because sight corresponded with hearing, and through both the tokens of the divine power shone forth upon him. For their hearing was overpowered by his words, and their eyes by his miracles of healing."[1]

Gregory's converts were possibly made too rapidly, and with too little real conviction. Perhaps he tempered the word of Christian discipline too tenderly to the shorn lambs of his flock. We are told that as a wise concession to those who had recently abandoned heathenism festivals were instituted on the anniversaries of martyrs to take the place of the heathen festivals to which they were accustomed, and that this concession was popular and these festivals kept with great rejoicings. The principle of claiming the heathen festivals, like the heathen philosophy for Christ, was sound; but human nature being what it is we may feel quite sure that an ignorant race made very much the same devotions at the Christian festivals as they had done before when they were heathen, even if they troubled to alter the names of those whose favour they were supplicating.

The Decian persecution tried his flock sorely. It raged in Pontus with especial fury, and stress is laid on the innumerable and exquisite forms of torture put in practise. Gregory's poor converts behaved very much as one might expect they would have done, but no worse. When it broke

[1] *Life*, by Gregory of Nyssa.

out we are told idolatrous worship had ceased, and the population was nominally Christian. There was now a division. Most seem to have been faithful, though many sacrificed. The prisons were full, houses were empty, and the deserts and solitary places were crowded with fugitives. Neither age nor sex was spared. Gregory advised flight, and himself set the example.

In A.D. 257 Gregory returned to Neocaesarea, and in A.D. 258 peace was restored to the Church. But it was short lived, as it was soon followed by an invasion of Goths, who ravaged Pontus and Asia Minor during the reign of Gallienus. An authentic letter from him " concerning those who had eaten things offered to idols and committed other sins during the incursion of the barbarians " has survived. It appears that some Christians had taken advantage of the general confusion to enrich themselves with the goods of their fellow-Christians who were fugitives ; others had forcibly detained escaped prisoners ; and some had even joined the army of the barbarians. Gregory insists that all such must be dealt with by the ecclesiastical discipline appropriate to their crimes. There is, however, no reason to infer, as some writers have done, that the number of such backsliders was large, or that there was a general collapse of Christian faith and morals.

Gregory was present with his brother Athenodorus at the council which met at Antioch in A.D. 264 to judge Paul of Samosata. There was a Theodorus present at the council which met in A.D. 269, and this Theodorus may possibly be Gregory. Before he died he expressed great anxiety for the conversion of the seventeen heathen who remained in his diocese, and ordered that no land should be bought for his grave, so that, as he had owned no property in life, he might not own any when dead. He was buried in the church of Neocaesarea which he had built.

GREGORY THE ILLUMINATOR

Nowhere was growth more rapid than in Armenia, the name given to that mountainous region lying between Persia and Asia Minor. Our information is scanty, but it seems certain that when Gregory the Illuminator first went there the king, Tiridates (who reigned A.D. 261–317), was decidedly hostile, and the Armenian Christians very few. But when the great persecution took place, not later than A.D. 309, we read that Maximin was forced to carry on a religious war against the Armenian king, to compel him to persecute his Christian subjects, which he was unwilling to do.[1] This is the first *war* in history in which the Christian religion is directly concerned.

Gregory, the principal agent in this conversion of a whole people, had been brought up in the

[1] Eusebius, *H. E.* ix. 8, 2.

Cappadocian Caesarea on the execution of his parents and all his relatives, who were people of high rank in Armenia. He was educated as a Christian, married, and had two children, one of whom succeeded him as Catholicos of Armenia, but was separated by consent from his wife, and then came to the court of Tiridates, who is said to have confined him in a dungeon for twelve years. We may take it that he was at first unfriendly. Later on he became a Christian, and his people followed him. This is the first instance on record of a whole nation becoming officially Christian. The Church was endowed as well as established, and the temple property was made over to the Church. Gregory was escorted by a retinue of nobles to Caesarea in Cappadocia, where he was consecrated Catholicos of Armenia by Leontius. This was A.D. 285–290.[1] He built his cathedral at Aschtischat, not far west of Lake Van. Aschtischat had been the principal seat of the Persian fire-worship, which had been imported into Armenia.[2]

Gregory is said to have consecrated twelve suffragans, and was succeeded by his son Aristakes. The office seems afterwards to have become hereditary and remained so for a considerable period. He was not present at the Council of Nicaea, A.D. 325, and Professor Harnack says that he was dead, but he is reported to have retired to lead a solitary life in the wilderness

---

[1] Harnack, *Expansion of Christianity*, ii. 203.
[2] Ibid., 302.

after consecrating his son as his successor, and this account seems probable enough.

Manes and Manicheeism

Manes was born about A.D. 240 at Ctesiphon, and seems to have derived his doctrines from Gnostic, Buddhist, and Christian sources. He claimed to be the Paraclete promised by Christ, and like Christ was accompanied by twelve disciples. After extensive travels he settled in Persia, taught under Sapor, and was finally put to death by one of his successors, A.D. 272–274. Eusebius, writing fifty years later, says that his doctrines had spread in Palestine like a deadly pestilence. S. Augustine, as he tells us in his *Confessions*, was for some time a Manichee, and it is evident that the teachers of the Manicheean tenets were numerous and influential in Africa in his time.

Manes seems to have taught a Gnostic dualism, man owing his body to the powers of darkness, and his soul to the Spirit of Light. All matter is the body, therefore including the body was evil. In organizing his society he borrowed from the Church. At the head were twelve apostles, with a thirteenth person as president, the first being Manes himself. Below there was a hierarchy of bishops, presbyters, deacons, and travelling missionaries. His followers were divided into Hearers, consisting of the main body of adherents, and the Perfect or the inner circle.

The Hearers had, among their other duties, to supply the Perfect with the necessaries of life. The Perfect led lives of extreme asceticism. They owned no property, neither drank wine nor ate meat. They did no work, but were occupied entirely in religious contemplation. They were forbidden to destroy life, and could only eat fruit and vegetables if gathered by some one else. S. Augustine says that a Manicheean saint might only eat a fig " if some one else had committed the sin of plucking it." [1] They kept Sunday as a fast day, baptized with oil instead of water, and celebrated the Communion, but with water instead of wine.

Diocletian issued a decree against them A.D. 287, addressed to the proconsul of Africa, where Manicheeism was especially strong, then and afterwards. However, up to the end of the period with which we are immediately concerned it does not seem to have come into conflict with the Church to any serious extent.

[1] Aug., *Con.* iii. 10.

XVI

THE FINAL STRUGGLE
A.D. 303–313

FORTY-THREE years of peace enabled the Church to grow in numbers, in influence, and in buildings, but relaxed its morals and left it ill-prepared for the last and fiercest persecution it ever had to face.

Christians were found in high positions in the imperial service, some were even governors of provinces, and the rulers of the Church were courted and honoured. "Who could describe those huge congregations which gathered in every city and the distinguished crowds in the churches? On whose account, not content with the ancient buildings, they erected spacious churches in all the cities."[1] No wonder if some of those who crowded in were unworthy, and if the heads of others were turned. "By reason of excessive liberty we sank into negligence and sloth; we envied and reviled one another, and were almost taking arms against each other, prelates inveighing against prelates, and people rising up against people."[2]

Diocletian was the son of Dalmatian slaves.

[1] Eusebius, *H. E.* viii. 1.   [2] Ibid.

He entered the Army and rose to the position of commander of the guard in the army of the East. When Numerian died at or near Chalcedon on his return from a successful Persian campaign, Diocletian was chosen emperor by the soldiers. Of all his predecessors he most resembled Augustus. He reorganized the Empire, though not always with the happiest results, and gave it a new lease of life. He was prudent, politic, and more of a statesman than a soldier. So far as we can judge he was a believing pagan with a special devotion to Jupiter as the patron of his fortunes, and to Aesculapius as the guardian of his health ; he was a believer in soothsaying and divination of many kinds. In A.D. 286 he associated another soldier of fortune, a rude and savage peasant called Maximian, with himself in the government of the Empire, both having the title of Augustus. In A.D. 293 he added two subordinate emperors or Caesars—Constantius for Gaul, Spain, and Britain, and Galerius for Illyricum ; while he himself retained Thrace, Egypt, and Asia, and Maximian Italy and Africa. He fixed his own capital at Nicomedia.

For many years Diocletian was very fully occupied in reorganizing the Empire and in defending his frontiers. The Persian War, which began A.D. 296 with the defeat of Galerius, was ended by the complete overthrow of Narses, the Persian king, in the following year. Diocletian was now for the first time at leisure to cope with the Christians. Hitherto he had let them be.

He could not have done anything else. To destroy the Church was a much more formidable task than it had been for Decius and Valerian, and Decius and Valerian had failed. Even after the termination of the Persian campaign and the success which attended him everywhere he may well have hesitated.

Maximian and Galerius hated the Christians. Galerius, according to Lactantius, was egged on by his mother, "who had conceived an ill-will against Christians because they would not take part in her sacrifices, and while she feasted with the Gentiles they continued in fasting and prayer." Galerius is described by the same writer as "of full stature; fat and swollen to a horrible degree of corpulence; by his speech, voice, and gestures a terror to all who come near." The weight of the soothsayers and Neoplatonists like Hierocles, "the author and adviser of the persecution," was thrown into the same scale.[1] A foretaste of what was to happen had been given in the East a year or two before the persecution broke out. An examination of some sacrificial victims proved unsatisfactory, and the soothsayers attributed their failure to the Christians present at the sacrifice who had made the sign of the Cross. Diocletian in a rage ordered every one in the palace at the time to sacrifice, or, if they refused, to be scourged. He also ordered that all soldiers should sacrifice or leave the Army. This seems to have been in the autumn A.D. 302.

[1] Lactantius, *On the Death of the Persecutors*, xvi.

Lactantius says that he had long withstood the persecuting zeal of Galerius, but at length gave way.[1] His hesitation may have been due to doubts about the success of policy, not about its essential appropriateness. The persecution when it came was evidently a deliberately and carefully planned attempt at the complete annihilation of Christianity.

The persecution began with the demolition of the great church at Nicomedia, where the emperors were staying.[2] Next day, February 24, A.D. 303, the edict of persecution was published. By this edict all churches were to be demolished[3]; all sacred writings burnt; the higher ministers of state, if Christian, to be outlawed, and subordinate officials, being Christians, to be reduced to slavery. Galerius wished to burn all who refused to sacrifice, but to this Diocletian would not consent. The edict was taken down and torn to pieces by a Christian of rank, said by one tradition to be S. George, who suffered the natural consequences of this daring act.[4]

The persecution went far beyond the letter of the edict from the first. Two outbreaks of fire at the imperial palace in Nicomedia, attributed by Galerius to the Christians, and by Lactantius to Galerius, brought about a holocaust of victims. One example from Eusebius will be enough. It is an account of the death of Peter, a palace

[1] Lactantius, *On the Death of the Persecutors*, x.
[2] Ibid., xii.   [3] Ibid., xiii.
[4] Eusebius, *H. E.* viii. 5.

domestic. "He was led into the middle of the aforesaid city before those emperors already mentioned. He was then commanded to sacrifice, but as he refused he was ordered to be raised in mid-air and scourged all over his naked body until he would obey. As he was immovable amid all these sufferings, his bones already appearing bared of the flesh, they mixed vinegar with salt and poured it upon the mangled parts of his body. But, as he bore these tortures, a gridiron and fire was produced, and the remnants of his body, like pieces of meat for roasting and eating, were placed in the fire, not at once so that he might expire, but little by little. He, however, persevered in his purpose, and gave up his life victorious in the midst of his tortures."[1]

The demand for the Scriptures led to some division among Christians. It was generally agreed that canonical writings must not be given up. Those who refused to surrender them were executed, but the magistrates were not particular, as a rule, about what books were given up, as long as some were handed over. Mensurius of Carthage filled his church library with heretical works, which were burnt instead of the Scriptures. Others adopted a stricter line. Felix, a bishop near by, refused to give up any books at all *Habeo sed non do*, he repeated. "It is better for me to be burnt than the Scriptures." Anulinus, the proconsul, said, "Why don't you surrender some worthless

[1] H. E. viii. 6.

books?" "No, I will not give them up," was his reply.

A second edict followed, ordering the imprisonment of the clergy. The prisons were, in consequence, so filled with bishops, presbyters, and deacons, readers and exorcists, that, we are told, there was no room left for criminals.

The second edict was succeeded by a third, which allowed prisoners to be liberated on condition of sacrificing, but ordered them to be tortured if they refused.

As in the Decian persecution, there were at first many apostates. Eusebius, a contemporary of these events, tells us that vast numbers endured the most appalling trials, but many gave way. Romanus, a deacon of the Church of Caesarea, was at Antioch when the churches were demolished, and saw men, women, and children approaching the idols in masses in order to sacrifice. He was moved to rebuke them, was seized, had his tongue cut out, and died.

It is also clear that the Roman officials no longer had much stomach for the work. We read of men being dragged to the altar by force, and allowed to go as though they had sacrificed; those who protested, were forced to silence by soldiers stationed there for the purpose, by whom they were struck and violently driven away.

Diocletian was incapacitated by sickness throughout A.D. 304. Maximian took advantage of his absence to issue a new edict, ordering that all persons of every city should sacrifice, and make libations to the gods."[1] The penalty of refusal was torture and death. For the account of what followed we are mainly indebted to Eusebius; it is confined principally to Egypt, Palestine, and Syria. In Egypt "thousands, men, women, and children, submitted to death in various shapes. Some, after being tortured with scrapings and the rack, and the most dreadful scourgings and other innumerable agonies, were finally committed to the flames. . . . Some were crucified as criminals usually were; others were nailed with the head downwards, and kept alive until they were destroyed by starving, on the cross itself."[2]

In Thebais as many as a hundred men with their wives and children were slain in one day. "We ourselves have observed when on the spot many crowded together in one day, some suffering decapitation, some burning, so that the weapon was completely blunted, and having lost its edge, broke to pieces, and the executioners themselves, wearied with slaughter, were obliged to relieve one another. Then, also, we were witnesses to the ardour of those that believed. As soon as the sentence was pronounced against the first, others rushed forward to the judge at the tribunal, and confessed that they were Christians. They received the sentence of death with gladness and exultation, so far as even to

---

[1] Eusebius, *On the Martyrs of Palestine*, iii.
[2] *H. E.* viii. 8.

sing and send up hymns of praise and thanksgiving until they breathed their last."[1]

The victims included Philoromus, a high official in the imperial service in Alexandria, and Phileas, a bishop distinguished "for his conduct and the services rendered to his country, as well as in the different branches of philosophy."

At Damascus certain women of the town were compelled under threat of torture to declare that they had once been Christians, and "that they were privy to the criminal acts among them; that in their very churches they committed licentious deeds, and innumerable other slanders which he made them utter against our religion."[2] This declaration the emperor had published abroad.

In Phrygia the most appalling outrage was perpetrated. "Soldiers surrounded a certain Christian town, together with the garrison, and, hurling fire into it, burnt them together with women and children, calling upon Christ the God of all. And this because all the inhabitants of the town, together with the town clerk and the governor, with all the magistrates of rank and the inhabitants of the surrounding country, confessed themselves Christians and would not sacrifice."[3] The town was Eumenea, and the story is corroborated by the discoveries of Sir William Ramsay. [4]

In Arabia Christians were slain with the axe;

[1] Eusebius, *H. E.* viii. 9.   [2] Ibid., ix. 5.   [3] Ibid., viii. 11.
[4] *Cities and Bishops of Phrygia*, ii, 505–508.

"some had their limbs fractured, as in Cappadocia; some were hung up by the feet and suffocated with the ascending smoke of a slow fire, as in Mesopotamia; some were mutilated by having their noses, ears, and hands cut off and the rest of their limbs and parts of their bodies cut to pieces, as in Mesopotamia."[1]

At Antioch they were roasted on grates over slow fires. In Pontus some had their fingers pierced with sharp reeds thrust under the nails. Others had masses of boiling lead poured down their necks.

In May, A.D. 305, the two Augusti, Diocletian and Maximian, abdicated. If we may believe Lactantius, they did so reluctantly under pressure from Galerius. Diocletian retired to Salona in Dalmatia, and occupied himself with building, planting, and gardening. Gibbon relates that, when pressed by Maxentius to resume the purple, he replied that "if he could show Maximian the cabbages which he had planted with his own hand he should no longer be urged to relinquish the enjoyment of happiness for the pursuit of power."

The abdication was followed by a long period of civil war. Galerius and Constantius became Augusti, and Severus and Daza, afterwards called Maximin, were made Caesars. To Maximin Daza was given the charge of Egypt and Syria; Severus had Italy and Africa; Constantius ruled Britain, Gaul, and Spain; while Galerius re-

[1] Eusebius, *H. E.* viii. 12.

served for himself the countries between Italy and Syria.

The arrangement was soon upset. Constantius died at York in A.D. 306, and was succeeded, in spite of Galerius, by his son Constantine. In the same year the Romans revolted from Severus; and Maxentius, son of the ex-emperor Maximian, with the assistance of his father, brought about the downfall and death of Severus and set himself up as Lord of Italy and Africa.

These changes had their effect on the persecutions. They had ceased altogether in Spain, Gaul, and Britain when Constantius became Augustus. And though, to quote Gibbon, he was "a tyrant as contemptible as he was odious," Maxentius allowed them to die out in Italy and Africa. Licinius, who had been given Illyria, was not an active persecutor, and Galerius himself seems to have tired of this work. But Maximin Daza, in Egypt and Syria, carried on the persecution with the enthusiasm of a neophyte. Lactantius says that he had been tending cattle not long before his elevation, and calls him "a person ignorant alike of war and of civil affairs." Eusebius, who had every reason for thinking ill of him, says that he was devoted to the pagan gods, and had temples built for them in every city, and would undertake nothing without soothsayers and oracles; that he was a drunkard, and indulged in every sort of dissipation, and was distinguished for his innumerable adulteries. However that may be, and his acts bear out the description, he was both shrewd and energetic, and perhaps the most formidable persecutor the Church has ever had.

Eusebius has left a graphic account of his doings in Palestine and Egypt. There is no reason to doubt its veracity. It would be only natural if it were highly coloured in places, but it is probably a case where the colours of nature are vivid enough. The intention, as in earlier persecutions, was to produce apostates not martyrs, and as compared with former persecutions this intention was carried out with far more logic and perseverance. Before Christians were tortured as part of the regular proceedings to make them recant, as slaves were tortured to make them confess, in order to overcome their obstinacy. When it was clear that they intended to remain obstinate they were put to death, usually in some painful manner. But now the torture was much more prolonged. Whether death was felt to be so light a punishment as to be useless, or they thought that the stoutest would break down under torture if only the torture were sufficiently prolonged, we do not know. Those whom we read of as being sentenced to death summarily are for the most part those who had made themselves conspicuous. Apphianus, for instance, on the day when every one in Caesarea was crowding to sacrifice in obedience to the edict, crept up behind Urbanus, the governor, as he was offering, and, seizing his right hand, exhorted him to desist. He was scourged, racked, his sides were scraped, he was beaten on the face and neck until unrecognizable, his feet were wrapped in linen bandages steeped in oil and then lighted, before he was thrown into the sea and drowned. His brother, Aedesius, met very much the same fate at Alexandria. "When he saw the judge at Alexandria condemning the Christians there and going beyond all bounds, sometimes insulting grave and decent men and women in various ways, sometimes consigning virtuous women and consecrated virgins to houses of ill fame, he tried to do what his brother had done, and with his words and acts covered the judge with shame."[1] The results also for himself were not dissimilar.

At Caesarea Theodosia approached some confessors, arraigned before the judgement-seat, and spoke to them. The judge seems to have regarded this as a provocation. "He had her tortured with dreadful and horrific cruelties, furrowing her sides and breasts with instruments to the very bones, and, while yet breathing and showing a serene and cheerful countenance, had her thrown into the sea." But the others were only condemned to the mines at Phoeno in Palestine. But one, Domninus, who had made himself known by his boldness, was condemned to be burned. "Others he made eunuchs and condemned to the mines; others after dreadful torture he cast into prison." Pamphilus, a friend of Eusebius, a learned philosopher, was

[1] Eusebius, *The Martyrs of Palestine*, v.

tortured with especial malignity and then cast into prison.

The intention seems to be to torture and not to kill. In the year A.D. 308 mutilation was substituted for capital punishment. Eusebius states that of a vast number of the confessors of the true religion confined in the porphyry quarry, ninety-seven men, women, and children were sent to the Governor of Palestine and had the ankles and sinews of their left legs scarred with a hot iron. Besides this they had their right eyes cut out. They were then committed to the mines in Palestine to drag out a miserable existence in constant and oppressive toil.

Late in the year A.D. 308 a new edict appeared ordering the magistrates in every city to restore the decayed temples ; to compel men, women, domestics, and even infants at the breast to sacrifice, and to cause all food offered for sale in the markets to be defiled with libations.[1] At Caesarea the bodies of martyrs were forbidden burial. "Beasts and dogs and birds of prey scattered the human limbs in all directions; and the whole city was spread with the entrails and bones of men, so that those who had been most opposed to us were outraged, not from any love of the martyrs, but because of the nuisance to themselves." We also read that some Egyptians who had travelled to Cilicia to minister to their brethren in the mines, and were on their way home, were detected, tortured,

[1] Eusebius, *The Martyrs of Palestine,* ix.

and burnt, as were others shortly afterwards for the same offence.[1]

In April, A.D. 311, an Edict of Toleration was issued in the names of Galerius, Constantine, and Licinius. Maximin's name may have appeared in the original document and been erased after his fall. It announced that as persecution had failed—"it has been impossible to induce them to abandon their obstinate way of life"—in order that men's lives should no longer be put in peril, the persecution was to cease. Prisoners were released, and convicts in the mines allowed to go home. "Joyous and cheerful they proceeded through every city. Numerous bodies pursued their journey through the public highways and markets, celebrating the praises of God in songs and psalms." Even their enemies congratulated them on their release.

Maximin was now emperor in the East, and did not issue the edict, though he gave orders for persecution to cease; but before the end of the year a fresh persecution began on new lines. Beginning with Antioch, he stirred up the municipalities to send delegates to him asking his permission to expel all Christians. This was graciously given. Further, he took steps to revive paganism by appointing a priesthood. In every city priests were appointed for the images, with high priests over them, by Maximin himself, from among the more distinguished inhabitants. So-called Acts of Pilate were forged

[1] Eusebius, *The Martyrs of Palestine*, xi.

and sent through the whole of the dominions subject to him. These were ordered to be published broadcast and to be given to schoolmasters to hand to their pupils to study and commit to writing as exercises for declamation.[1] We are told that "schoolboys had the names of Jesus and Pilate and the forged Acts in their mouths the whole day."[2]

At Tyre the letter of Maximin, in answer to the municipal petition against the Christians, was engraved on bronze. He begins by assuming that Christianity is exploded. He congratulates them on their renewed devotion to the gods, and pointed to the flourishing crops, the excellence of the season, and the prevailing peace as a proof that their devotion had been rewarded. It ends by ordering the restitution of apostates and the expulsion of those who remain obdurate. Only the leaders of the Church seem to have been put to death. Peter of Alexandria and several other Egyptian bishops and Lucian, a learned presbyter of Antioch, were among the slain.

But the end was to come soon. Civil war broke out between the emperors. Constantine and Licinius combined against Maxentius, ruler of Italy and Africa. Constantine, who was at Colmar, moved at once against Maxentius. Somewhere, after leaving Colmar, he had his vision of the Cross. In October, A.D. 312, Constantine defeated Maxentius at Saxa Rubra,

[1] Eusebius, *H. E.* ix. 5.   [2] Ibid., 7.

and entered Rome with his victorious army. Maximin, on hearing the news, thought it prudent to stop his persecution, and issued his own Edict of Toleration. That was before the end of A.D. 312. In January of the next year Constantine met Licinius at Milan, and together they issued the Edict of Milan. The edict is lost, but it seems to have granted universal toleration. This edict did not cover the East. But Maximin was defeated by Licinius in A.D. 313 and died. Licinius issued an edict from Nicomedia in June, A.D. 313, which repeated the provisions of the Edict of Milan and restored their lands and buildings to the Church.

A similar rescript to Anulinus, Proconsul of Africa, ordered the restoration of houses and lands to the Catholic Church of the Christians, to the exclusion of heretical bodies.

The long struggle was over and the victory was won. The Galilean had conquered, but at a heavy cost. Sir William Ramsay, judging by the inscriptions found in south-west Phrygia belonging to the third century and the suddenness with which they break off, thinks that the Church and State in the East never recovered from the destruction of the energetic and progressive elements in the population which took place. He draws a poignant contrast between the rich political and intellectual life of Christians of the third century and the pathetic silence which succeeded. There are also moral losses to which Eusebius alludes, but he very honestly lets us know that it is no part of his purpose to enlarge on scandals. It is a travesty of justice on the part of Gibbon to accuse him of deliberately concealing the truth. We learn that many unsuitable persons were ordained during the troubles, that ambitious people aspired to office, and that quarrels took place among the confessors. After all this was inevitable. The Church was, to a great extent, deprived of its rulers, and ecclesiastical discipline was relaxed, and it must have been very hard for those who had endured much not to exhibit some degree of pride and contempt in their attitude to those who had endured less, as well as to those who had failed altogether. These quarrels were to bear their evil fruits when peace was established.

It is not however proposed to carry on this history beyond the age of persecution. That age forms a distinct epoch during which the Church had to face trials and difficulties of an exceptionally intimidating character, though less dangerous to its spiritual welfare than the patronage of the State and the influx of hordes of unconverted barbarians afterwards proved to be. To this epoch the inquirer must turn who wishes to know what the Church was like, and for what principles it stood when it was nearer to the Church of the New Testament in its doctrine and its life than it has ever been since. When the age of persecution was over the New Testament conditions were altered. The Church was no longer despised and disregarded, but dominant and envied. Its danger was no longer in the enmity but in the friendship of the world. There is no such break in the history of the Church until we come to the Reformation. The point therefore at which it began to take effect seems to afford an appropriate terminus for this work.

Below is a list of the chief modern authorities consulted:

"Ante-Nicene Christian Library," edited by A. Roberts and J. Donaldson.
Anon—The Works of Apuleius, translated, published 1853 by H. G. Bohn.
Batiffol, P.—*Primitive Catholicism.*
Berwick, E.—*Philostratus' Apollonius of Tyana.*
Benson, E. W.—*Cyprian.*
Bigg, C.—*The Christian Platonists of Alexandria; Chief Ancient Philosophies; The Church's Task under the Roman Empire.*
Brightman, F. E.—"Terms of Communion" (in *The Early History of the Church and the Ministry*).
Cabrol, F., Leclercq, H.—*Monumenta Ecclesiae Liturgica*, i.
Conolly, R. H.—"The So-called Egyptian Church Order" (in *Texts and Studies*, viii. 4.)
Conybeare, F. C.—*Monuments of Early Christianity.*
Duchesne, L.—*Early History of the Church; Liber Pontificalis, with Introduction and Commentary.*
Frere, W. H.—"Early Ordination Services." (*Journal of Theological Studies*, xvi. 1915.) "Early Forms of Ordination," (in *The Early History of the Church and the Ministry*).
Friedlander, L.—*Roman Life and Manners.*
Funk, F. X.—*Didascalia et Constitutiones Apostolorum.*
Gibbon, E.—*Decline and Fall of the Roman Empire.*
Gibson, Miss Margaret Dunlop.—*Didascalia Apostolorum*, trans.
Gore, C.—*The Church and the Ministry*; new edition, revised by C. H. Turner.
Gwatkin, H. M.—*Early Church History.*
Harnack, A.—*The Expansion of the Church.*
Hauler, E.—*Didascaliae Apostolorum Fragmenta Veronensia Latina.*
Hamilton, C. F.—*The People of God.* ii.
Harris, J. R.—"Apology of Aristides," (in *Texts and Studies*), i.
Horner, G.—*The Statutes of the Apostles*, or *Canones Ecclesiastici.*

Inge, W. R.—*The Philosophy of Plotinus.*
Lightfoot, J. B.—*Dissertation on the Christian Ministry*, (appended to *The Epistles to the Philippians*) ; *The Apostolic Fathers.*
Maclean, A. J.—*The Ancient Church Orders.*
Phillimore, J. S.—*Philostratus in Honour of Apollonius of Tyana.*
Ramsay, Sir William.—*The Church in the Roman Empire; Cities and Bishopricks in Phrygia.*
Robinson, J. A.—"The Passion of S. Perpetua and her Companions" (in *Texts and Studies*, i.) ; "The Christian Ministry in the Apostolic and sub-Apostolic Periods," (in *The Early History of the Church and the Ministry*).
Turner, C. H.—"Apostolic Succession," (in *The Early History of the Church and the Ministry*) ; Notes in *The Church and the Ministry* (Gore).

CHRONOLOGICAL TABLE

YEAR.	EMPEROR.	POPE.	WRITERS.	EVENTS.
64	Nero.			Burning of Rome. Beginning of Persecution.
67				Martyrdom of S. Paul?
68	Galba.	Linus.		Martyrdom of S. Peter? Flight of Church of Jerusalem to Pella.
69	Otho. Vitellius. Vespasian.			
70			Gospel of S. Mark (not later than).	Fall of Jerusalem.
75-80			Gospel of S. Luke and Acts.?	
79	Titus.			
80		Anencletus or Cletus.?	Gospel of S. Matthew.?	Birth of Polycarp.
81	Domitian.			
85-90			Gospel and Epistles of S. John.	
91		Clement.?		
94-95				Renewed outbreak of Persecution. Execution of Flavius Clemens, consul A.D. 95, and banishment of his wife Domitilla on charge of Atheism.
95			Apocalypse.? Clement's Epistle to Corinthians.?	
96	Nerva.			Recall of Domitian's exiles.
98	Trajan.		Suetonius and Tacitus wrote during this reign.	
99		Evarestus.?	Didache.?	
101				1st Decian War. Trajan leaves Rome.
103				Return and Triumph of Trajan.
103-105			Juvenal's 1st Satire.	Martyrdom of Symeon of Jerusalem.

YEAR.	EMPEROR.	POPE.	WRITERS.	EVENTS.
105-107			Epistle of Barnabas. ?	2nd Dacian War. Trajan leaves Rome.
111		Alexander. ?		Pliny goes to Bithynia.
113-117				Trajan starts for East and winters at Antioch; invades Armenia and Mesopotamia and advances to Persian Gulf. Parthian War. Rising of Jews who massacre in Egypt, Greece, Cyrene, Osrrhene, suppressed by Lusius. Trajan dies in Cilicia on way back to Italy.
107-116			Epistles of Ignatius. ? Epistle of Polycarp. ?	Martyrdom of Ignatius. ?
117	Hadrian.	Sixtus or Xystus.		
125				Hadrian visits Athens. Building of Aelia Capitolina on site of Jerusalem begun.
127		Telesphorus?		Rescript to Minucius Fundanus.
132-135				Jewish rebellion under Bar-Cochba. Christians persecuted by Jews for refusing to join.
137 138	Antoninus Pius.	Hyginus.	Apology of Aristides. ?	Martyrdom of Telesphorus.?
145				Marcion arrives in Rome. ?
145			Shepherd of Hermas. ?	Justin arrives in Rome. ?
146		Pius. ?		
150		Anicetus. ?		Hegesippus visits Corinth and Rome.
152			1st Apology of Justin. ?	
154				Polycarp visits Rome. ? Beginnings of Montanism.
150-175			Lucian's period of greatest literary productiveness.	
161	Marcus Aurelius.			
163-167				Parthian War.
165				Capture of Seleucia and Ctesiphon.
167		Soter		Martyrdom of Justin.

Chronological Table

YEAR.	EMPEROR.	POPE.	WRITERS.	EVENTS.
174				War against Germans. Campaign against the Quadi. Incident of the Thundering Legion. ?
175			Hegesippus. The True Word of Celsus.	
177		Eleutherus.	Apology of Athenagoras.	Persecution in Lyons and Vienna.
179				Martyrdoms in Madaura and Scili.
180	Commodus.		Irenaeus against Heresies. Octavius of Minucius Felix ?	Death of Marcus Aurelius at Vienna, March 17, during campaign against Marcomanni and Quadi.
180				Peace with Marcomanni and Quadi.
183				Martyrdom of Apollonius at Rome.
185				Birth of Origen and Philostratus.
190				Amnesty to exiled Christians.
192	Pertinax.	Victor.		Assassination of Commodus.
193	Didius Julianus. Septimus Severus.			Pertinax murdered. Empire sold to D. Julianus.
193-197			Apology of Tertullian.	Civil War. Severus defeats Niger and the army of Syria on the Hellespont and in Cilicia, and Albinus the army of Britain at Lyons. Byzantium surrendered and fortifications dismantled.
198		Zephyrinus.?		Parthians defeated. Ctesiphon taken by Severus.
200			Clement's Strumateis. ?	Martyrdom of Perpetua and her companions.
200-222			Dio Cassius' History written.	
202				Persecution at Alexandria Clement forced to flee.
203				Origen takes charge of Catechetical School.

YEAR.	EMPEROR.	POPE.	WRITERS.	EVENTS.
207				Tertullian becomes a Montanist.
208				Caledonian War.
211	Geta and Caracalla.			Death of Severus at York. Murder of Geta by Caracalla.
213				Death of Clement of Alexandria.
214-215			Philostratus writes "On Apollonius of Tyana."	
217	Macrinus.	Callistus.	Apollonius of Tyana published at Tyre.	Julia Domna at Antioch. Murder of Caracalla. Suicide of Julia.
218	Heliogabalus.			Revolt of Syrian army. Defeat and death of Macrinus.
222	Severus Alexander.	Urbanus.		Alexander Severus declared Caesar. Murder of Elagabalus by Praetorians.
225			Approximate date of so-called Egyptian Church Order.	
226				Artaxerxes of Persia, founder of dynasty of Sassanides, overthrew Parthians.
230		Pontianus.		Artaxerxes declared war against Roman Empire.
231				Origen moves from Caesarea to Alexandria.
233				Porphyry born.
235	Maximinus Thrax.	Anteros.	Origen's Exhortation to Martyrs.	Pontianus and Hippolytus exiled to Sardinia where they both die. Severus Alexander and Mammaea murdered by soldiers at Mainz.
236 August 237 or 238		Fabian.		Bodies of Pontianus and Hippolytus buried in Rome.
238				Maximinus killed by soldiers.
238	Gordian I and Gordian II.			Defeat and death of Gordians. Murder of Maximin.

Chronological Table 341

YEAR.	EMPEROR	POPE.	WRITERS.	EVENTS.
238	Pupienus and Balbinus. Gordian III.			Murder of Pupienus and Balbinus.
240				Sapor succeeds Artaxerxes as King of Persia.
242				Persian War. Victory over Persians.
244	Philip the Arabian.		Plotinus began to lecture in Rome.	Murder of Gordian III.
247			Origen against Celsus.	Dionysius, Bishop of Alexandria.
248	Decius.			1000th Anniversary of Founding of Rome. Cyprian, Bishop of Carthage.
250				Persecution began. Fabian martyred.
251	Gallus.	Cornelius.		Decius defeated and slain in battle with Goths. Persecution continued.
252				Gallus makes peace with Goths by payment of annual subsidy.
253				Aemilianus defeats Goths. Also defeats and slays Gallus. In turn defeated and killed.
247–264				Dionysius, Bishop of Alexandria.
253	Valerian.	Lucius.		
254		Stephen.		Death of Origen in Tyre.
258–260				Persecution of Valerian.
257		Xystus or Sixtus } II.		
258				Martyrdom of Sixtus.
259		Dionysius.		Martyrdom of S. Cyprian.
260	Gallienus.			Valerian defeated and made prisoner by Sapor, who invaded Cappadocia.
262				Porphyry arrives in Rome, attaches himself to Plotinus. Edict of Toleration. Odenathus appointed Augustus by the Senate.
265			Death of Dionysius of Alexandria.	Alemanni invade Italy. Goths invade Greece after ravaging Pontus and Bithynia.

YEAR.	EMPEROR.	POPE.	WRITERS.	EVENTS.
267				Assassination of Odenathus.
268	Claudius.			Zenobia rules alone.
269		Felix.		Defeat of Goths by Claudius.
270	Aurelian.			
273			Approx. date of Didascalia.	Paul of Samosata deposed. Aurelian makes peace with Goths and defeats Alemanni on the Danube and exterminates their army in Italy. Death of Gregory Thaumaturgus. Aurelian takes Palmyra and captures Zenobia.
275	Tacitus.	Eutychianus.		
276	Probus.			
277				Germans defeated in Gaul by Probus, who invades Germany and imposes peace.
282	Carus Carinus. Numerian.			Carus defeats Sarmatians and invades Persia, where he died.
283		Gaius.		
284–305	Diocletian.			
285–305	Maximian (in the west).			
293–306	Constantius (in Gaul and Britain).			
286				Tiridates restored to Armenia by Romans, but driven out again by Narses, King of Persia.
287–294				Revolt of Britain under Carausius suppressed by Constantius.
296		Marcellinus.		Rebellion in Egypt suppressed by Diocletian. Edict against Manichees. War with Persia. Galerius defeated.
297				Victory over Persians. Peace imposed on Narses. Tiridates restored to Armenia. Christian officers removed from the army by Galerius
293–311	Gallerius (in Illyricum and from 305 in Asia).			

Chronological Table 343

YEAR.	EMPEROR.	POPE.	WRITERS.	EVENTS.
300				Death of Porphyry.
302				All Christians ordered to sacrifice or leave the army.
303				Diocletian's first edict of persecution issued, Feb. 24. Second edict ordering imprisonment of the clergy. Third edict permitting release of clergy on sacrificing, Nov. Diocletian celebrates triumph at Rome.
304				Fourth edict, by Maximian, ordering all persons to sacrifice on pain of death.
305	Severus in Italy, Africa, Spain. Maximin Daza in Egypt and Syria.			Diocletian reappears in March after fourteen months sickness. Diocletian abdicates in May and retires to Salona. Maximian also abdicates. Constantius becomes Augustus. End of persecution in Gaul and Britain. Synod of Elvira.
306	Constantine in Britain.	Marcellus. ?		End of persecution in Italy and Africa.
307				Severus put to death.
308				Fifth edict in Palestine substituting mutilation and mines for public execution.
309	Maxentius in Italy. Licinius in Illyria (in place of Severus).			
310		Eusebius.		
311		Miltiades.		Edict of Toleration by Galerius.
312				End of persecution in Asia. Constantine's vision of the Cross. Defeats Maxentius at Saxa Rubra.
313				Edict of Milan. Maximin's defeat. End of persecution in Syria and Egypt. Death of Maximin in June. New Edict of Toleration by Licinius published at Nicomedia.
314		Silvester.		

INDEX

Acilius Glabrio, death of, 21–2.
Acolytes, 271.
Aedesius, martyrdom of, 328.
Agape, 232–8.
Almsgiving, 243–9.
Anicetus, Bishop of Rome, 30, 207.
Antoninus Pius, policy towards Church of, 29–30.
Anulinus, 332.
Apollonius, martyrdom of, 115.
Apollonius of Tyana, 160–8.
Apologies, 68–72.
Apphianus, martyr, 327–8.
Apuleius, *Golden Ass* of, 5–6, 175.
Aristides, Apology of, 68–9.
Armenia, conversion of, 313–15.
Arrius Antoninus, 115.
Athenagoras, plea for the Christians by, 39.
Aurelian, Emperor, 306.

Baptism, 219–26; by blood, 222.
Barnabas, Epistle of, 62–3.
Basilides, Gnostic, 48–9.
Basilides, martyr, 118.
Begging, 246–7.
Bishop, 231, 259–63, 273, 275, 279–98.
Blandina, martyrdom of, 43–5.
Burial, Christian, 242.

Callistus, Bishop of Rome, 211–12.
Caracalla, Emperor, 128.
Carpocrates, 49.
Celsus, 53, 152–60.
Cerinthus, 47–8.
Charismatic theory of ministry, 279–83.
Charity, organization of, 243–9.
Church: belief of, 11–12, 54, 66–9, 225; creation of, by Jesus, 10–11; local Churches, 12. Its relation to amusements, 93–5; business, 90–3; citizenship, 95–9; family life, 85–90; marriage, 242–3; military service, 99–103; slavery, 103–4. Spread of, 13–14, 298, 317.
Clemens, Flavius, death of, 21, 22.
Clement of Alexandria, 133–42.
Clement of Rome, 61.
Commodus, 114–16.
Communion: fasting, 229; first, 227; frequency of, 229; of sick, 301.
Confessors, claims of, 193–7.
Confirmation, 226–7.
Constantine, 326, 331.
Constantius, 318, 325–6.
Conybeare, F. C., 84, 115.
Cornelius, Bishop of Rome, 213.

Cyprian, 189, 199–202, 295.

Deaconess, 275–6.
Deacons, 267–9.
Decius, 185.
Diadoché, 74.
Didaché, 61–2, 218, 280.
Dinocrates, 123.
Diocletian, 317–25.
Dionysius of Alexandria, 197–8, 248, 299–303.
Discipline, 193–6, 249–58.
Doctor, 222.
Domitian, 20–2.
Domitilla, banishment of, 21.

Easter, date of, 207–10.
Egyptian Church Order, see Orders, Church.
Elagabalus, 129.
Eleutherus, Bishop of Rome, 208.
Empire, Roman: communication in, 1–3; religion of, 3–7.
Eucharist, 227–9; validity of, 291; daily, 229.
Eumenea, destruction of, 324.
Exorcism, 223–4.

Fasting, 238–40.
Felicissimus, 214.
Felicitas, martyrdom of, 119–27.
Fortunatus, 214.

Galerius, Emperor, 318–20, 325–6, 330.
Germanicus, 31.
Gnostics, 46–54.

Gregory of Nyssa, 307, 310.
Gregory Thaumaturgus, 306–13.
Gregory the Illuminator, 313–15.

Hadrian, policy towards Christians, 28–9.
Healing, gift of, 241.
Hegesippus, *Hypomnemata* of, 73, 292–3.
Heraclas, 300.
Hermes, *Shepherd* of, 72.
Herod, 32.
Higher Criticism, anticipations of, 301, 302.
Hilarianus, 121.
Hippolytus, 210–12, 295.
Hospitality, 205, 246–7.

Ignatius, martyrdom of, 27–8; letters of, 64–7.
Internationalism, 1, 8.
Irenaeus, 74–5; on Apostolic succession, 207–8, 293–5.
Isis, worship of, 174–7.

Jews: numbers of, 7–8; opposition to Christianity of, 9–10, 34; tolerated by Empire, 15.
Julia Domna, 117, 128–9, 161–2.
Julia Moesa, 128–9.
Justin, martyrdom of, 40–2; writings of, 69–70.
Lapsed, treatment of, 193–6, 213, 300–1.

Index

Laurence, martyrdom of, 201.
Lent, suggested origin of, 240.
Leonides, 118.
Licinius, 326, 330.
Lights, ceremony of bringing in of, 234–6.
Lucian the Confessor, 194–5.
Lucian the Philosopher, 4–6, 152.

Manes and Manicheeism, 315–16.
Marcion, 49–51.
Marcus Aurelius, 36–40.
Marriage, 242–3.
Martyrs, commemoration of, 193.
Maxentius, 325, 326.
Maximian, 318, 319, 325.
Maximilla, 57.
Maximinus, 130.
Maximin Daza, 325, 326, 330–1.
Melito, 71.
Milan, Edict of, 332.
Mines, Christians condemned to, 328, 329.
Minucius Felix, the *Octavius* of, 71.
Minucius Fundanus, rescript of Hadrian to, 29.
Mithraism, 177–84.
Montanus and Montanists, 54–60.

Neocaesarea, conversion of, 307–13.
Neoplatonism, 169–72.
Nero, 17–19.

Nerva, 22.
Nicetes, 32.
Nicolaitanes, 48.
Nicomedia, 318, 320.
Novatian, 196, 212–13.
Novatus, 196, 213.

Orders, Church, 62, 218–19.
Origen, 118, 129, 142–51.
Orphans, care of, 247–8.

Paganism, attempts to revive, 330–1.
Papias, 63–4.
Paul of Samosata, 304–6.
Paul, S.: martyrdom of, 19–20; missionary journeys of, 13.
Penance, *see* Discipline.
Perpetua, 119–27.
Persecution: causes of, 15–17, 112–13; effect of, 332, 333. In Alexandria, 186–9, 193, 198, 301, 328; Caesarea, 329; Carthage, 189–201; Egypt, 323–4; Lyons and Vienne, 42–5; Phrygia, 324; Pontus, 311–12; Rome, 17–22, 201; Syria, 324. Under Antoninus Pius, 29–36; Caracalla, 128; Commodus, 114–16; Decius, 185–93; Diocletian, 317–25; Domitian, 20–2; Galerius, 319–32; Hadrian, 28–9; Marcus Aurelius, 36–45; Maximian, 320–5; Maximin Daza, 325–32; Nero, 17–19; Severus, 117–28; Trajan, 22–8; Valerian, 197–202.

Peter, S.: first visit to Rome of, 13–14, 203–4; martyrdom of, 19–20.
Philomelium, letter from Church of Smyrna to Church at, 31.
Philostratus, 162, 168.
Plague, behaviour during, 248–9.
Pliny, elder, on immortality, 3; younger, as , 4; as persecutor, 22–6.
Plotinus, 169–72.
Polycarp: martyrdom of, 31–6; visit to Rome, 30, 207; youth, 30.
Pomponius, 122.
Pontianus, Bishop of Rome, 210.
Porphyry, 170–2.
Pothinus, 44.
Presbyters, 263–7.
Priscilla, 57.
Prison, support of martyrs in, 245–6.
Prophets, 54–6, 246, 259, 280–2.
Pudens, 123.

Quadratus, Apology of, 68.
Quintus, apostasy of, 31.

Reader, 269–70.
Re-baptizing heretics, question of, 215–16, 300.
Religion, demands of, 173–4.
Rome, Church of, 203–17.
Rusticus, Christian, 127.
Rusticus, Prefect of Rome, 40–2.
Salona, 325.

Saturninus, Gnostic, 48.
Saturninus, martyrdom of, 119–28.
Seating of congregation, 229–32.
Secundulus, martyrdom of, 119–28.
Severus, Alexander, 129.
Severus, Septimius, 117–18, 127–8.
Sick, care of, 241–2.
Simeon, son of Cleophas, martyrdom of, 27.
Simon Magus, 47, 204.
Sixtus, martyrdom of, 201.
Slaves, position of, in the Church, 103–4, 221.
Soldiers, Christian, 319.
Soter, Bishop of Rome, 205–6, 207.
Stephen, Bishop of Rome, 214, 215, 216, 217, 300.
Subdeacon, 270–1.
Succession, Apostolic doctrine of, 290–8.
Suffering, indifference of Christians to, 45.

Tatian, 48.
Tertullian: Apology of, 72; on Montanism, 56–9, 208, 239; writings of, 75–83.
Theophilus, 70.
Thundering Legion, 39–40.
Tiridates, 313–14.
Trades forbidden to Christians, 221.
Trajan, policy towards Christians, 22–7.

Unction, 224, 226, 227, 241.
Urbanus, 327.

Valentinus, 51–2.
Valerian, Emperor, 192–701.
Victor, Bishop of Rome, 208–10.
Virgins, 276–8.

Widows, order of, 241, 271–5.

Xystus, *see* Sixtus.

Zenobia, 305–6.
Zephyrinus, Bishop of Rome, 210.

Printed by A. R. Mowbray & Co. Ltd.
London and Oxford

ADVERTISEMENT

SECOND EDITION, REVISED

A DICTIONARY OF ENGLISH CHURCH HISTORY

Edited by the Rev. S. L. Ollard, M.A.
Rector of Bainton; Examining Chaplain to the Archbishop of York,
and Hon. Canon of Worcester.

Assisted by Gordon Crosse, M.A.
New College, Oxford, and of Lincoln's Inn, Barrister-at-Law.

With an Appendix and Three Maps.

Cloth, 15/- net.

In the new edition some articles have been rewritten and others revised, and such events as the creation of new dioceses since the "Dictionary" was first published are recorded in an Appendix. A new map shows the effect of these changes on the diocesan boundaries.

"A MAGNUM OPUS.—The warmest congratulations are due to all concerned in the production of this large and admirable book. It is a remarkable illustration of Anglican scholarship, and a book of which the English Church may well be proud."—*Church Times.*

"The work has been well done. . . . It is so brightly written that we feel sure it will be used not only for reference but for continuous reading as well. The editors have been fortunate in securing an excellent list of contributors."—*The Times.*

"Its editors are to be congratulated on the result of their labours . . . which contains as much information as one could reasonably expect to find in such a work. The articles are for the most part short, they are never immoderately long; and in spite of the fact that they contain a great deal of matter in a very small space, they are always readable."—*English Historical Review.*

A. R. MOWBRAY & CO. LTD.
28 Margaret Street, Oxford Circus, London, W. 1; 9 High Street, Oxford

ADVERTISEMENTS

The Art of Public Worship
By the Rev. Percy Dearmer, D.D.
Professor of Ecclesiastical Art, King's College, London.
Cloth, 4/6 net.

Second Impression.
Letters of Richard Meux Benson
Founder and First Superior of the Society of S. John the Evangelist, Cowley.

Selected and Arranged by the late Rev. G. Congreve, M.A., and the Rev. W. H. Longridge, M.A.

With Memoir and Reminiscences by BISHOP HALL, BISHOP GORE, DR. DARWELL STONE, and others.
Cloth, 6/- net.

Sixteenth Thousand.
Everyman's History of the Prayer Book
By the Rev. Percy Dearmer, D.D.
With Ninety-nine Illustrations.
Paper boards, 2/6 net ; Cloth boards, 3/- net ; Cloth boards, gilt, 3/6 net.

Fifty-sixth Thousand.
Everyman's History of the English Church
By the Rev. Percy Dearmer, D.D.
With 112 Illustrations.
2/6 net ; Cloth, 3/- net.

A. R. MOWBRAY & CO. LTD.
28 Margaret Street, Oxford Circus, London, W. 1 ; 9 High Street, Oxford

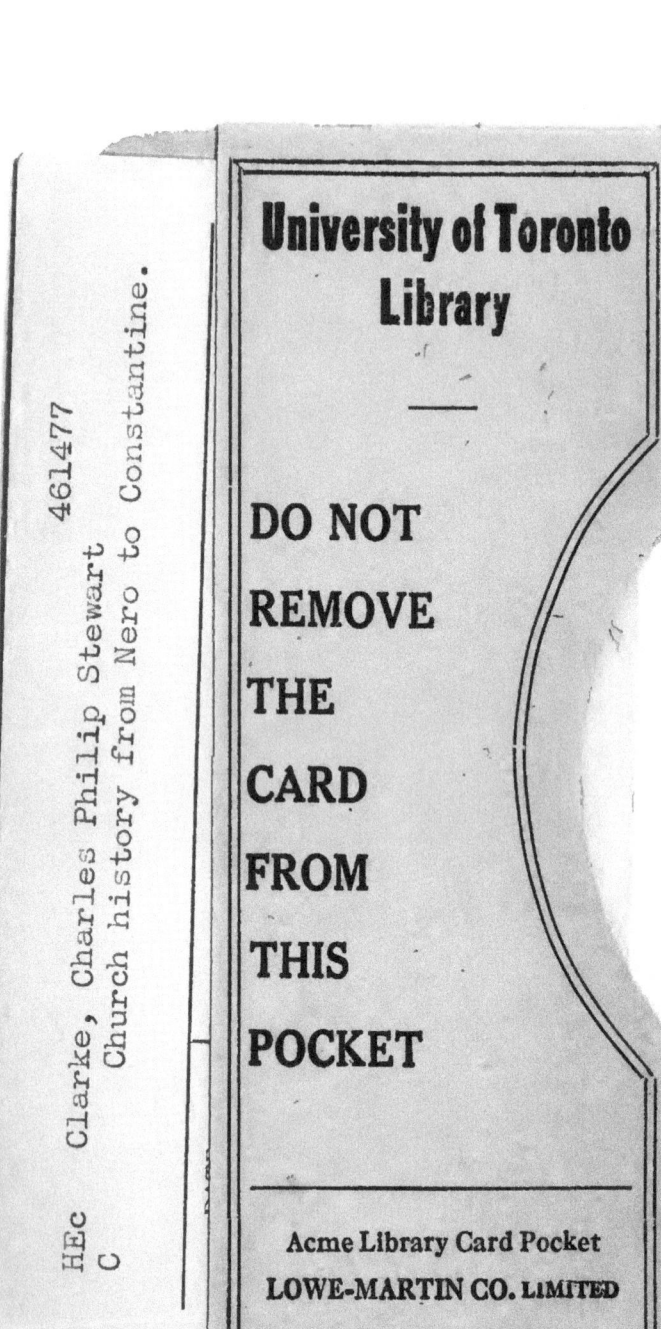

HEc Clarke, Charles Philip Stewart 461477
C Church history from Nero to Constantine.

University of Toronto Library

DO NOT REMOVE THE CARD FROM THIS POCKET

Acme Library Card Pocket
LOWE-MARTIN CO. LIMITED

ImTheStory.com

Personalized Classic Books in many genre's

Unique gift for kids, partners, friends, colleagues

Customize:

- Character Names
- Upload your own front/back cover images (optional)
- Inscribe a personal message/dedication on the inside page (optional)

Customize many titles Including
- Alice in Wonderland
- Romeo and Juliet
- The Wizard of Oz
- A Christmas Carol
- Dracula
- Dr. Jekyll & Mr. Hyde
- And more...

CPSIA information can be obtained at www.ICGtesting.com
Printed in the USA
LVOW011849061212